DDC®

Internet in an Hour

Investing & Personal Finance

Matt Burke, CFP
Don Mayo
Kathy Berkemeyer

Acknowledgements

To my father who taught me the importance of integrity, honesty, and a good name; and my precious wife who sacrificially cares for our quiver of arrows.

Matt Burke

To my family of friends—thanks for everything.

Don Mayo

Dedicated to the memory of my parents, John and Gert Madden.

Kathy Berkemeyer

Project Manager
Monique Peterson

Editorial Assistants
Emily Hay
Jacinta O'Halloran

Technical and English Editors
David Sheptock
Jacinta O'Halloran

Contributing Author
Cathy Vasecky

Research
Brian Young

Design and Layout
Maria Kardasheva
Elviro Padro
Shu Y. Chen

Cover Design and Layout
Amy Capuano

Illustrations
Ryan Sather

Published by DDC Publishing, Inc.

ISBN: 1-56243-758-5
Cat. No. HR11
DDC Publishing, Inc. Printing:
10 9 8 7 6 5 4 3 2 1
Printed in the United States of America.

Contents

Introduction

This Book is Designed for You . . .

if you are ready to explore the rapidly growing World Wide Web of finance. You'll learn how to get online and get the search results you want quickly. Find answers to all your questions about investing online and managing personal finance safely and securely.

Internet in an Hour for Investing & Personal Finance is divided into two main sections: Basics and Finance.

Basics

In Internet Basics, you can learn how to:

- Use Netscape Navigator to browse the World Wide Web.
- Use Internet Explorer to browse the World Wide Web.
- Access the Internet using America Online.
- Find information on the Web with search engines.

Finance

In the Finance section, you'll find the best investment sites the Web has to offer. Find out how and where to do all your personal banking online, answer questions about debt management and estate planning, keep up-to-date with financial news and online trading, learn the best ways to finance a home or car, and save for college and retirement. We've also included top-rated financial super sites, complete with tools, resources, and up-to-the minute information on money matters.

Disclaimer

Although we have thoroughly researched all the Web sites listed in this book, we do not guarantee the performance of any of them. Furthermore, the investment sites listed are neither a solicitation nor recommendation to buy or sell any specific investments.

What Do I Need to Use This Book?

This book assumes that you have some general knowledge and experience with computers and that you already know how to perform the following tasks:

- Use a mouse (double-click, etc.).
- Make your way around Microsoft Windows 95.
- Install and run programs.

If you are completely new to computers as well as the World Wide Web, you may want to refer to DDC's **Learning Microsoft Windows 95** or **Learning the Internet**.

This book also assumes that you have an Internet connection and access to browser applications such as Microsoft Internet Explorer 4.0, Netscape Navigator 4.0, or America Online.

✔ *If you do not currently have these applications, contact your Internet Service Provider for instructions on how to download them. You can also use other browsers or previous versions such as Explorer 3.0 and Navigator 3.0 to browse the Web.*

✔ *This book does not cover how to get connected to the Internet.*

Please read over the following list of "must haves" to ensure that you are ready to be connected to the Internet.

- A computer (with a recommended minimum of 16 MB of RAM) and a modem port.
- A modem (with a recommended minimum speed of 14.4kbps, and suggested speed of 28.8kbps) that is connected to an analog phone line (assuming you are not using a direct Internet connection through a school, corporation, etc.).
- Established access to the Internet through an online service, independent Internet Service Provider, etc.
- Patience. The Internet is a fun and exciting place, but getting connected can be frustrating at times. Expect to run into occasional glitches, get disconnected from time to time, or experience occasional difficulty in viewing certain Web pages and features. The more up-to-date your equipment and software are, however, the less difficulty you will probably experience.

Internet Cautions

ACCURACY:

- Be cautious not to believe everything on the Internet. Almost anyone can publish information on the Internet, and since there is no Internet editor or monitor, some information may be false. All information found on the World Wide Web should be checked for accuracy through additional reputable sources.

SECURITY:

- When sending information over the Internet, be prepared to let the world have access to it. Computer hackers can find ways to access anything that you send to anyone over the Internet, including e-mail. Be cautious when sending confidential information to anyone.

VIRUSES:

- These small, usually destructive computer programs hide inside of innocent-looking programs. Once a virus is executed, it attaches itself to other programs. When triggered, often by the occurrence of a date or time on the computer's internal clock/calendar, it executes a nuisance or damaging function, such as displaying a message on your screen, corrupting your files, or reformatting your hard disk.

BASICS

Netscape Navigator: 1

◆ About Netscape Navigator
◆ Start Netscape Navigator ◆ The Netscape Screen
◆ Exit Netscape Navigator

About Netscape Navigator

- This chapter focuses on Netscape Navigator 4.0, the Internet browser component of Netscape Communicator. Netscape Messenger, the e-mail component, is covered in Chapters 4-6.

Start Netscape Navigator

1. Click the Start button .
2. Click Programs, Netscape Communicator, Netscape Navigator.
   OR

   If you have a shortcut to Netscape Communicator  on your desktop, double-click it to start Netscape Navigator.

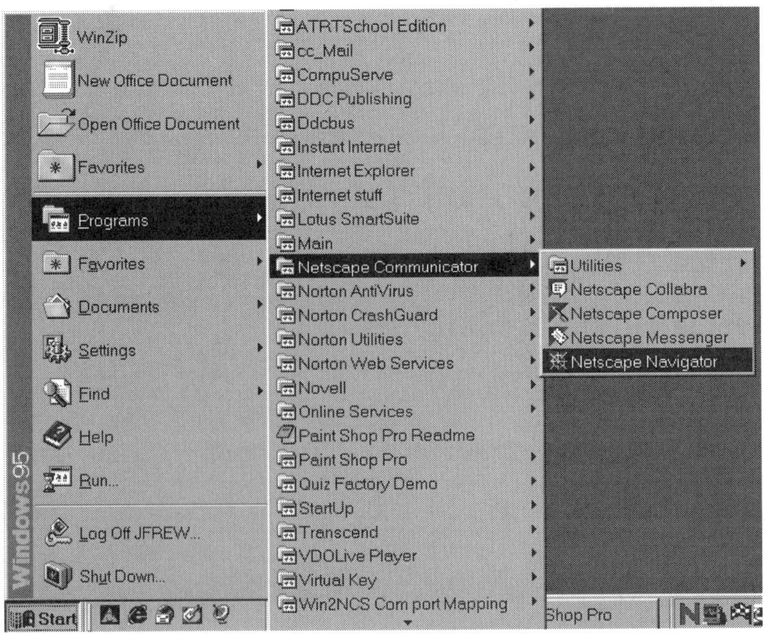

✔ *The first time you start Netscape Communicator, the New Profile Setup dialog box appears. Enter e-mail and service provider information in the dialog boxes that appear. If you do not know the information, you can leave it blank until you are ready to fill it in. See the sections on Netscape Messenger in this book for more information.*

The Netscape Screen

- The Netscape Navigator screen contains features that help you explore the Internet. Some of these features are constant and some change depending on the task attempted or completed.

Title bar

Displays the name of the program (Netscape) and the current Web page (Welcome to Netscape).

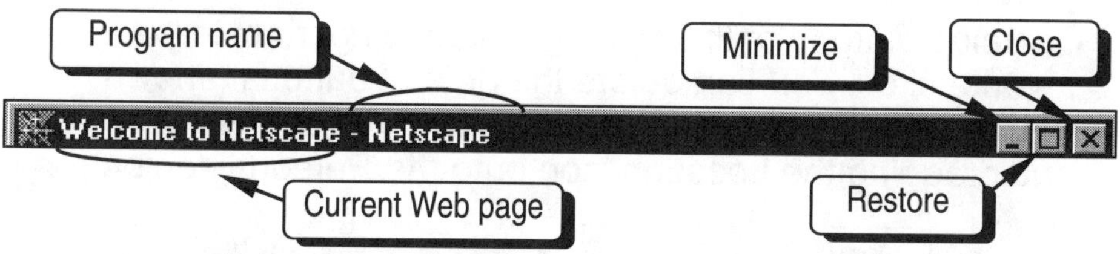

Menu bar

Displays drop-down lists of Netscape commands.

Navigation toolbar

Contains buttons for online activity. The name and icon on each button identify the command.

✔ *If the toolbar buttons are not visible, open the View menu and click Show Navigation Toolbar.*

Location toolbar

The electronic address of the current Web page displays in the Location field. You can also type the Web page address, called a Uniform Resource Locator (URL), in the Location field and press Enter to access it.

✔ *If the Location toolbar is not visible, open the View menu and click Show Location Toolbar.*

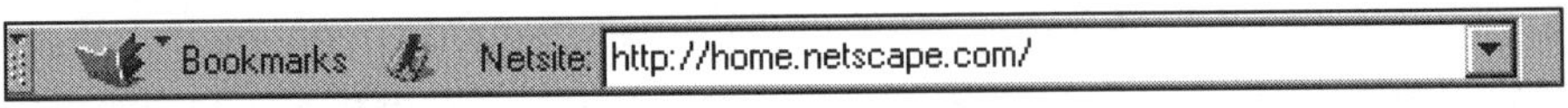

The Bookmarks QuickFile button is also on the Location toolbar. Click to view a list of sites that you have bookmarked for quick access. (For more on Bookmarks, see page 10.)

Personal toolbar

Contains buttons or links that you add to connect to your favorite sites. You can delete the default buttons (shown below) and add your own by displaying the desired Web site and dragging the Location icon onto the Personal toolbar.

Netscape's status indicator

Netscape's icon pulses when Netscape is processing a command. Click to return to Netscape's home page.

Status bar

When a Web page is opening, the Status bar indicates the downloading progress and the security level of the page being loaded. When you place the cursor over a hyperlink, the Status bar displays the URL of the link.

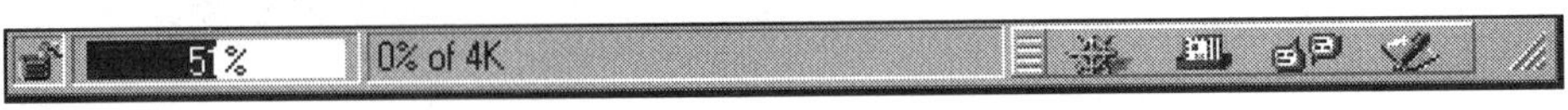

Component toolbar

The buttons on this toolbar link to other Netscape components: Navigator, Messenger Mailbox, Collabra Discussions, and Page Composer.

Exit Netscape Navigator

- Exiting Netscape Navigator and disconnecting from your Internet Service Provider (ISP) are two separate steps. You can disconnect from your service provider and still have Netscape Navigator open. You can also disconnect from Navigator and still have your ISP open.
- You may want to disconnect from your ISP and keep Netscape open to:
  - Read information obtained from the Web
  - Access information stored on your hard disk using Netscape
  - Compose e-mail to send later
- If you don't disconnect from your ISP and you pay an hourly rate, you will continue incurring charges.

✔ *You can disconnect from your ISP and still view Web information accessed during the current session by using the Back and Forward toolbar buttons. Your computer stores the visited sites in its memory.*

Netscape Navigator: 2

◆ The Navigation Toolbar
◆ Open World Wide Web Sites

The Navigation Toolbar

- The Netscape Navigation toolbar displays buttons for Netscape's most commonly used commands. Note that each button contains an icon and a word describing the button's function. Choosing any of these buttons activates the indicated task immediately.
- If the Navigation toolbar is not visible, select Show Navigation Toolbar from the View menu.

Moves back through pages previously displayed. Back is available only if you have moved around among Web pages in the current Navigator session; otherwise, it is dimmed.

Moves forward through pages previously displayed. Forward is available only if you have used the Back button; otherwise, it is dimmed.

Reloads the currently displayed Web page. Use this button if the current page is taking too long to display or to update the current page with any changes that may have occurred since the page was downloaded.

Displays the home page.

Displays Netscape's Net Search Page. You can select one of several search tools from this page.

Displays a menu with helpful links to Internet sites that contain search tools and services.

Prints the displayed page, topic, or article.

Displays security information for the displayed Web page as well as information on Netscape security features.

Stops the loading of a Web page.

Open World Wide Web Sites

- There are several ways to access a Web site. If you know the site's address, you can enter the correct Web address (URL) on the Location field on the Location toolbar.

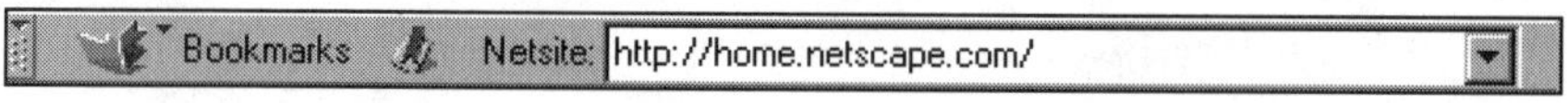

- If the address you are entering is the address of a site you have visited recently or that you have bookmarked (see page 10 for more information on Bookmarks), you will notice as you begin to type the address that Netscape attempts to complete it for you. If the address that Netscape suggests is the one you want, press Enter.
- If the address that Netscape suggests is not correct, keep typing to complete the desired address and then press Enter. Or, you can click the down arrow next to the Location field to view a list of other possible matches, select an address, and press Enter.

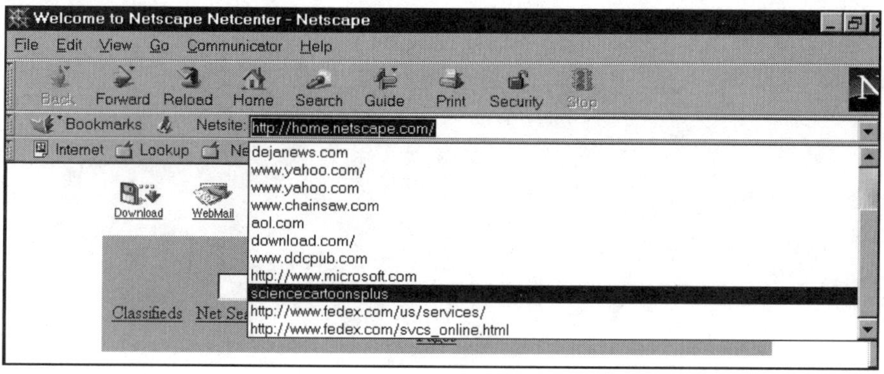

- There are a couple of shortcuts for entering URL addresses. One shortcut involves omitting the **http://www**. prefix from the Web address. Netscape assumes the **http://** protocol and the **www** that indicates that the site is located on the Web.
- If you are trying to connect to a company Web site, entering the company name is generally sufficient. Netscape assumes the **.com** suffix. For example, entering **ddcpublishing** on the location line and pressing Enter would reach the **http://www.ddcpub.com** address.

✔ *Don't be discouraged if you can't connect to the World Wide Web site immediately. The site may be offline temporarily. The site may also be very busy with other users trying to access it. Be sure the URL is typed accurately. Occasionally, it takes several tries to connect to a site.*

Netscape Navigator: 3

◆ History List ◆ Bookmarks ◆ Add Bookmarks ◆ Delete Bookmarks ◆ Print Web Pages

History List

- While you move back and forth among Web sites, Netscape automatically records each of these site locations in a History list, which is temporarily stored on your computer.
- You can use the History list to track or view sites that you have recently visited. The History list is an easy way to see the path you followed to get to a particular Web page.
- To view the History list, click History on the Communicator menu, or press Ctrl+H. To link to a site shown in the History list, double-click on it.

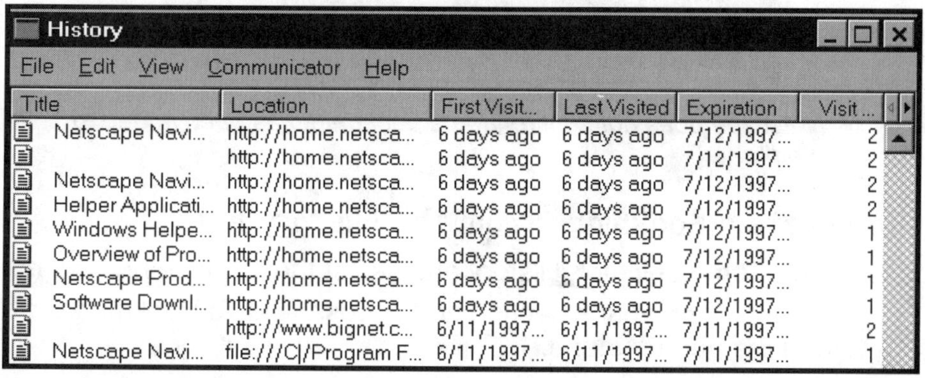

Bookmarks

- A Bookmark is a placeholder containing the title and URL of a Web page that, when selected, links directly to that page. If you find a Web site that you like and want to revisit, you can create a Bookmark to record its location. (See **Add Bookmarks** on the following page.)
- The Netscape Bookmark feature maintains permanent records of the Web sites in your Bookmark files so that you can return to them easily.

- You can view the Bookmarks menu by selecting Bookmarks from the Communicator menu or by clicking on the Bookmarks QuickFile button 

on the Location toolbar. The drop-down menu shown below appears.

Add Bookmarks

To add a Bookmark from an open Web page:

- Display the Web page to add, go to Bookmarks on the Communicator menu and click Add Bookmark.

✔ *Netscape does not confirm that a bookmark has been added to the file.*

To create a Bookmark from the History list:

1. Click Communicator, History and select the listing to bookmark.
2. Right-click on your selection and choose Add To Bookmarks from the pop-up menu.

Delete Bookmarks

- Bookmarks may be deleted at anytime. For example, you may wish to delete a Bookmark if a Web site no longer exists or is no longer of interest to you.

To delete a Bookmark:

1. Click Communicator.
2. Click Bookmarks.
3. Click Edit Bookmarks.

4. In the Bookmarks window, select the Bookmark you want to delete by clicking on it from the Bookmark list.
5. Press the Delete key.

   OR

   Right-click on the Bookmark and select Delete Bookmark from the pop-up menu as shown in the following illustration.

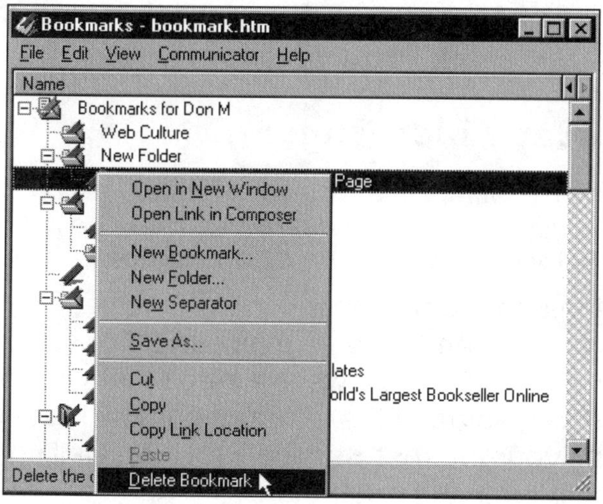

Print Web Pages

- You can print all information you find on the Internet.

To print a Web page:

✔ *Only displayed pages can be printed.*

1. Click the Print button 

 on the Navigation toolbar.

   OR

   Click File, Print.

2. In the Print dialog box that displays, select the desired print options and click 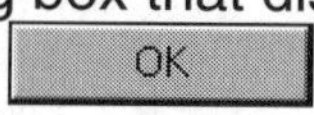

.

- In most cases, the Web page will be printed in the format shown in the Web page display.

Netscape Messenger: 4

◆ Start Netscape Messenger
◆ Configure Netscape Messenger
◆ The Message List Window ◆ Get New Mail
◆ Read Messages ◆ Delete a Message
◆ Print Messages

Start Netscape Messenger

✔ *This section assumes that you have already set up an e-mail account with a service provider. If you do not have an e-mail address, contact your Internet Service Provider.*

- Establishing a modem connection and configuring your computer to send and receive mail can be frustrating. Don't be discouraged. What follows are steps that will get you connected, but some of the information may have to be supplied by your Internet Service Provider. Calling for help will save you time and frustration.

  - Click the Mailbox icon 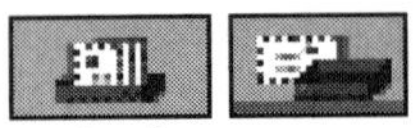 on the Component bar from the Navigator window.

    OR

    Start Netscape Messenger from the Netscape Communicator submenu on the Start, Programs menu.

Configure Netscape Messenger

- Using Netscape Messenger you can send, receive, save, and print e-mail messages and attachments. First, you must configure the program with your e-mail account information.
- You may have already filled in this information if you completed the New Profile Setup Wizard when you installed Netscape Communicator.
- If not, follow these steps to get connected. You can also use these steps to change your e-mail setting.

Step 1: Identity Settings

- From the Navigator or Messenger menu:

1. Click Edit and select Preferences.
2. Double-click the Mail & Groups Category to display the list and click Identity.
3. Enter your name, e-mail address, and any optional information in the Identity dialog boxes.

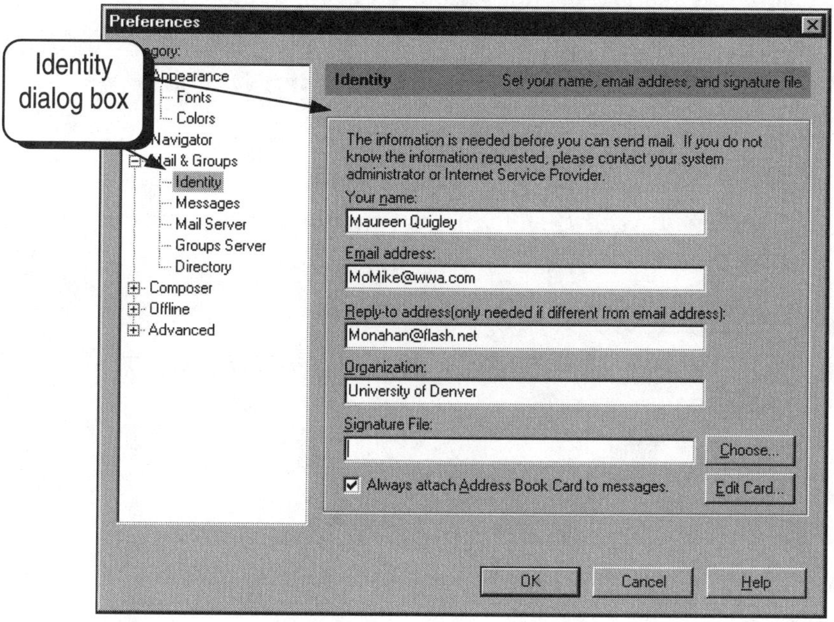

Step 2: Mail Server Preference Settings

- Completing this step will allow you to send and receive mail.

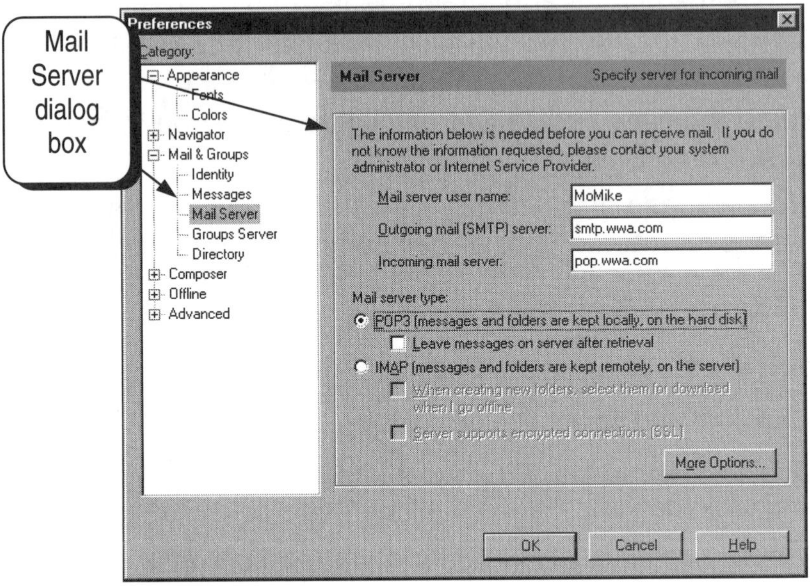

1. Click Mail Server from the Mail & Groups Category.
2. Enter your mail server user name. This is the part of your e-mail address that appears in front of the @ sign.
3. Enter your outgoing and incoming mail server address information.

✔ *Check with your ISP if you don't already have this information.*

4. Click OK to save and close the preference settings.

✔ *You should now be able to send and receive e-mail messages.*

The Message List Window

- After you launch Messenger, a message list window will open, displaying the contents of the e-mail Inbox folder. You can retrieve, read, forward, and reply to messages from this window.

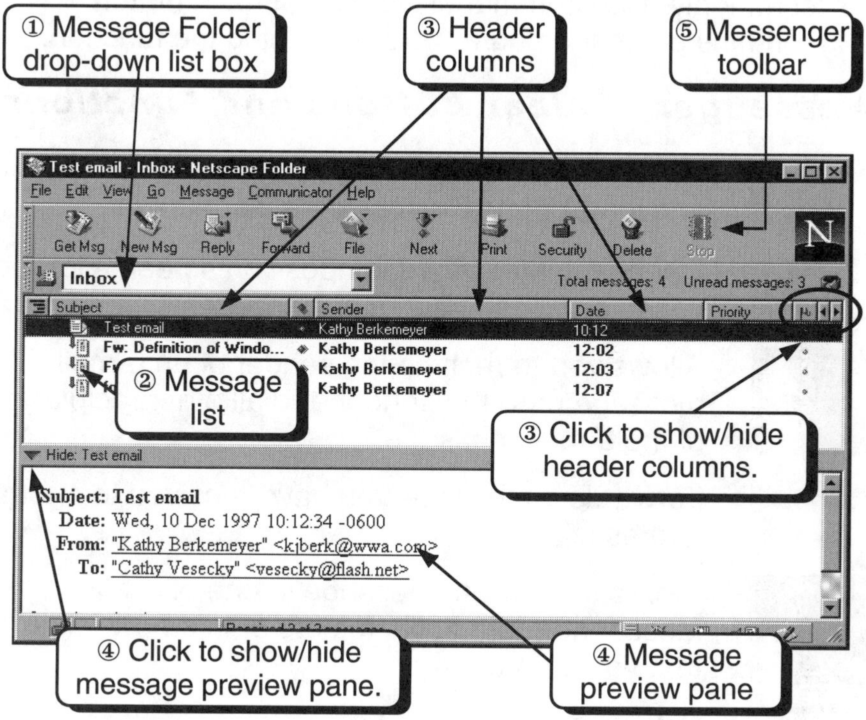

- The message list window includes the following:

  ① The Message Folder drop-down list box displays the currently selected message folder. Click the down arrow to display a list of other message folders.

  ② The message list displays header information for each of the messages contained in the selected folder.

  ③ Header columns list the categories of information available for each message, such as subject, sender, and date.

④ The message preview pane displays the content of the message currently selected from the message list. You can show/hide the preview pane by clicking on the blue triangle icon in the bottom-left corner of the message list pane.

⑤ The Messenger toolbar displays buttons for activating commonly used commands. Note that each button contains an image and a word describing the function.

Messenger Toolbar Buttons and Functions

Retrieves new mail from your Internet mail server and loads it into the Inbox message folder.

Opens the Message Composition screen allowing you to compose new mail messages.

Allows you to reply to the sender of an e-mail message or to the sender and all other recipients of the e-mail message.

Forwards a message you have received to another address.

Stores the current message in one of six Messenger default file folders or in a new folder that you create.

Selects and displays the next of the unread messages in your Inbox.

Prints the displayed message.

Displays the security status of a message.

Deletes the selected message. Deleted messages are moved to the Trash folder.

Get New Mail

- You must be connected to your ISP to access new e-mail messages.

To retrieve new messages:

1. Click the Get Msg button 

on the Messenger toolbar. (If you do not know your e-mail password, contact your ISP.)
2. If you have not instructed Netscape Messenger to save your password, you will have to enter it in the Password Entry dialog box that follows.

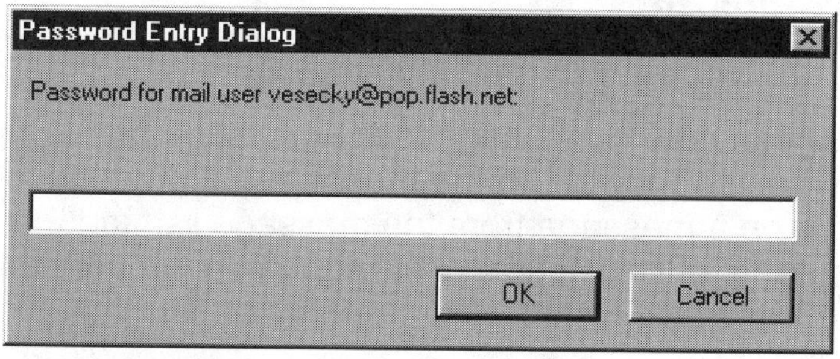

3. Click 

.

- The Getting New Messages box opens, displaying the status of your message retrieval.

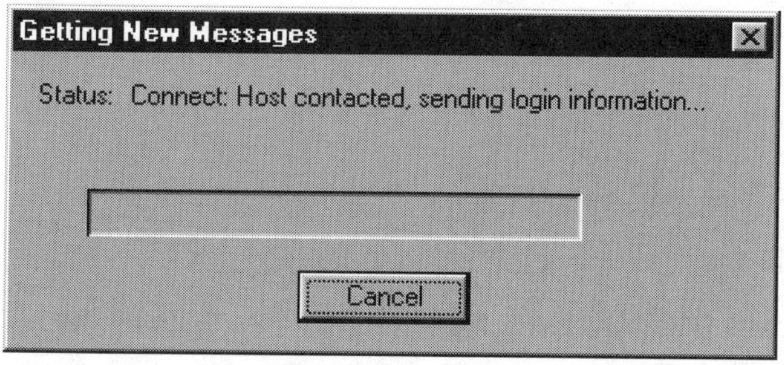

- Once your new messages are retrieved, they are listed in the message list window. By default, Messenger stores new mail messages in the Inbox folder.

To save your Password permanently in Messenger:

1. Click Edit, Preferences.
2. Click on Mail Server under the Mail & Groups Category to select it.

   ✔ *If the Mail & Groups menu is not displayed, expand the list by clicking the + sign next to the Mail & Groups category.*

3. Click the More Options button More Options... .
4. Select the Remember my mail password check box and click OK twice to save and exit Preferences.

Read Messages

- There are two ways to read messages:
  - You can read a message in the message preview pane located directly below the message list window. Single-click on a message from the message list and the contents of the message will appear in the preview pane.

    ✔ *If the message does not appear, the preview pane may be hidden. Click on the blue triangle icon at the bottom of the message list window to show the preview pane.*

    OR

    Double-click on the message from the message list to open it in its own window.

To close a message:

- Click File, Close.

  OR

  Click on the Close button (X) in the upper-right corner of the window.

To read the next unread message:

- Click the Next button  on the Messenger toolbar.

  OR

  If you have reached the end of the current message, you can press the spacebar to proceed to the next unread message.

- Once you have read a message, it remains stored in the Inbox folder until you delete it or file it in another folder. (See **Delete a Message** below.)

  ✔ *You do not have to be online to read e-mail. You can reduce your online time by disconnecting from your ISP after retrieving your messages.*

  ✔ *Icons located to the left of message headers in the message list identify each message as either unread*  *(retrieved during a previous Messenger session), new*  *(and unread), or read* *.*

Delete a Message

- There are two steps required to delete a message permanently. Deleting a message from the message list moves the message to the Trash folder. You must then delete it from the Trash folder to remove it permanently from your hard disk.

  1. To delete a message, click on the message to select it from the message list window.
  2. Click the Delete button  on the Messenger toolbar.

To delete messages from the Trash folder:

- Click Empty Trash Folder from the File menu to delete all items stored there.

  OR

  Delete the desired message by selecting it and pressing the Delete key.

✔ *To select more than one message to delete, hold the Ctrl button while you click each message to delete. Once all the desired messages are selected, press the Delete key.*

Print Messages

■ The message must first be open in order to print it.

1. Click the Print button  on the Messenger toolbar.
2. In the Print dialog box that appears, select the desired print options and click OK.

Netscape Messenger: 5

◆ New E-Mail Messages
◆ The Message Composition Toolbar
◆ Compose and Send Messages
◆ Reply to Mail ◆ Forward Mail
◆ Add Entries to the Personal Address Book
◆ Address a New Message Using the Personal Address Book

New E-Mail Messages

- You can compose an e-mail message in Netscape Messenger on- or offline.
- After composing an e-mail message online, you have three choices:
  - send the message immediately
  - store the message in the Unsent Messages folder to be sent later (File, Send Later)
  - save the message in the Drafts folder to be finished and sent later (File, Save Draft)
- After composing a message offline (which frees up your phone line and also reduces any hourly ISP charges), store the message in your Unsent Messages folder until you are online and can send it.

The Message Composition Toolbar

- The toolbar in the Message Composition window has several features that are specific only to the message composition screen.

Message Composition Toolbar Buttons and Functions

Button	Function
Send	Immediately sends current message.
Quote	Used when replying to a message, the Quote feature allows you to include text from the original message.
Address	Select an address from the addresses stored in your personal Address Book to insert into address fields.
Attach	By clicking the Attach button, you can send a file, a Web page, or your personal address card along with your e-mail message.
Spelling	Checks for spelling errors in the current message.
Save	Lets you save your message as a draft for later use.
Security	Sets the security status of a message.
Stop	Stops the display of an HTML message or a message with an HTML attachment.

Compose and Send Messages

- There are four steps to composing and sending a basic e-mail message using Netscape Messenger:

Step 1: New Message

1. Click the New Message button 

from the Messenger main screen.

   OR

   Press Ctrl+M.

   ✔ *The Message Composition window displays.*

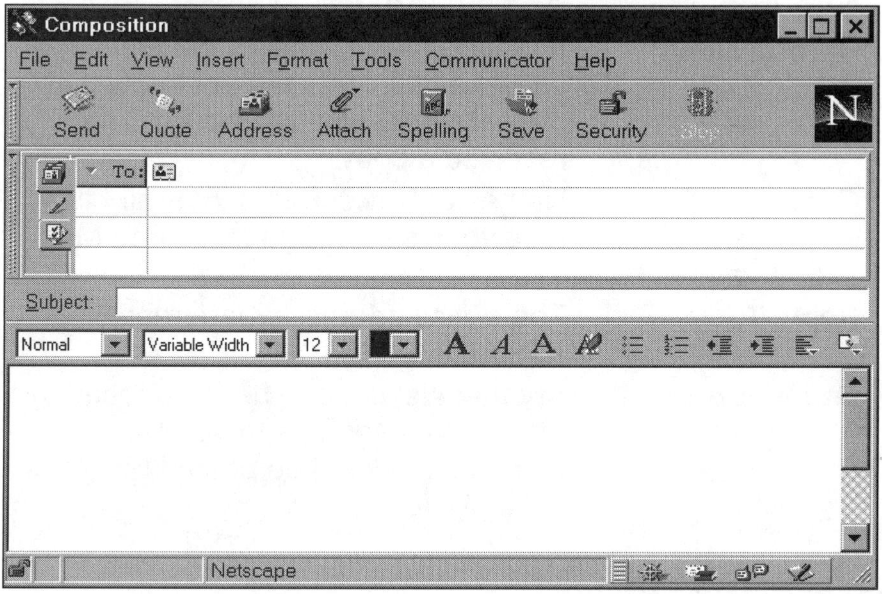

2. In the Message Composition window, type the e-mail address(es) of the message recipient(s) in the To field.

   ✔ *If you are sending the message to multiple recipients, press Enter after typing each recipient's address to move to the next address line.*

   OR

   Click the Address button 

on the Message Composition toolbar and select an address to insert from the Address Book (see pages 27-30 for more information on using the Address Book).

- Click the To button 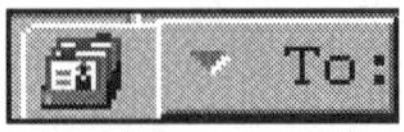

to display a drop-down menu of addressee options. Click on any of following options to enter the recipient information indicated:

To	The e-mail address of the person to whom the message is being sent.
CC (Carbon Copy)	The e-mail addresses of people who will receive copies of the message.
BCC (Blind Carbon Copy)	Same as CC, except these names will not appear anywhere in the message, so other recipients will not know that the person(s) listed in the BCC field received a copy.
Group	Names of Newsgroups that will receive this message (similar to Mail To).
Reply To	The e-mail address where replies should be sent.
Follow-up To	Another Newsgroup heading; used to identify Newsgroups to which comments should be posted (similar to Reply To).

Step 2: The Subject

- Click in the Subject field (or press Tab to move the cursor there) and type a banner for your message. This is the first thing the recipient will see announcing your e-mail message. The subject should be a few-word summation of your message.

Step 3: The Message

- Click to or Tab down to the blank composition area below the Subject field and type the body of your message.

To spell-check your e-mail message:

- Check the spelling of your message by clicking on the Spelling button  on the Message Composition toolbar and respond to the dialog prompts that follow.

Step 4: Sending the Message

To send a message immediately:

- Click the Send button  on the Message Composition toolbar.

To send a message later:

- Use these procedures to send message that you compose offline or that you wish to send later.
  - Click File, Send Later.

  OR

  Click File, Save Draft.
- Saving the message in the Drafts folder lets you finish and then send it later.

Reply to Mail

- Select the message from the message list or open the message in its own window:

1. Click the Reply button .

   ✔ *The Reply submenu displays*
2. Click Reply to Sender to reply to the original sender only.

   OR

   Select Reply to Sender and All Recipients to send a reply to the sender and all other recipients of the original message.

- Selecting one of these options automatically inserts the recipient's name or e-mail address in the address fields.

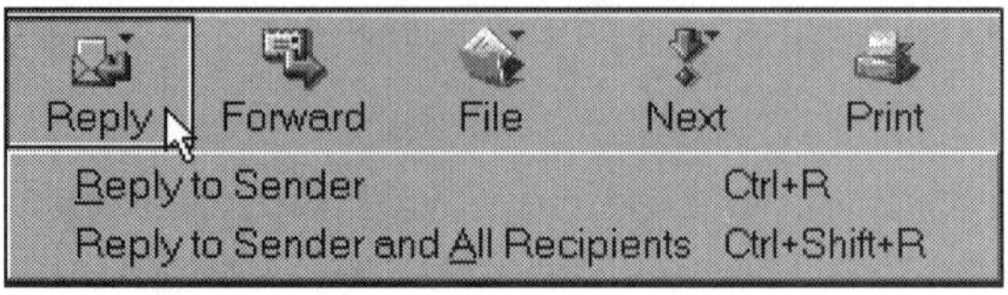

✔ *The Message Composition window opens, with the To, Cc, and Subject fields filled in for you.*

- Compose your reply as you would a new message.

To include a copy of the original message with your reply:

1. Select the original message from the message list.
2. Click the New Msg button 

on the Messenger toolbar.
3. Click the Quote button 

on the Message Composition toolbar.

   ✔ *The entire message will be automatically inserted in the body of your new message. You can edit the original message and header text as you wish.*

4. When you are finished, click the Send button 

to send the message immediately.

Forward Mail

- To forward a message:

1. Select the message from the message list or open the message to forward.
2. Click the Forward button 

from the toolbar.

   ✔ *The Message Composition window opens, with the Subject field filled in for you.*

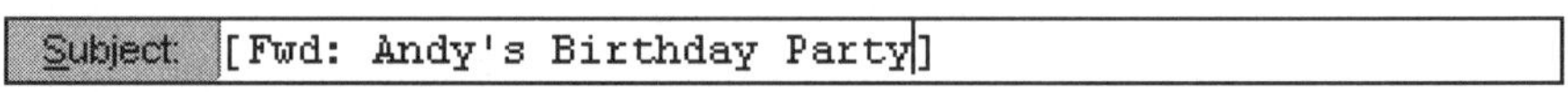

3. Type the e-mail address of the new recipient in the To field.

✔ *If the original message does not appear in the composition area, click the Quote button* 

on the Message Composition toolbar to insert it.

4. Click in the composition area and edit the message as desired. You can also type any additional text you want to include with the forwarded message.

5. When you are done, click the Send button 

to send the message immediately.

   OR

   Select File, Send Later to store the message in the Unsent Messages mailbox to be sent later.

   OR

   To save the reply as a draft to be edited and sent later, select Save Draft from the File menu.

Add Entries to the Personal Address Book

- You can compile a personal Address Book to store e-mail addresses that you use often. Click on entries from the Address Book to insert an e-mail address automatically into the e-mail message header.

To add a name to the Address Book:

1. Click Communicator, Address Book.

   ✔ *The Address Book window displays.*

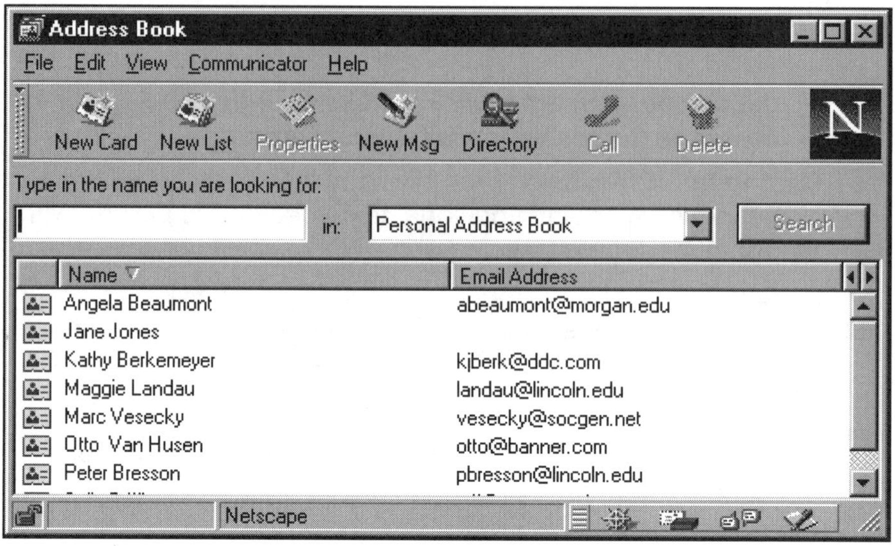

2. Click the New Card button 

on the Address Book toolbar.
3. In the New Card box that appears, enter the recipient's first name, last name, organization, title, and e-mail address.

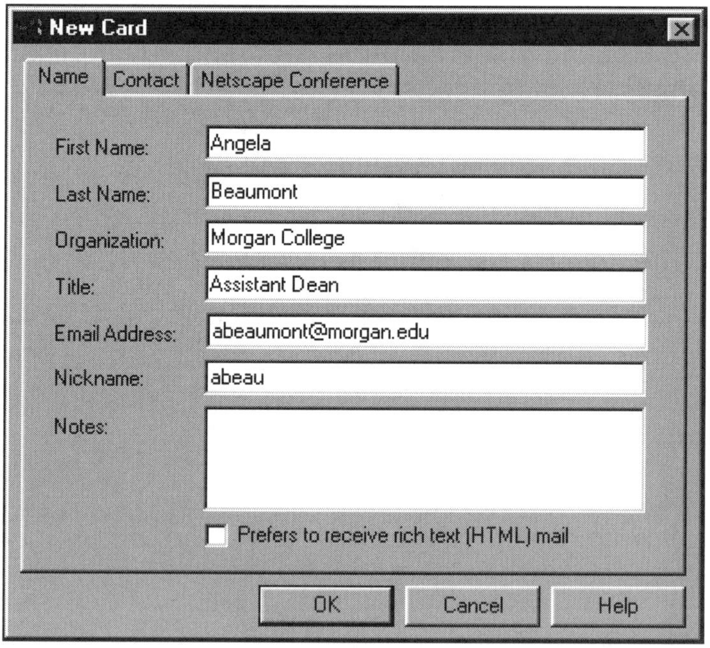

- In the Nickname field, if desired, type a unique nickname for the recipient. When addressing a message, you can use the recipient's nickname in the To field and Messenger will automatically fill in the full e-mail address.
- In the Notes field, type any notes you want to store about the recipient.
- Click the Contact tab, if desired, and enter the recipient's postal address and phone number.

4. Click OK.

- You can edit an address book entry at any time by double-clicking on the person's name in the Address Book window.
- To add the name and address of the sender of a message you are reading:
  - Click Message, Add to Address Book.

Add a name to the Address Book from the Add to Address Book submenu:

1. Right-click on unopened message.
2. Click Add to Address Book.
3. Click Sender to add the sender name to your address book.

   OR

   Click All to add all names from the addressee fields to the Address Book (e.g., everyone from the cc: field).

- The New Card dialog box opens, with the sender's name and e-mail address filled in for you. You can enter a nickname and any other information you want in the remaining fields.

Address a New Message Using the Personal Address Book

1. Click the New Msg button  to open the Message Composition window.
2. Click on the Address button  on the Message Composition toolbar and select a recipient(s) from the list in the Address Book window.
3. Double-click on the name from the list of addresses.
4. Click  to close the Address Book. The name(s) are automatically inserted in the address field.

Netscape Messenger: 6

◆ Attached Files ◆ View File Attachments
◆ Save Attached Files ◆ Attach Files to Messages

Attached Files

- Sometimes an e-mail message will come with a separate file(s) attached. Messages containing attachments are indicated when you display a message and it contains a paperclip icon to the right of the message header. Attachments can be used when you want to send someone a document, a spreadsheet, a video clip, or any other type of file.
- With Messenger, you can view both plain text attachments and binary attachments. Binary files are files containing more than plain text (i.e., images, sound clips, and formatted text, such as spreadsheets and word processor documents).
- Almost any e-mail program can read plain text files. Binary files, however, must be decoded by the receiving e-mail program before they can be displayed in a readable form. When a binary attachment arrives, Messenger automatically recognizes and decodes it.

View File Attachments

- E-mail attachments are displayed in one of two ways.

View attachments Inline:

- If you select View, Attachments, Inline, you see the attachment in a separate attachment window below the message. If there is more than one attachment, you will see a series of sequential windows—one with the message and the other with the attachments.

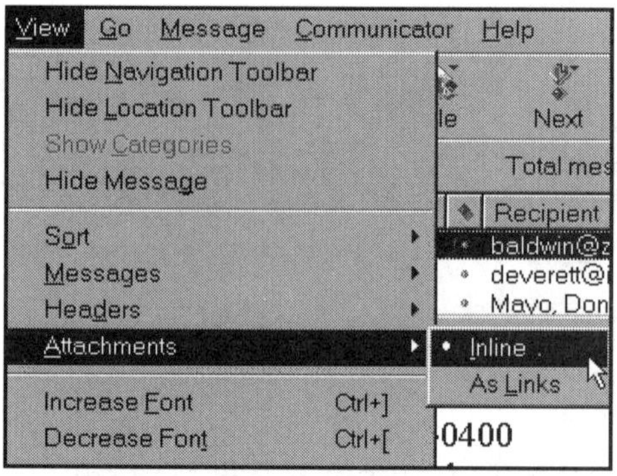

✔ *Only plain text, images, and Web page attachments can be viewed Inline.*

View attachments As Links:

- If you select View, Attachments, As Links, the window below the message displays an attachment box listing the details of the attachment. It also serves as a link to the attachment.

✔ *Viewing attachments as links reduces the time it takes to open a message on screen.*

- Click on the blue-highlighted text in the attachment box to display the attachment.

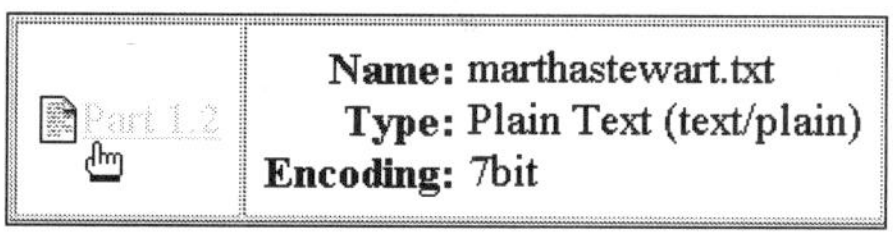

- You can right-click on the attachment icon portion of the attachment box to display a menu of mail options such as forwarding, replying, or deleting the message.
  - By right-clicking on the actual attachment, you can choose from several save options.
  - If you open a Web page attachment while online, you will connect to that Web site. If you are not online, the Web page will display fully formatted, but it will not be active.

- If an attached image displays as a link even after you select View, Attachments, Inline, it is probably because it is an image type that Messenger does not recognize. In this case, you need to install and/or open a plug-in or program with which to view the unrecognized image.

Save Attached Files

- You can save an attached file to your hard drive or disk for future use or reference.

To save an attachment:

1. Open the message containing the attachment to save.
2. If the attachment is in Inline view, convert it to a link (View, Attachments, As Links).
3. Right-click on the link and select Save Link As.

   OR

   Click on the link to open the attachment. Select File, Save As, or, if Messenger does not recognize the attachment's file type, click the Save File button in the Unknown File Type dialog box.

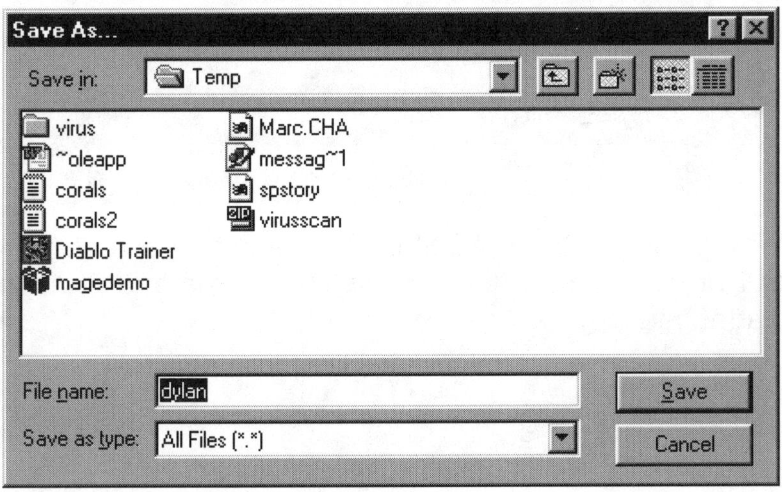

4. In the Save As dialog box that follows, click the Save in drop-down list box and select the drive and folder in which to save the file.
5. Click in the File name text box and type a name for the file.
6. Click Save.

Attach Files to Messages

- Any type of file can be sent as an attachment to an e-mail message—including text files, graphics, spreadsheets, and HTML documents.

To attach a file to an e-mail message:

1. Click the Attach button 

on the Message Composition toolbar, and select File from the drop-down menu that appears.
2. In the Enter file to attach dialog box that follows, click the Look in drop-down list box and select the drive and folder containing the file to attach.
3. Then select the file to attach and click Open.

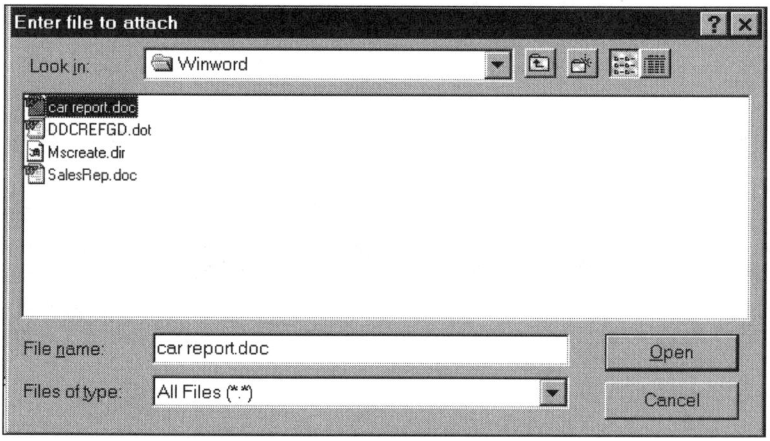

- After you have attached a file, the Attachments field in the Mail Composition window displays the name and location of the attached file.

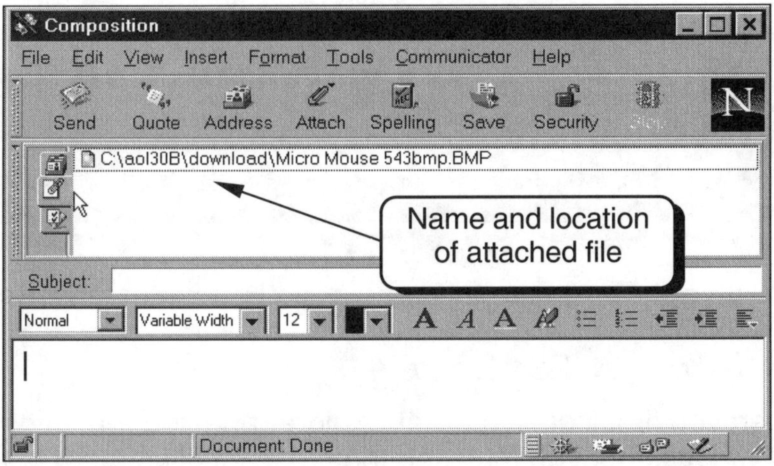

✔ *Messages containing attachments usually take longer to send than those without attachments. When attaching very large files or multiple files, you may want to zip (compress) the files before attaching them. To do so, both you and the recipient need a file compression program, such as WinZip or PKZip.*

- Once you have attached the desired files and finished composing your message, you can send the e-mail, save it in the Unsent Messages folder for later delivery, or save it as a draft for later editing.

Microsoft Internet Explorer: 7

◆ Start Internet Explorer 4
◆ Internet Explorer Screen ◆ Exit Internet Explorer

Start Internet Explorer 4

- When you first install Internet Explorer and you are using the Active Desktop, you may see the message illustrated below when you turn on your computer. If you are familiar with Explorer 3, you may want to select 1 to learn the new features in Explorer 4. Select 2 to learn about Channels.

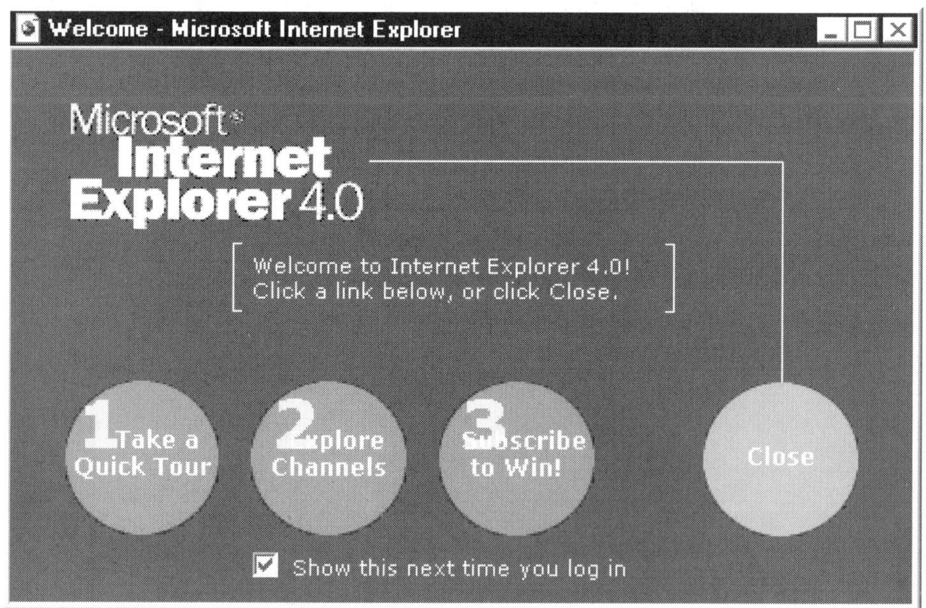

To start Internet Explorer:

- Click on the Desktop.

  OR

  Click on the Taskbar.

  OR

  Click the Start button, then select Programs, Internet Explorer, and click Internet Explorer.

Internet Explorer Screen

- When you connect to the World Wide Web, the first screen that displays is called a home page. The home page is the first page of any World Wide Web site.
- You can change the first page that you see when you connect to Explorer.

To change the home page:

1. Click View, Internet Options.
2. Enter a new address in the Address text box.

   ✔ *The page that you see when you are connected may differ from the one illustrated below.*

3. Click OK.

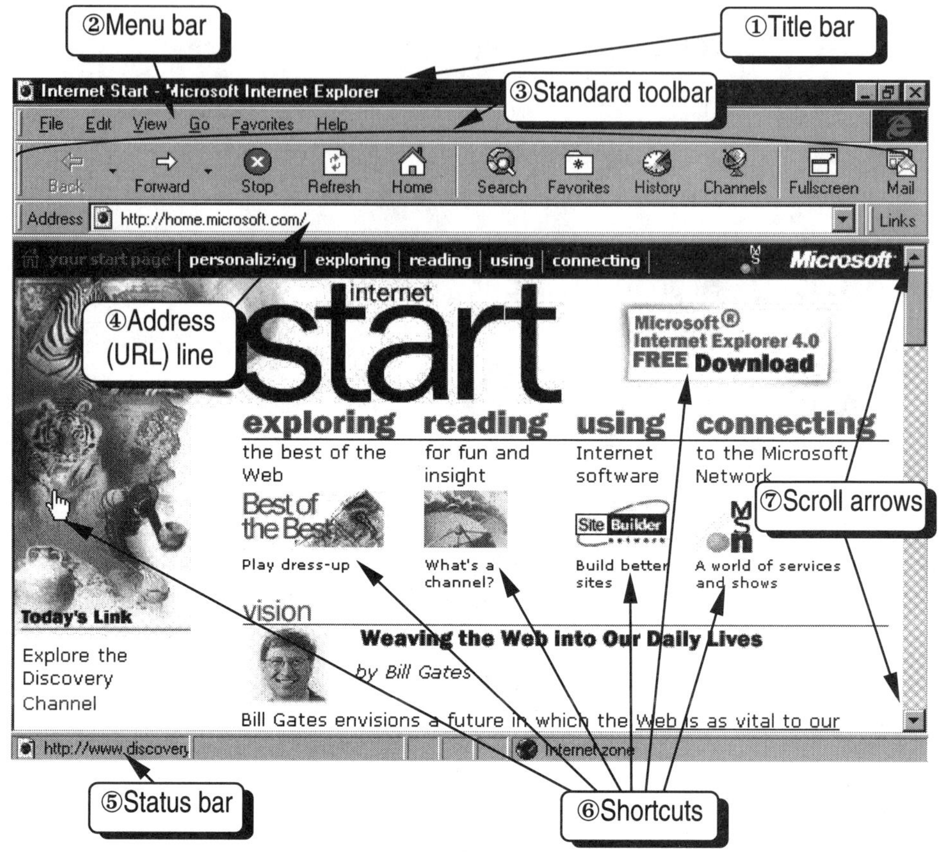

① Title bar Displays the name of the program and the current Web page. You can minimize, restore, or close Explorer using the buttons on the right side of the Title bar.

② **Menu bar** Displays menus currently available, which provide drop-down lists of commands for executing Internet Explorer tasks.

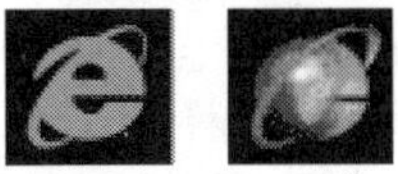

The Internet Explorer button on the right side of the Menu bar rotates when action is occurring or information is being processed.

③ **Standard toolbar** Displays frequently used commands.

④ **Address (URL) line** Displays the address of the current page. You can click here, type a new address, press Enter, and go to a new location (if it's an active Web site). You can also start a search from this line.

The Links bar contains links to various Microsoft sites. Drag the split bar to the left or somewhere else on the screen to display current Links. You can add or delete links.

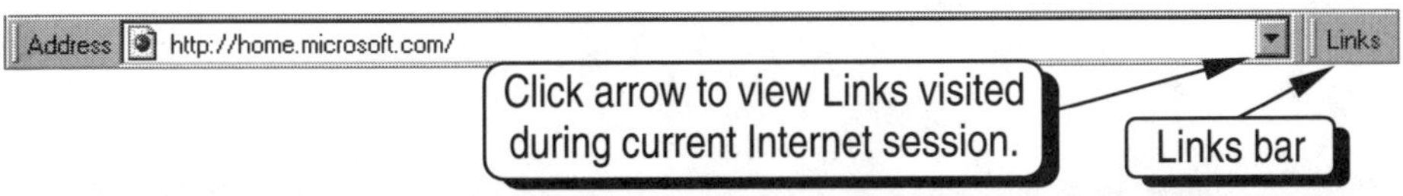

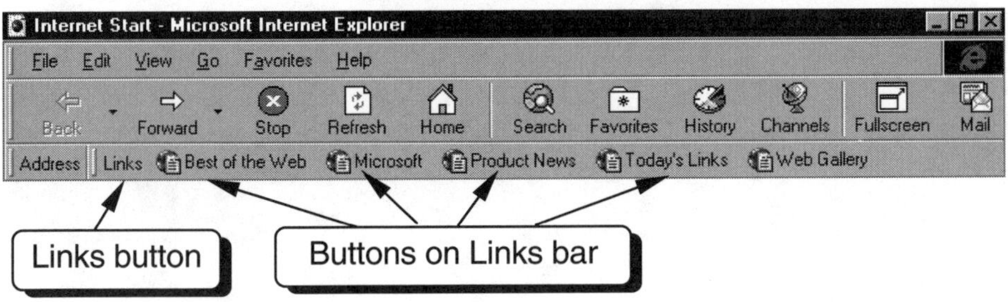

⑤ **Status bar**	Displays information about actions occurring on the page and the Security Level. Internet Security Properties lets you control content that is downloaded on to your computer.
⑥ **Shortcuts**	Click on shortcuts (also called hyperlinks) to move to other Web sites. Shortcuts are usually easy to recognize. They can be underlined text, text of different colors, "buttons" of various sizes and shapes, or graphics. You are pointing to a shortcut when the mouse pointer changes to a hand, and the full name of the Web site appears on the Status bar.
⑦ **Scroll arrows**	Scroll arrows are used to move the screen view, as in all Windows applications.

Exit Internet Explorer

- Exiting Internet Explorer and disconnecting from your service provider are two separate steps. It is important to remember that if you close Internet Explorer (or any other browser), you must also disconnect (or hang up) from your service provider. If you don't disconnect, you'll continue incurring any applicable charges.

Microsoft Internet Explorer: 8

- ◆ Standard Toolbar Buttons
- ◆ Open a Web Site from the Address Bar

Standard Toolbar Buttons

- The Internet Explorer Standard toolbar displays frequently used commands. If the Standard toolbar is *not* visible when you start Explorer, open the View menu, select Toolbars, then select Standard Buttons.

Internet Explorer Toolbar and Functions

Moves back through pages previously displayed. Back is available only if you have moved around among Web pages in the current Explorer session.

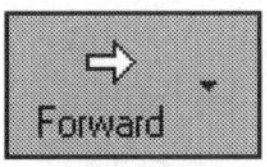

Moves forward through pages previously displayed. Forward is available only if you have used the Back button.

Interrupts the opening of a page that is taking too long to display.

Reloads the current page.

Returns you to your home page. You can change your home page to open to any Web site or a blank page (View, Internet Options, General).

Allows you to select from a number of search services with a variety of options.

Displays the Web sites that you have stored or bookmarked using the Favorites menu.

Displays links to Web sites that you have visited in previous days and weeks. You can change the number of days that sites are stored in your History folder (View, Internet Options, General).

Displays the list of current channels on the Explorer bar.

Conceals Menu, titles, Status bar, and Address bar to maximize your screen for viewing a Web page. Click it again to restore your screen.

Displays a drop-down menu with various Mail and News options. You will learn about Outlook Express e-mail options in Chapters 10-12.

Open a Web Site from the Address Bar

1. Click in the Address bar and start typing the address of the Web site you want to open.
2. If you have visited the site before, Internet Explorer will try to complete the address automatically. If it is the correct address, press Enter to go to it. If it is not the correct address, type over the suggested address that displayed on the line.

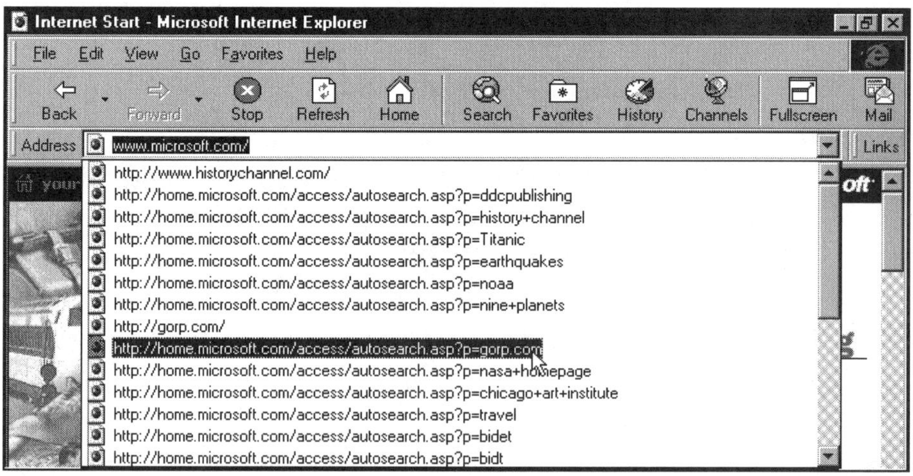

✔ *To turn off the AutoComplete feature, open the View menu, select Internet Options, and click the Advanced tab. Deselect Use AutoComplete in the Browsing area of the dialog box.*

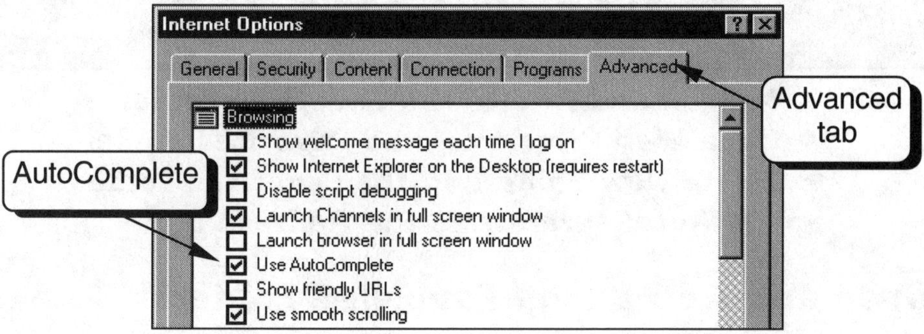

Microsoft Internet Explorer: 9

◆ Open and Add to the Favorites Folder
◆ Open Web Sites from the Favorites Folder
◆ Create New Folders in the Favorites Folder
◆ AutoSearch from the Address Bar

Open and Add to the Favorites Folder

- As you spend more time exploring Web sites, you will find sites that you want to visit frequently. You can store shortcuts to these sites in the Favorites folder.

To add a site to the Favorites folder:

1. Go to the desired Web site.
2. Open the Favorites menu or right-click anywhere on the page and select Add To Favorites.

   ✔ *The Add Favorite dialog box appears*

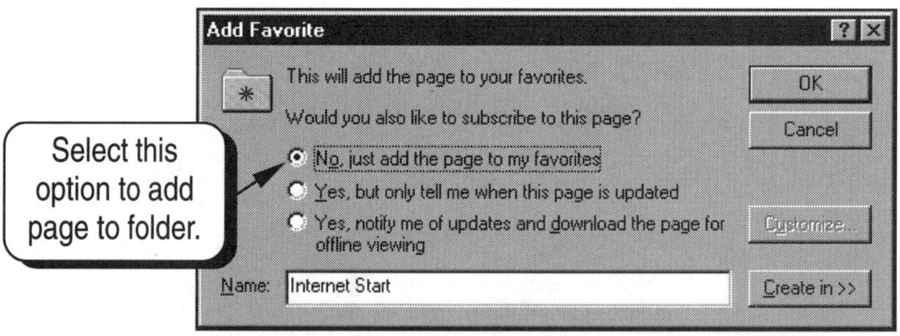

3. The name of the Page you have opened appears in the Name box. You may also choose to subscribe to a page. Subscribing to a page means you can schedule automatic updates to that site. Choose from the following options:
   - No, just add the page to my favorites.

   ✔ *Choose this option to put a shortcut to the Web site in your Favorites folder.*

- Yes, but only tell me when this page is updated.

✔ *Explorer will alert you when an update to the site is available.*

- Yes, notify me of updates and download the page for offline viewing

✔ *Explorer will automatically download and update to your computer.*

4. Click OK to add the Web address to the Favorites folder.

Open Web Sites from the Favorites Folder

- Click the Favorites button Favorites on the Standard toolbar to open Web sites from the Favorites folder. The Explorer bar will open on the left side of the Browser window.

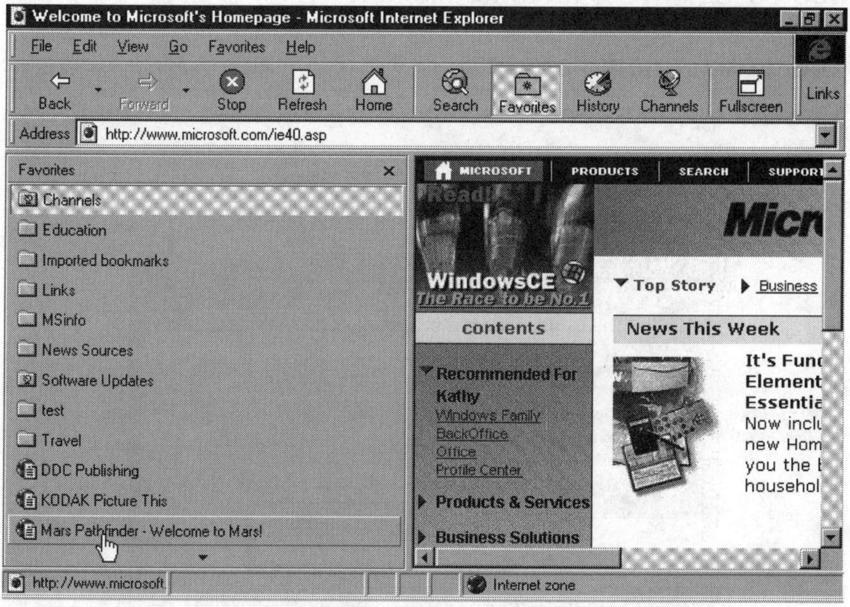

- Click on an address or open a folder and select a site. Close the Explorer bar by clicking the Close button ☒ or the Favorites button Favorites on the toolbar.

- You can also open the Favorites menu and select a site from the list or from a folder.

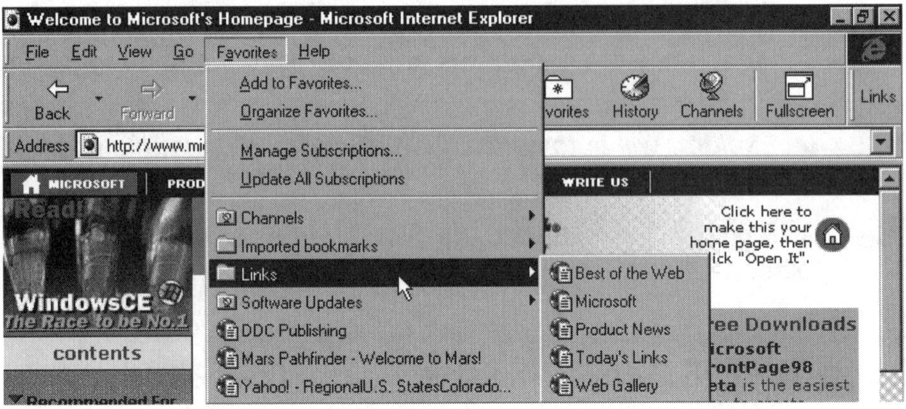

Create New Folders in the Favorites Folder

- You can create new folders before or after you have saved addresses in your Favorites folder.

To create a new folder:

1. Click Favorites and select Organize Favorites.
2. Click the Create New Folder button .
3. Type the name of the new folder and press Enter.

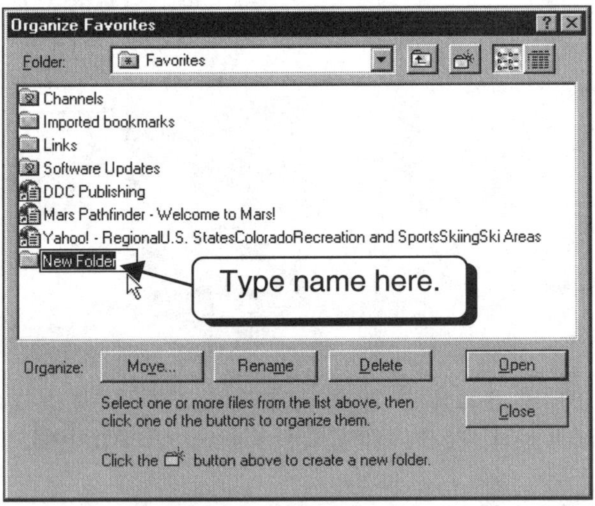

AutoSearch from the Address Bar

- In addition to displaying and entering addresses in the Address bar, you can use AutoSearch to perform a quick search directly from the Address bar.
- Click once in the Address bar and type *go*, *find,* or *?* and press the spacebar once. Enter the word or phrase you want to find and press Enter. For example, if you want to search for information about the year 2000, type *find the year 2000* on the Address bar and press Enter.

Outlook Express: 10

◆ Start Outlook Express
◆ Configure Outlook Express
◆ Outlook Express Main Window
◆ Retrieve New Messages ◆ The Mail Window
◆ Read Messages ◆ Delete a Message
◆ Print a Message ◆ Save a Message

Start Outlook Express

- Click the Mail icon  on the Taskbar.

  OR

  Click Go, Mail.

✔ *Clicking the Mail icon from the Explorer main window may take you to the Microsoft Outlook organizational program. To use the more compact Outlook Express as your default mail program, click View, Internet Options from the Explorer main window. Click the Programs tab and choose Outlook Express from the Mail pull-down menu.*

✔ *If you downloaded Internet Explorer 4, be sure that you downloaded the standard version, which includes Outlook Express in addition to the Web browser.*

Configure Outlook Express

✔ *This section assumes that you have already set up an e-mail account with a service provider.*

- Establishing a modem connection and configuring your computer to send and receive mail can be frustrating. Don't be discouraged. What follows are steps that will get you connected, but some of the information may have to be supplied by your Internet Service Provider.
- Before you can use Outlook Express to send and receive e-mail, you must configure the program with your e-mail account information.

- You may have already filled in this information if you completed the Internet Connection Wizard when you started Internet Explorer for the first time. If not, you can enter the information by running the Internet Connection Wizard again.

Using Internet Connection Wizard

1. Launch Outlook Express.
2. Open the Tools menu, select Accounts.
3. Click the Mail tab.
4. Click Add and select Mail to start the Connection Wizard.

   ✔ *The Internet Connection Wizard will ask for information necessary to set up or add an e-mail account.*

5. Enter the name you want to appear on the "From" line in your outgoing messages. Click Next.

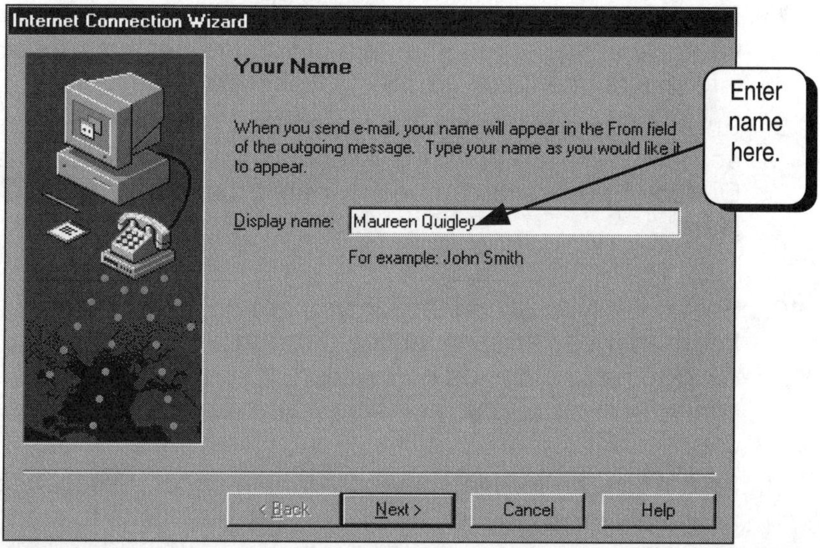

6. Type your e-mail address. This is the address that people use to send mail to you. Click Next.
7. Enter the names of your incoming and outgoing mail servers. Check with your Internet Service Provider if you do not know what they are. Click Next.

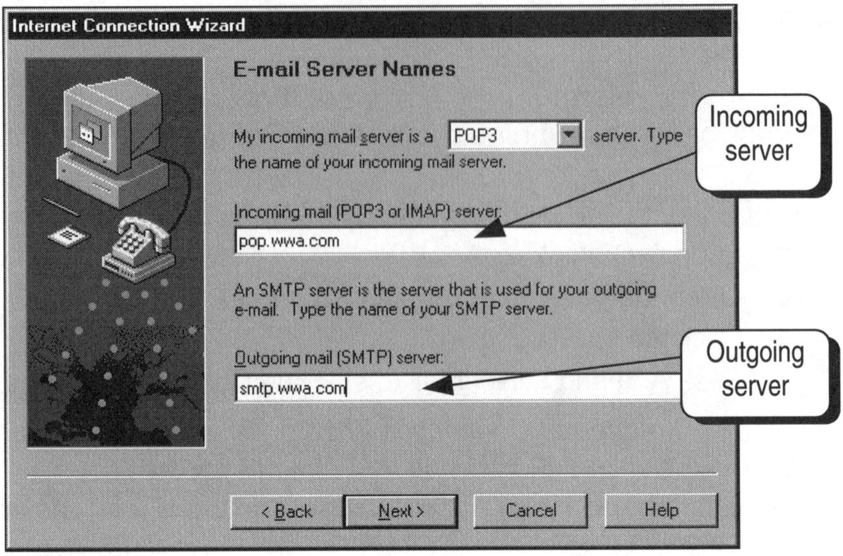

8. Enter the logon name and password that your ISP requires for you to access your mail. Again, if you are not sure about this information, contact your ISP. Click Next.
9. Enter a name for your e-mail account. The name you enter will appear when you open the Accounts list on the Tools menu in Outlook Express. It can be any name that you choose. Click Next.

10. Select the type of connection you are using to reach the Internet. If you are connecting through a phone line, you will need to have a dial-up connection. If you have an existing connection, click Next and select from the list of current connections.
11. Select Use an existing dial-up connection, or select Create a new dial-up connection and follow the directions to create a new one.

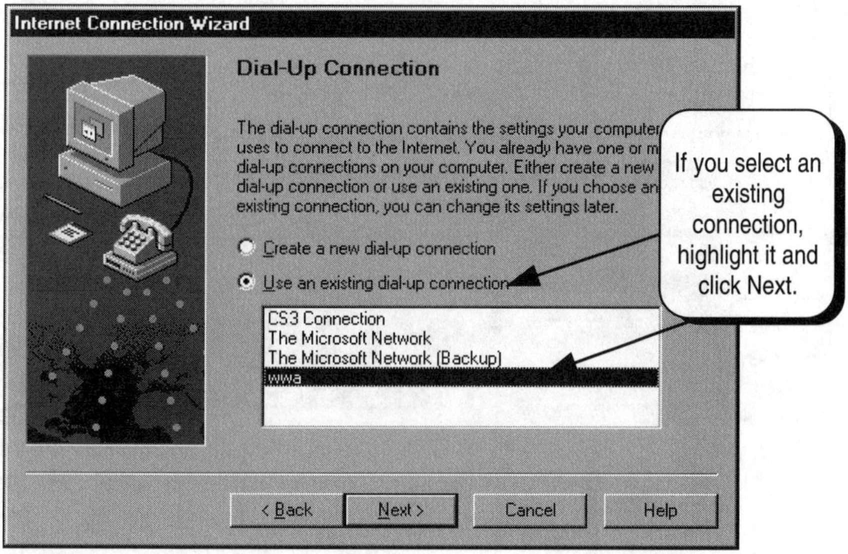

12. If you select Use an existing dial-up connection, click Finish in the last window to save the settings.

    ✔ *You should then be able to launch Outlook Express and send and receive mail and attachments.*

Outlook Express Main Window

- After you launch Outlook Express, the main Outlook Express window opens by default. You can access any e-mail function from this window.

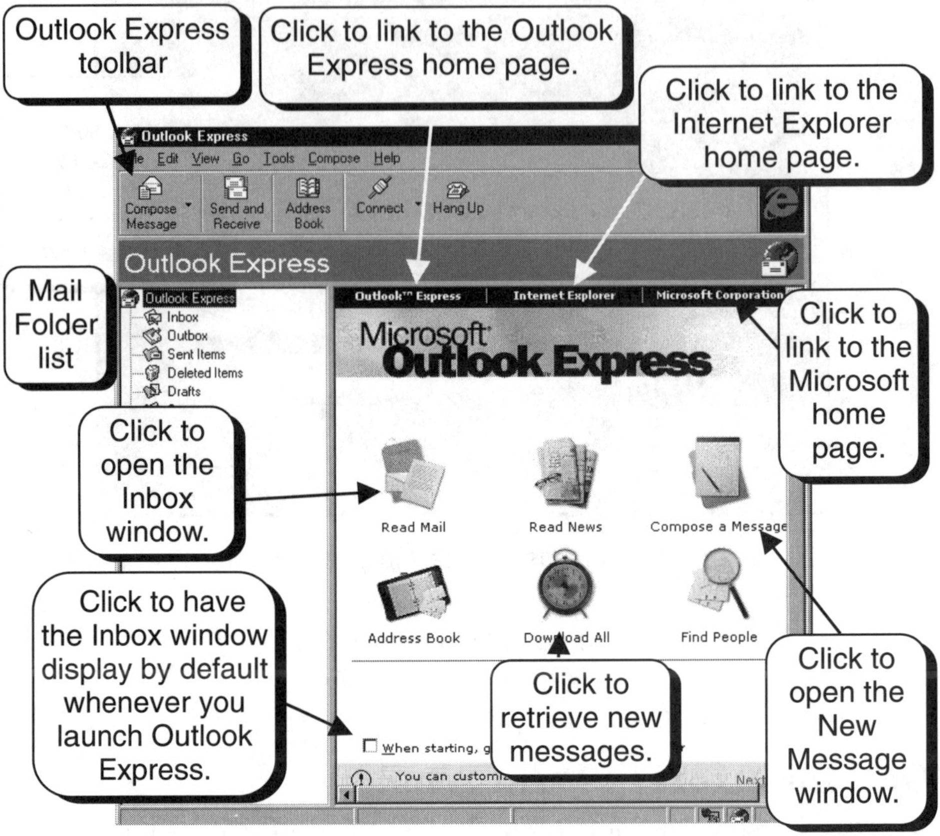

- Descriptions of items in the main window follow below:
  - The Mail Folder list displays in the left column of the window, with the Outlook Express main folder selected. To view the contents of a different folder, click on the desired folder in the folder list.
  - Shortcuts to different e-mail functions are located in the center of the window. Click on a shortcut to access the indicated task or feature.
  - Hyperlinks to Microsoft home pages are located at the top of the window. Click on a link to connect to the indicated home page.

- The Outlook Express toolbar displays buttons for commonly used commands. Note that each button contains an image and text that describes the button function. Clicking any of these buttons will activate the indicated task immediately.

Retrieve New Messages

- You can retrieve new mail from any Outlook Express window.

1. Click the Send and Receive button 

on the toolbar.
2. In the Connection dialog box that displays, enter your ISP user name in the User Name text box and your password in the Password text box. Click OK. (If you do not know your user name or password, contact your ISP.)

✔ *You must re-enter your password each time you reconnect to the Internet unless you set Outlook Express to save your password permanently. To do so, select the Save Password check box in the connection dialog box and click OK.*

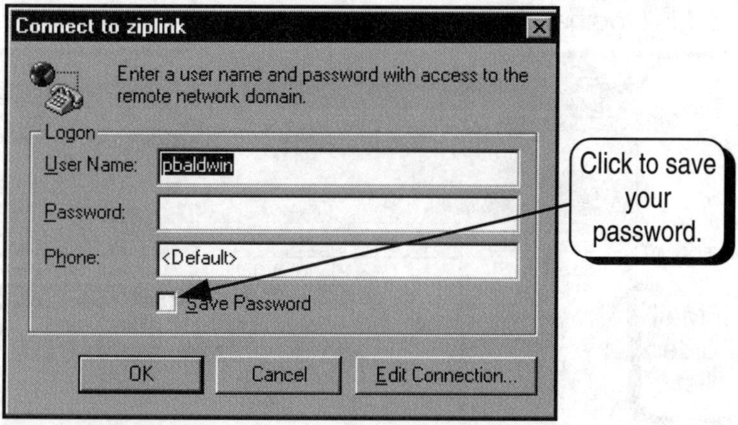

3. Once you are connected to the Internet and Outlook Express is connected to your ISP mail server, new mail messages will begin downloading from your ISP mail server.

✔ *A dialog box displays the status of your retrieval.*

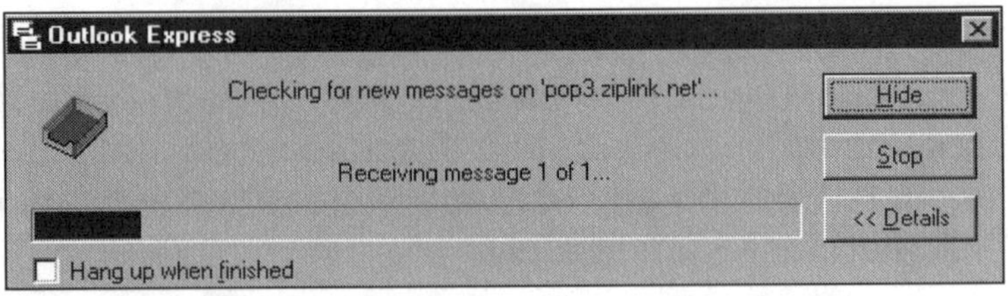

The Mail Window

- After retrieving new messages, Outlook Express stores them in the Inbox folder.
- To view your new messages, you must open the Mail window and display the contents of the Inbox folder.

1. Click the Read Mail shortcut 

in the Outlook Express main window.
2. The Mail window opens with the Inbox folder displayed. A description of the items in the Mail window appears on the following page.

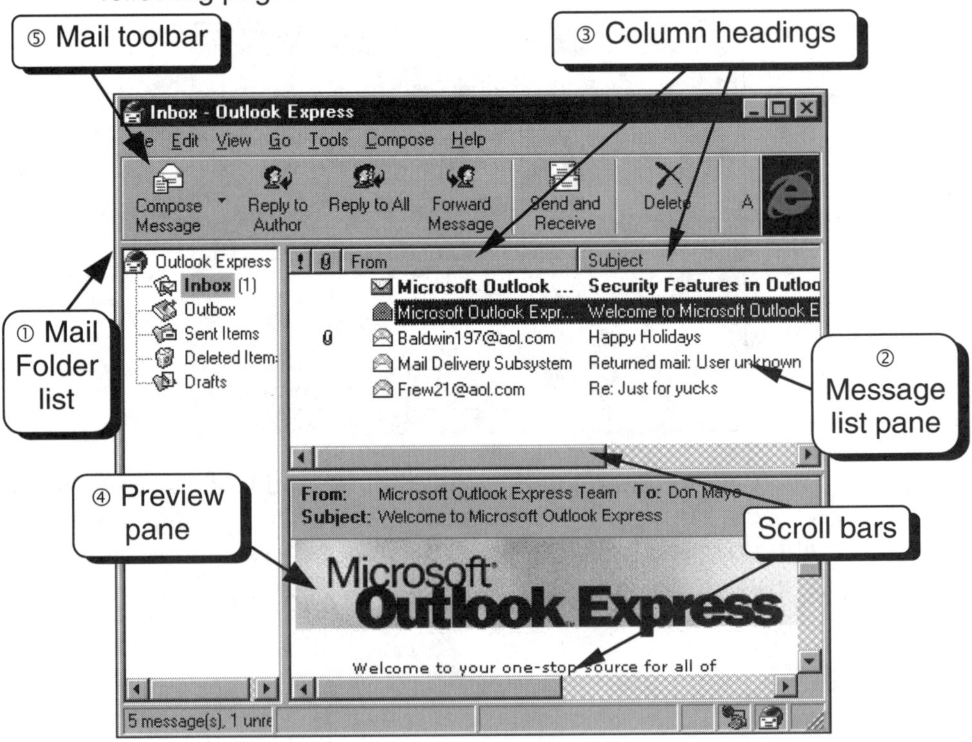

✔ *In the message list, unread messages are displayed in bold text with a sealed envelope icon . Messages that have been read are listed in regular text with an open envelope icon .*

① The Mail Folder list displays the currently selected message folder, the contents of which are displayed in the mail list. Click on another folder to display its contents in the mail list.

② The message list pane displays a header for each of the messages contained in the currently selected mail folder.

③ Column headings list the categories of information included in each message header, such as subject, from, and date received.

④ The preview pane displays the content of the message currently selected from the message list. You can show/hide the preview pane by selecting View, Layout and clicking on the Use preview pane check box.

⑤ The Mail toolbar displays command buttons for working with messages. These commands vary depending on the message folder currently displayed (Inbox, Sent, Outbox, etc.).

Read Messages

✔ *You do not have to be online to read e-mail. You can reduce your online time if you disconnect from your ISP after retrieving your messages and read them offline.*

■ You must have the Mail window open and the mail folder containing the message to read displayed.

To read messages:

- To read a message in the preview pane, click on the desired message header in the message list. If the message does not appear, select View, Layout, Use preview pane.

  OR

To open and read a message in a separate window, double-click on the desired message header in the message list.

✔ *The Message window opens displaying the Message toolbar and the contents of the selected message.*

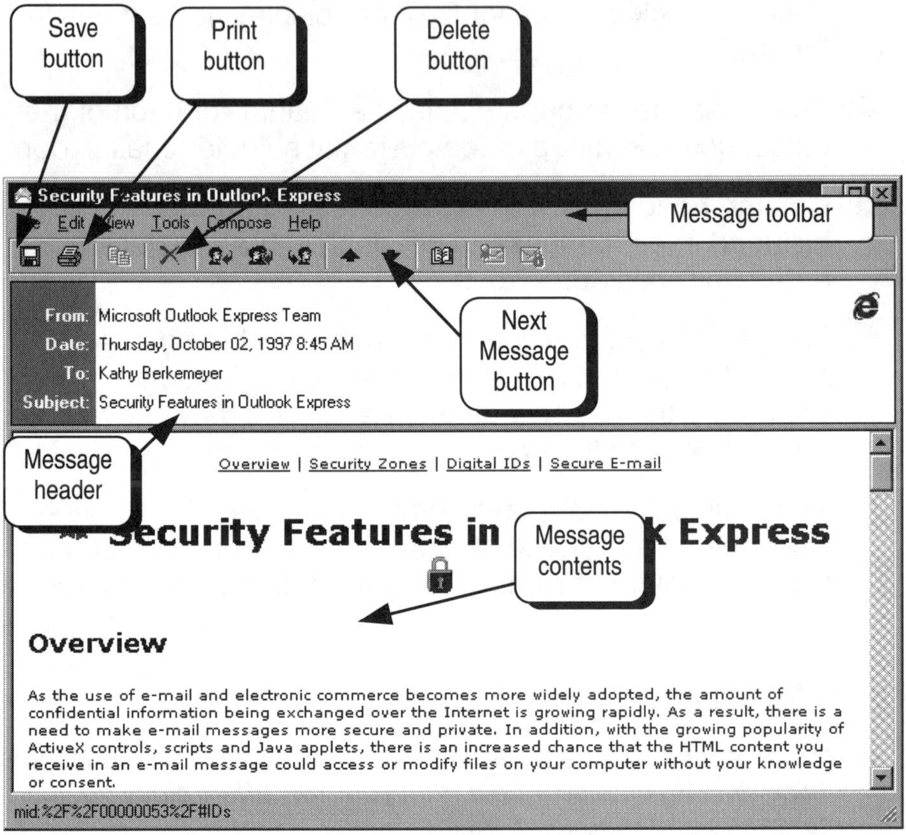

To close the Message window:

- Click File, Close.

  OR

  Click on the Close button (X) in the upper-right corner of the window.

✔ *Use the scroll bars in the Message window or the preview pane to view hidden parts of a displayed message. Or, press the down arrow key to scroll down through the message.*

To read the next unread message:

- Select View, Next, Next Unread Message.

  OR

  If you are viewing a message in the Message window, click the Next button on the Message toolbar.

- Once you have read a message, it remains stored in the Inbox folder until you delete it or file it in another folder.

Delete a Message

1. Select the desired header from the message list in the Mail window.
2. Click the Delete button in the Mail toolbar, or select Edit, Delete.

   OR

1. Open the desired message in the Message window.
2. Click the Delete button on the Message toolbar.

✔ *To select more than one message from the message list to delete, press the Ctrl button while you click each message header.*

Print a Message

1. Select the message you want to print from the message list in the Mail window or open the message in the Message window.
2. Select Print from the File menu.
3. In the Print dialog box that opens, select the desired print options and click OK.

- You can send the message to the printer using the most recently used print settings by opening the message in the Message window and clicking the Print button on the Message toolbar.

Save a Message

1. Open the desired message in the Message window and click the Save button  on the Message toolbar.
2. In the Save Message As dialog box that opens, click the Save in drop-down list box and select the drive and folder in which to store the message file.

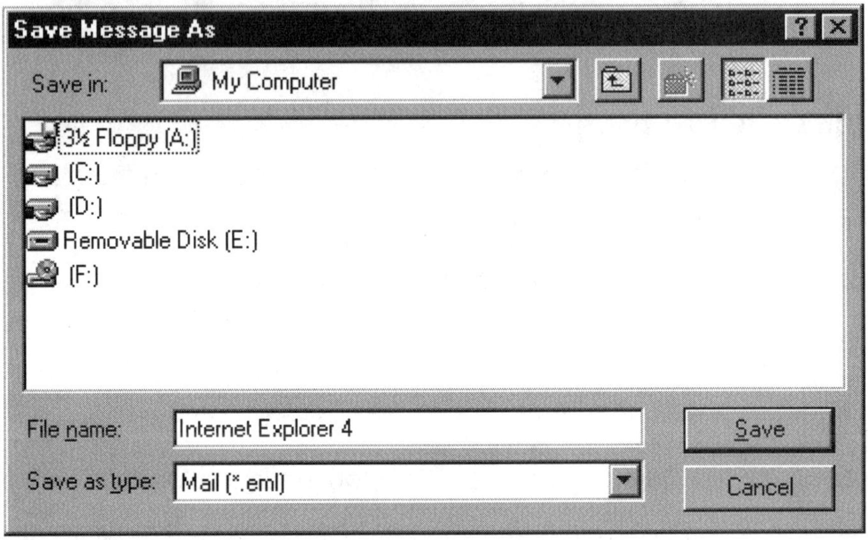

3. Click in the File name box and enter a name for the message.
4. Click Save.

Outlook Express: 11

◆ Compose New Messages ◆ Send Messages
◆ Reply to Mail ◆ Forward Mail
◆ Add Entries to the Personal Address Book
◆ Address a New Message Using the Personal Address Book

Compose New Messages

- You can compose an e-mail message in Outlook Express online or offline. When composing an e-mail message online, you can send the message immediately after creating it.
- When composing a message offline, you will need to store the message in your Outbox folder until you are online and can send it. (See **Send Messages** on page 60.)

To create a message:

1. Open the New Message window.
2. Click the Compose Message button on the toolbar in either the Mail window or the Main window.

   ✔ *The New Message window displays.*
3. In the New Message window, type the e-mail address(es) of the message recipient(s) in the To field.

   ✔ *If you type the first few characters of a name or e-mail address that is saved in your Address Book, Outlook Express will automatically complete it for you.*

   OR

   Click the Index Card icon in the To field or the Address Book button on the New Message toolbar and select an address to insert from your personal Address Book. (See page 64 for information on using the Address Book.)

   ✔ *If you are sending the message to multiple recipients, insert a comma or semicolon between each recipient's address.*

4. After inserting the address(es) in the To field, you may click in either of the following fields and enter the recipient information indicated:

CC (Carbon Copy)	The e-mail addresses of people who will receive copies of the message.
BCC (Blind Carbon Copy)	Same as CC, except these names will not appear anywhere in the message, so other recipients will not know that the person(s) listed in the BCC field received a copy.

5. Click in the Subject field and type the subject of the message. An entry in this field is required.
6. Type your message in the blank composition area below the Subject field.

   ✔ *You can check the spelling of your message by selecting Spelling from the Tools menu and responding to the prompts that follow.*

Send Messages

- Once you have created a message, you have three choices:
  - to send the message immediately
  - to store the message in the Outbox folder to be sent later
  - to save the message in the Drafts folder to be edited and sent later

To send a message immediately:

✔ *In order to send messages immediately, you must first select Options from the Tools menu in the Mail window. Then click on the Send tab and select the Send messages immediately check box. If this option is not selected, clicking the Send button will not send a message immediately, but will send the message to your Outbox until you perform the Send and Receive task.*

1. Click the Send button  on the New Message toolbar.

   OR

   Click File, Send Message.

2. Outlook Express then connects to your ISP's mail server and sends out the new message. If the connection to the mail server is successful, the sending mail icon displays in the lower-right corner of the status bar until the transmittal is complete.

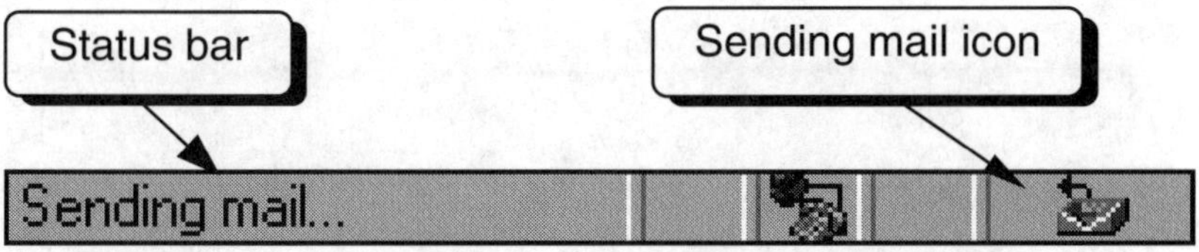

- Sometimes, however, Outlook Express cannot immediately connect to the mail server and instead has to store the new message in the Outbox for later delivery. When this happens, the sending mail icon does not appear, and the number next to your Outbox folder increases by one 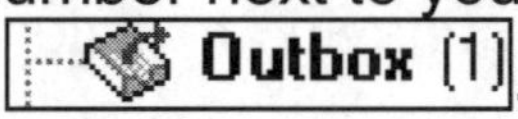.
- Outlook Express does not automatically reattempt to send a message after a failed connection. Instead, you need to send the message manually from the Outbox (see **To send messages from your Outbox folder** below).

To store a message in your Outbox folder for later delivery:

1. Select File, Send Later in the New Message window.

   ✔ *The Send Mail prompt displays, telling you that the message will be stored in our Outbox folder.*

2. Click .

   ✔ *The message is saved in the Outbox.*

To send messages from your Outbox folder:

- Click on the Send and Receive button  on the toolbar.

  OR

  Click Tools, Send and Receive, All Accounts.

✔ *When you use the Send and Receive command, Outlook Express sends out all messages stored in the Outbox and automatically downloads any new mail messages from the mail server.*

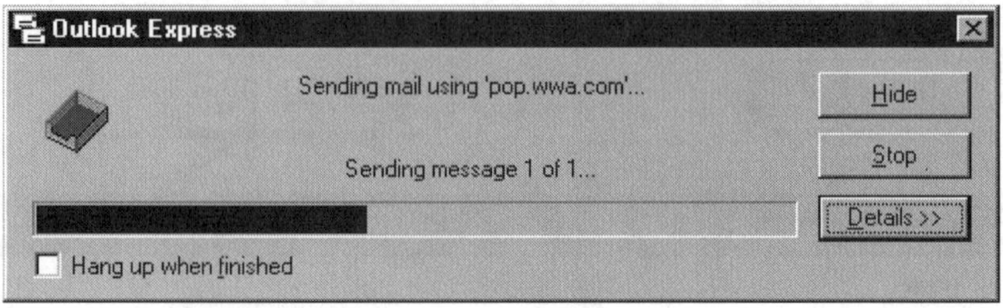

Reply to Mail

- In Outlook Express, you can reply to a message automatically, without having to enter the recipient's name or e-mail address.
- When replying, you have a choice of replying to the author and all recipients of the original message or to the author only.

To reply to the author and all recipients:

1. Select the message you want to reply to from the message list in the Mail window.
2. Click the Reply to All button  on the Mail toolbar.

To reply to the author only:

- Click the Reply to Author button  on the Mail toolbar.

- Once you have selected a reply command, the New Message window opens with the address fields and the Subject filled in for you.

✔ *You can access all of the mail send commands by right-clicking on the message in the Message list.*

- The original message is automatically included in the body of your response. To turn off this default insertion, select Options from the Tools menu, click on the Send tab, deselect the Include message in reply check box, and click OK.
- To compose your reply, click in the composition area and type your text as you would in a new message.
- When you are done, click the Send button  on the New Message toolbar to send the message immediately. Or, select Send Later from the File menu to store the message in the Outbox folder for later delivery. To save the reply as a draft to be edited and sent later, select Save from the File menu.

Forward Mail

- There are times when you will want to forward mail that you have received.
  1. Select the message to forward from the message list in the Mail window.
  2. Click the Forward Message button  on the Mail toolbar.

     ✔ *The New Message window opens with the original message displayed and the Subject field filled in for you.*

3. Fill in the e-mail address information by either typing each address or selecting the recipients from your Address Book. (See **Address a New Message Using the Personal Address Book** on page 66.)

   ✔ *If you are forwarding the message to multiple recipients, insert a comma or semicolon between each recipient's address.*

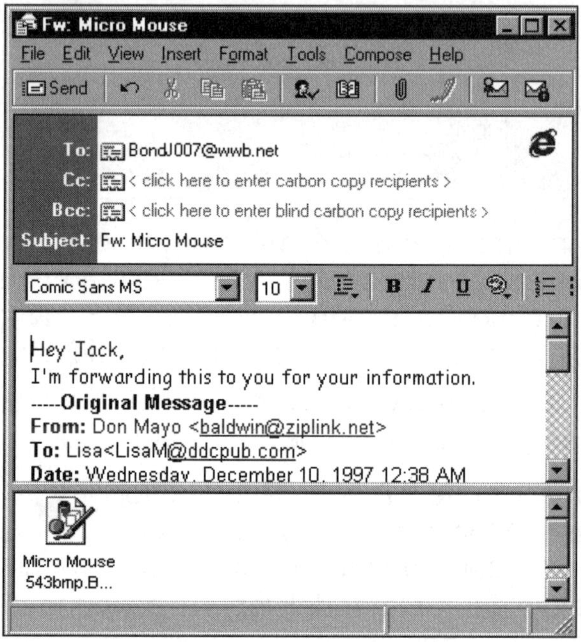

4. Click in the composition area and type any text you wish to send with the forwarded message.

5. When you are done, click the Send button [Send] on the New Message toolbar to send the message immediately.

   OR

   Select Send Later from the File menu to store the message in the Outbox folder for later delivery.

Add Entries to the Personal Address Book

- In Outlook Express, you can use the Windows Address Book to store e-mail addresses. You can then use the Address Book to find and automatically insert addresses when creating new messages.

To add an entry to the Address Book:

1. Click the Address Book button  on the toolbar in the Mail window or the Main window.

   ✔ *The Address Book window opens.*

2. Click the New Contact button  on the Address Book toolbar.

   ✔ *The Contact Properties dialog box displays.*

3. In the Properties dialog box, type the First, Middle, and Last names of the new contact in the appropriate text boxes.
4. Type the contact's e-mail address in the Add new text box and then click the Add button.

   ✔ *You can repeat this procedure if you wish to list additional e-mail addresses for the contact.*

5. In the Nickname text box, you can enter a unique nickname for the contact.

   ✔ *When addressing a new message, you can type the nickname in the To field, rather than typing the entire address, and Outlook Express will automatically complete the address.*

To add an Address Book entry from an e-mail message:

- You can automatically add the name and address of the sender of a message.

  1. Open the message in the Message window.
  2. Right-click on the sender's name in the To field.
  3. Select Add to Address Book from the shortcut menu.

- You can also set Outlook Express to add the address of recipients automatically when you reply to a message.

  - Select Options from the Tools menu and select the Automatically put people I reply to in my Address Book check box on the General tab.

✔ *You can edit an Address Book entry at any time by double-clicking on the person's name in the contact list in the Address Book window.*

Address a New Message Using the Personal Address Book

1. Click the Select Recipients button on the New Message toolbar.
2. In the Select Recipients dialog box that follows, select the address to insert from the contact list.

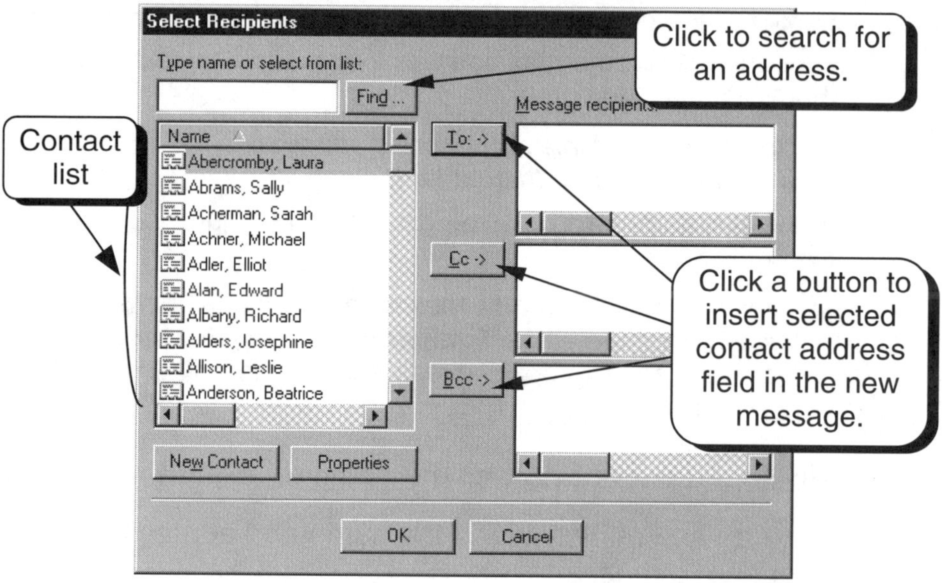

3. Click the button for the field in which you want to insert the address (To, Cc, or Bcc).
4. Click OK to return to the New Message window when you are finished.

Outlook Express: 12

◆ View Attached Files ◆ Save Attached Files
◆ Attach Files to a Message

View Attached Files

- Sometimes e-mail messages come with separate files attached. Messages containing attachments show a paperclip icon to the left of the message header.
- If the selected message is displayed in the preview pane, a larger paper clip attachment icon will appear to the right of the header at the top of the preview pane.

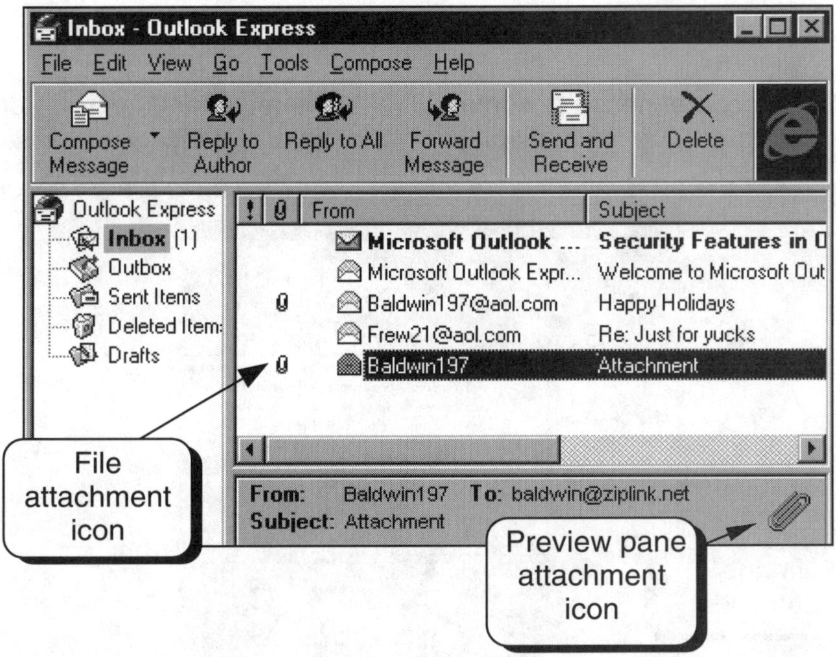

- If you open the selected message in its own window, an attachment icon will appear in a separate pane below the message.

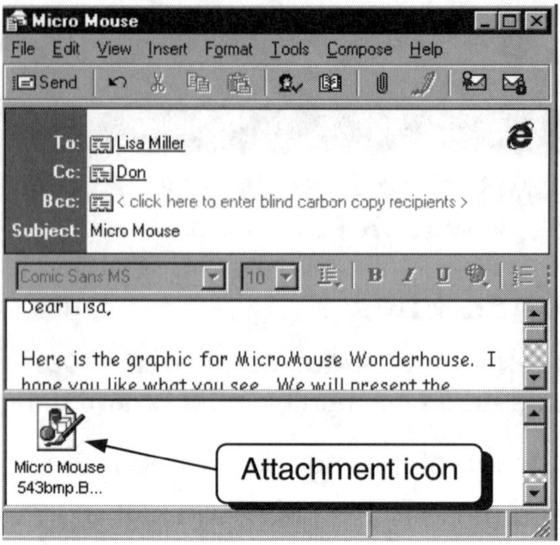

To view an attachment:

1. Open the folder containing the desired message in the Mail window.
2. Select the message containing the desired attachment(s) from the message list to display it in the preview pane.

✔ *If the attachment is an image, it will display in the message.*

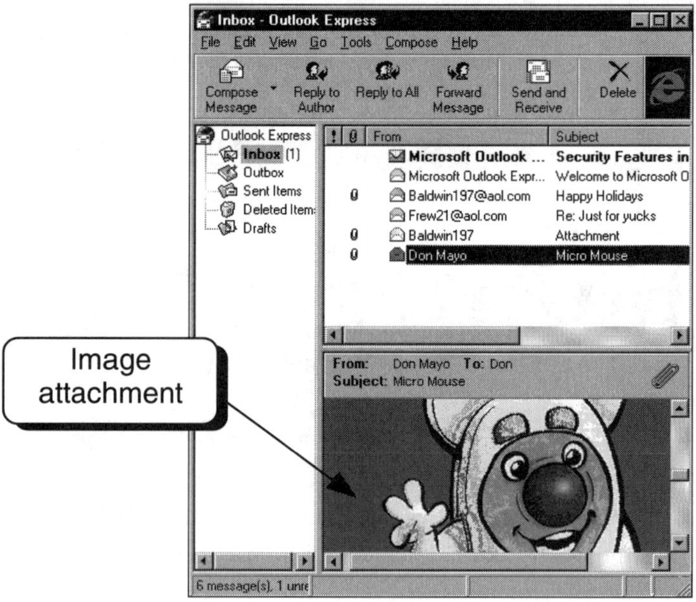

✔ *If the image does not display, click Tools, Options, click the Read tab, select the Automatically show picture attachments in messages check box, and click OK.*

- Other types of attachments, such as programs, word processor documents, or media clips, do not display in the message, but have to be opened in a separate window.

To open an attachment in a separate window:

1. Click on the attachment icon  in the preview pane. A button will display with the file name and size of the attachment.

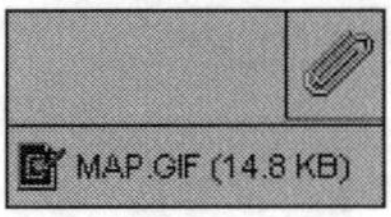

2. Click on this button.
3. If the Open Attachment Warning dialog box displays, select the desired option and click 
.

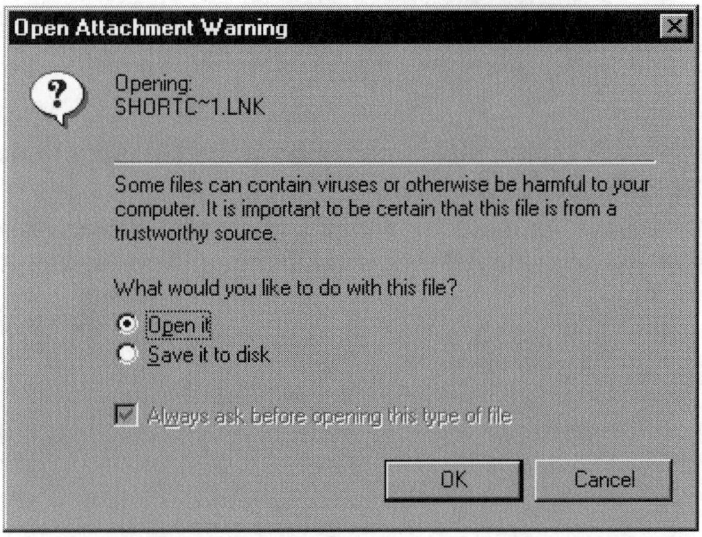

✔ *If you are not sure of the source of the attachment, you may want to save the attachment to a disk and run it through an anti-virus program.*

- Outlook Express will open the attached file or play the attached media clip.
- If the attached file does not open, Outlook Express does not recognize the file type of the attached file. Your computer may not contain the necessary plug-in or application to view it.
- To view an unrecognized attachment, you have to install and/or open the application or plug-in needed to view it.

Save Attached Files

- If desired, you can save an attached file to your hard drive or disk for future use or reference.

To save an attachment:

1. Select Save Attachments from the File menu, and select the attachment to save from the submenu that displays.

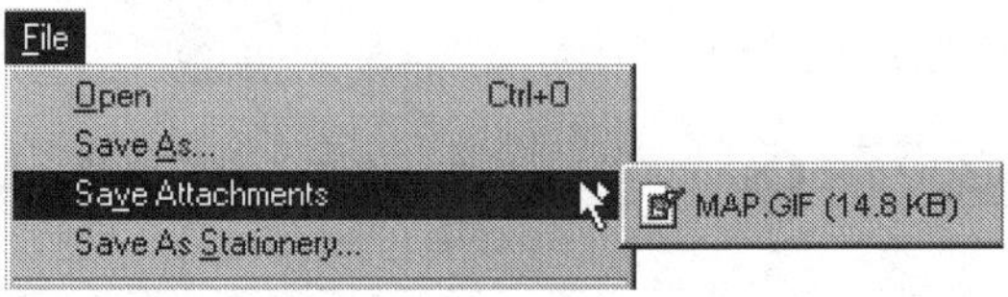

   OR

   Right-click on the attachment icon in the Message window and select the Save As option.

2. In the Save As dialog box that follows, click the Save in drop-down list box and select the drive and folder in which to save the file.

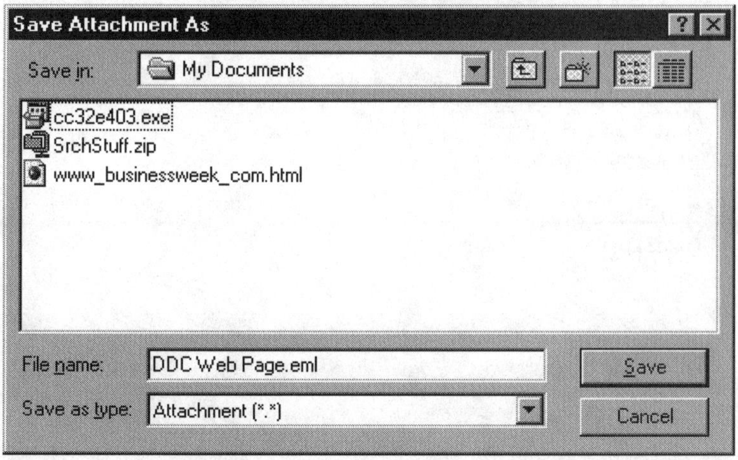

3. Click in the File name text box and type a name for the file.
4. Click Save.

Attach Files to a Message

- You can attach a file to an e-mail message.

  ✔ *When attaching very large files or multiple files, you may want to zip (compress) the files before attaching them. To do so, both you and the recipient need a file compression program, such as WinZip or PKZip.*

To add an attachment:

1. Click the Insert File button  on the New Message toolbar.

   OR

   Click Insert, File Attachment.
2. In the Insert Attachment dialog box that appears, click the Look in drop-down list box and select the drive and folder containing the file to attach. Then select the file and click Attach.

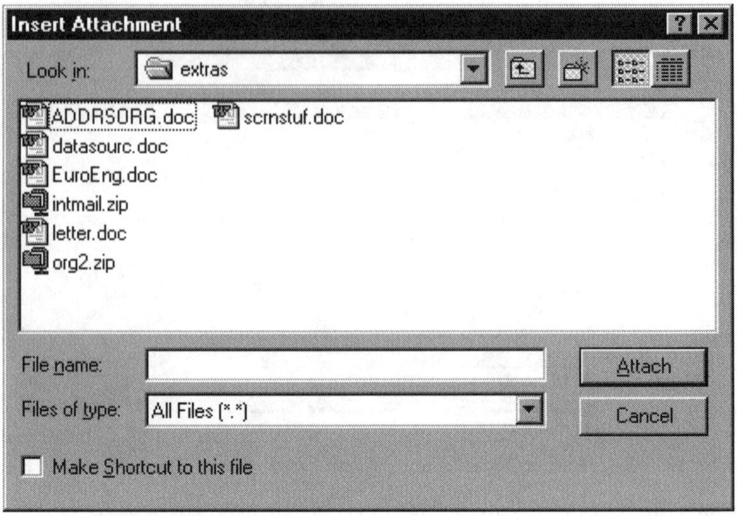

✔ *The attachment will appear as an icon in the body of the message.*

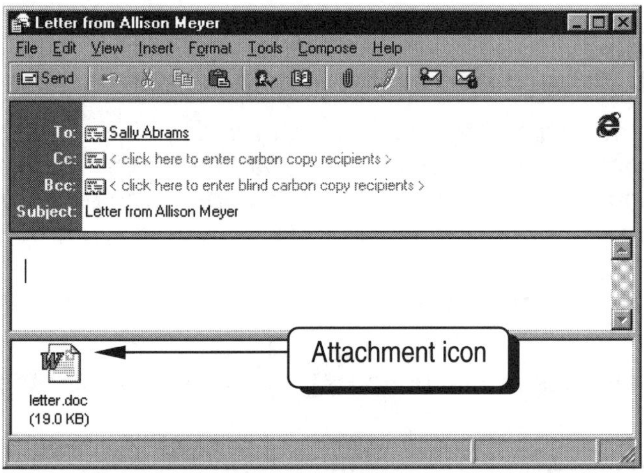

✔ *You can add multiple attachments by repeating the procedure as many times as you like.*

✔ *Before you send a message containing an attachment, you should make sure the recipient's e-mail program can read the attachment.*

America Online: 13

◆ About America Online ◆ Start America Online 4.0
◆ The AOL Home Page, Menu, and Toolbar
◆ AOL Help ◆ Exit AOL

About America Online

- America Online (AOL) is an all-purpose online service. Unlike Netscape Navigator or Microsoft Internet Explorer, AOL is not an Internet browser, yet you can browse the Internet using AOL navigation features.
- Unlike Internet browsers, AOL does not require a separate Internet Service Provider for Internet access, nor does it require a separate mail server connection to access e-mail from the AOL Mail Center.

Start America Online 4.0

1. Click the AOL icon on your desktop. This icon should display on your desktop after you install AOL.

   OR

   Click the Start button, Programs, America Online, America Online 4.0.
2. Make sure your screen name is displayed in the Select Screen Name box and type your password in the Enter Password box.
3. Click the Sign On button SIGN ON to connect to the AOL server.

The AOL Home Page, Menu, and Toolbar

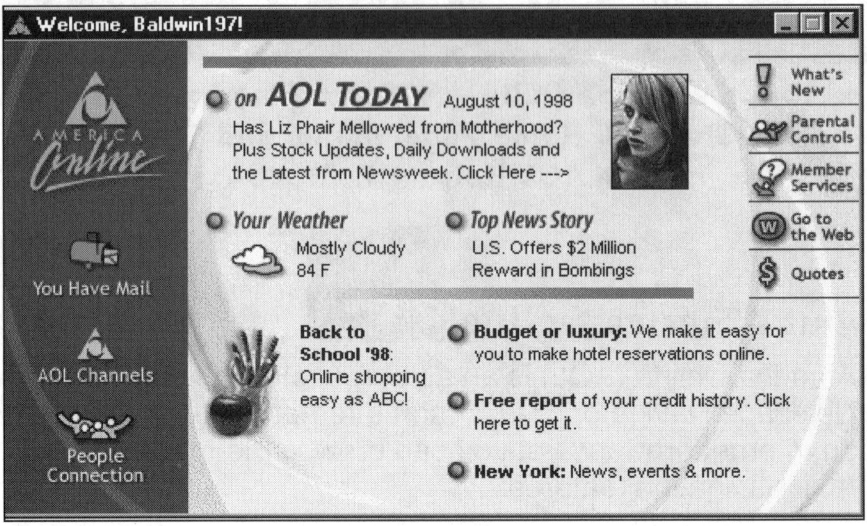

- After you log on to America Online, you will see a series of screens. The final first screen you see is the AOL home page or start page. The AOL home page contains links to daily AOL featured areas and constant AOL areas such as *Channels* and *What's New*. You can also access your mailbox from the home page.

- The AOL menu displays currently available options. Click the menu item to display a drop-down list of links to AOL areas and basic filing, editing, and display options.

- The AOL toolbar contains buttons for AOL's most commonly used commands. Choosing a button activates the indicated task immediately.

	You have new mail if the flag on the mailbox is in the up position. Click to display your mailbox.
	Click to compose new mail messages.
	Click to read new, old, or sent mail; to set mail preferences; and to activate Flashsessions.
	Click to open the Print dialog box, where you can select from the standard print options.
	Click to access the Personal Filing Cabinet, where you can store e-mail messages, Newsgroup messages, and other files.
	Click to set AOL preferences, check personalized stock portfolios, read news and current events, set parental controls, passwords, and Buddy lists.
	Click this button to create links or shortcuts to your favorite Web sites or AOL areas.
	Click to connect to the Web, Internet directories, and Newsgroups.
	Click to access AOL's 21 channels, AOL areas, and Web site connections.
	Click to access the AOL Community Center, Chat Rooms, and meet the stars in the Live chat forum.
	Click to move to keywords or information entered on the URL line.
	Each AOL area has a keyword. Enter the keyword for immediate access to the desired AOL area.

AOL Help

- AOL offers extensive Help so that you can learn to use AOL effectively.
- To access Help, click Help and the help topic of choice from the menu.

Exit AOL

- To exit AOL, click the close window button in the upper-right corner of the AOL screen.

  OR

  Click Sign Off, Sign Off on the menu bar.

  OR

  Click File, Exit.

America Online: 14

◆ Access the Internet from AOL
◆ Open a Wold Wide Web Site
◆ The AOL Browser Screen ◆ Stop a Load or Search

Access the Internet from AOL

- Click the Internet button 

on the AOL main screen.

  OR

  Press Ctrl+K, type the word *internet* in the Keyword box and press Enter.

  ✔ *The Internet Connection window displays.*

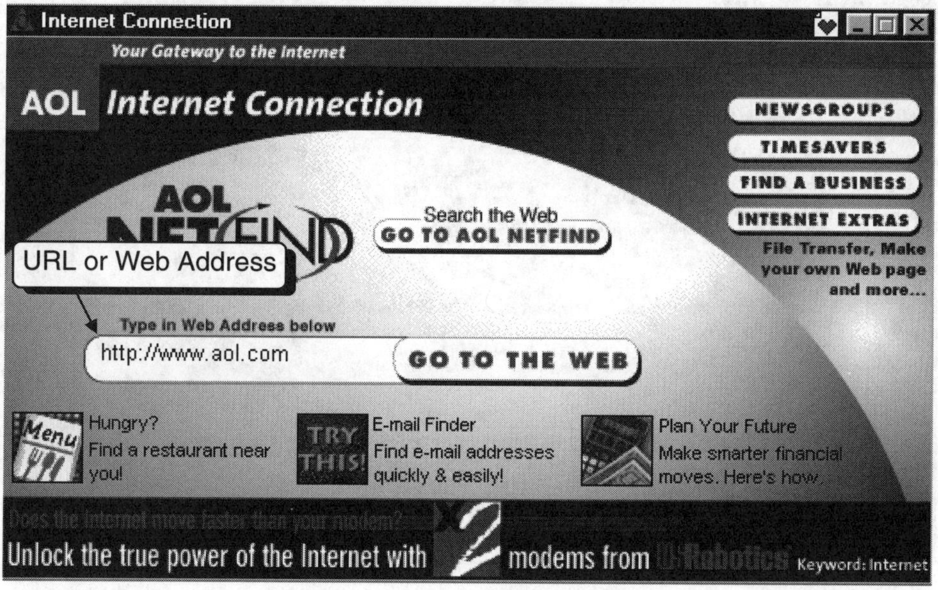

Open a World Wide Web Site

- If you know the Web address (URL), type it into the Type in Web Address below box and click the GO TO THE WEB button GO TO THE WEB or press Enter. If the Web address is correct, you will be connected to the Web site.
- If you wish to search the Internet, click the GO TO AOL NETFIND button Search the Web GO TO AOL NETFIND.

The AOL Browser Screen

- Once you are connected to the Web, the screen below displays.

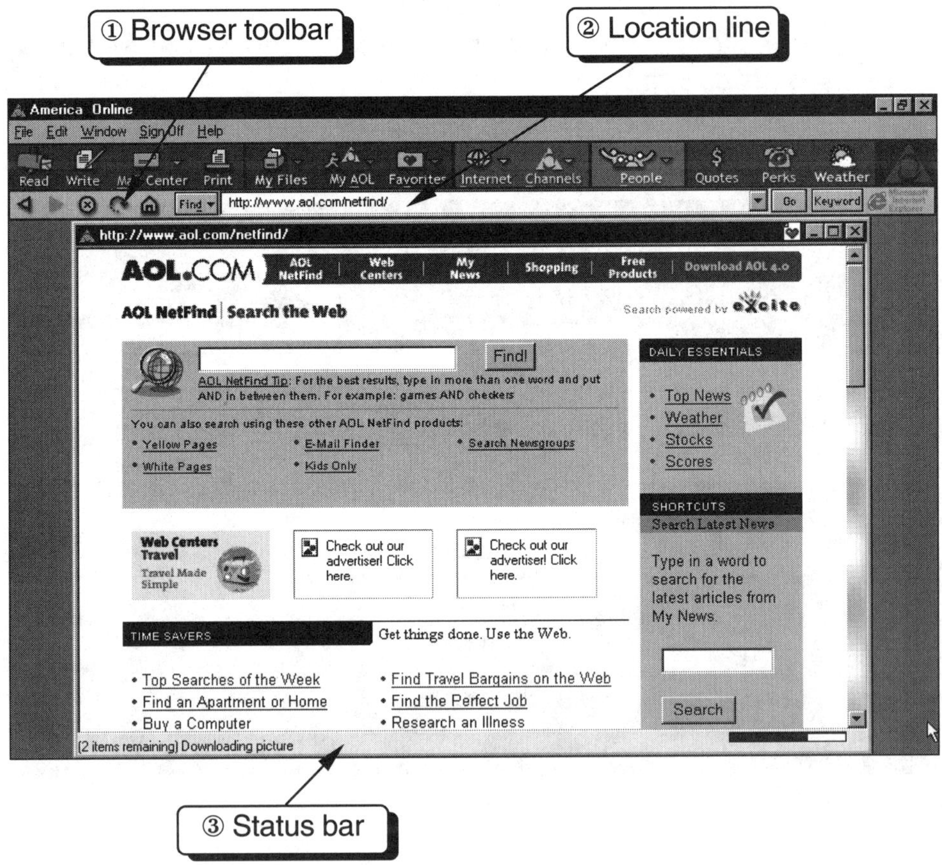

① Browser toolbar

- The AOL Browser toolbar will help you navigate through sites you visit on the Web. Buttons on the Browser toolbar also connect you to search and Internet preference areas.

	Moves back through pages previously displayed.
	Moves forwards through pages previously displayed.
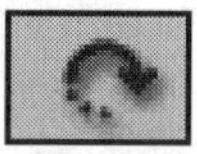	Reloads an image that has been downloaded or restarts a load that has been interrupted. Since the image is stored in the computer's memory, it reloads much faster.
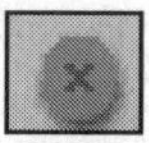	Stops the loading of a Web page.
	Returns to your home page.
	Go here to search the AOL directory using keywords or phrases, to search the Internet, or to find AOL access numbers.

② Location line

- AOL stores each Web address you visit during each AOL session. If you wish to return to an address you have visited during the current session, you can click the location box arrow and click the address from the drop-down list.

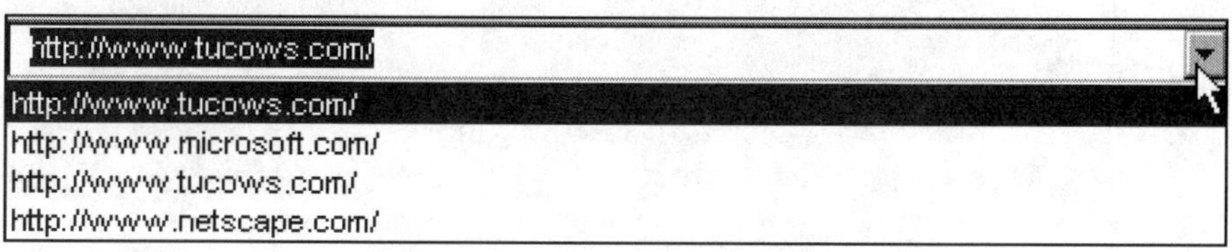

③ Status bar

- The Status bar, located at the bottom of the screen, is a helpful indicator of the progress of the loading of a Web page. For example, if you are loading a Web site, you will see the byte size of the page, the percentage of the task completed, and the number of graphics and links yet to load. In many cases the time it will take to load the page will display.

Stop a Load or Search

- Searching for information or loading a Web page can be time consuming, especially if the Web page has many graphic images, if a large number of people are trying to access the site at the same time, or if your modem and computer operate at slower speeds. If data is taking a long time to load, you may wish to stop a search or the loading of a page or large file.

  - To stop a search or load click the Stop button  on the Navigation toolbar.
  - If you decide to continue the load after clicking the Stop button , click the Reload button .

America Online: 15

◆ Favorite Places ◆ Add Favorite Places
◆ View Favorite Places ◆ Delete Favorite Places
◆ AOL History List ◆ Save Web Pages
◆ Print Web Pages

Favorite Places

- A Favorite Place listing is a bookmark that you create containing the title, URL, and direct link to a Web page or AOL area that you may want to revisit.
- The AOL Favorite Place feature allows you to maintain a record of Web sites in your Favorite Places file so that you can return to them easily.

Add Favorite Places

- There are several ways to mark an AOL area or Web site and save it as a Favorite Place. Once the page is displayed:

  1. Click the Favorite Place icon  on the Web site or AOL area title bar.

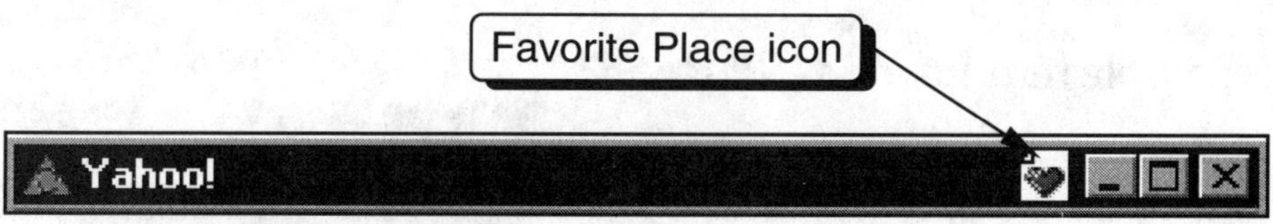

  2. Click on one of three options that display:

✔ *The site will automatically be added to your Favorite Places list.*

OR

✔ *The site will automatically generate an Instant Message screen with a link to the site inserted.*

OR

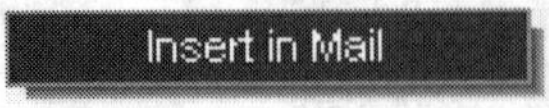

✔ *The site will automatically generate an e-mail composition screen with a link to the site inserted. Complete this as you would any e-mail message.*

OR

Display the Web page to add, right-click anywhere on the page and select Add to Favorites from the shortcut menu.

View Favorite Places

- You can view the Favorite Places file by clicking the Favorites button  on the AOL toolbar and selecting Favorite Places. Click on any listing from the list to go directly to that page.
- The details of any Favorite Place listing can be viewed or modified by using the buttons on the Favorite Places screen.

Delete Favorite Places

- You may wish to delete a Favorite Place if a Web site no longer exists or an AOL area no longer interests you.

To delete a Favorite Place:

1. Click the Favorite Places button  on the toolbar.
2. Click Favorite Places.
3. Click on the listing to delete.
4. Click the Delete button  from the Favorite Places screen.

   OR

   Right-click on the listing and select Delete from the pop-up menu.

   OR

   Press the Delete key.

5. Click Yes to confirm the deletion.

AOL History List

- While you move back and forth within a Web site, AOL automatically records each page location. The History is only temporary and is deleted when you sign off. AOL areas are not recorded in the History list.
- To view the History list, click on the arrow at the end of the URL line. You can use History to jump back or forward to recently viewed pages by clicking on the page from the list.

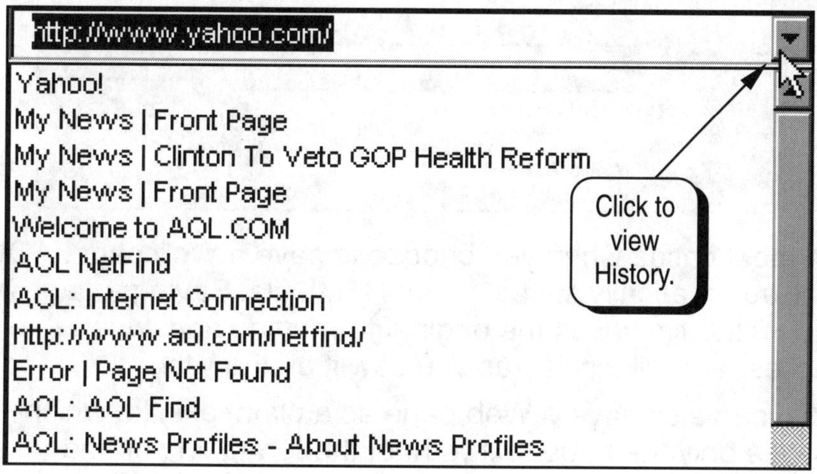

Save Web Pages

- When you find a Web page with information that you would like to keep for future reference or to review later offline, you can save it.

To save a Web page:

1. Click File, Save.
2. Type a filename in the File name box.

   ✔ *When you save a Web page, often the current page name appears in the File name box. You can use this name or type a new one.*

3. Choose the drive and folder in which to store the file from the Save in drop-down list.
4. Click Save.

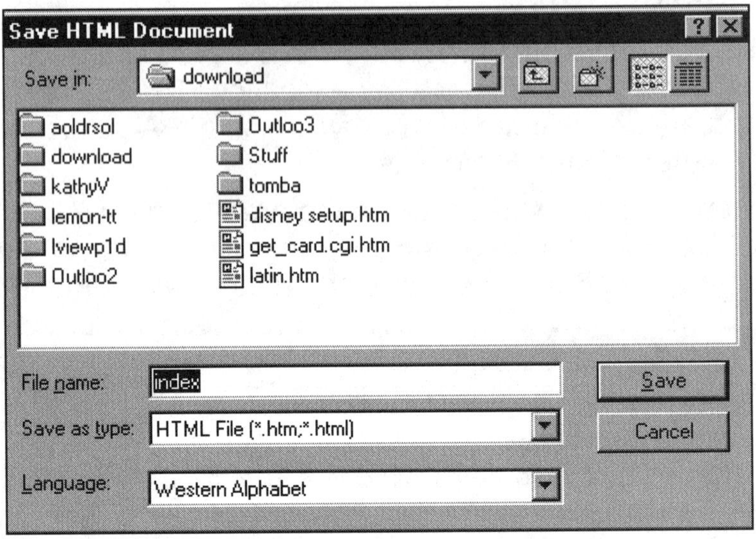

- In most cases when you choose to save a Web page, AOL will automatically save it as an HTML file. Saving a page as an HTML file saves the original formatting and, when accessed, will display as you saw it on the Web.
- You can also save a Web page as a plain text file, which saves only the page text without the formatting or images and placeholders. You might want to do this when saving a very large file, such as a literary work or multiple-page article. To save in plain text format, click the Save as type down arrow in the Save As dialog box and select plain text from the list.
- You can view a saved Web page by clicking File, Open. In the Open a file dialog box, choose the location from the Look in drop-down list and double-click the file name.

Print Web Pages

- One of the many uses of the Internet is to find and print information.

To print a Web page, display it and do the following:

1. Click the Print button 

on the AOL toolbar.

   OR

   Click Print on the File menu.
2. In the Print dialog box that displays, select the desired print options and click OK.

- In most cases, the Web page will be printed in the format shown in the Web page display.

America Online E-mail: 16

◆ Read New Mail ◆ Compose a New Mail Message
◆ Send Messages ◆ Reply to Mail
◆ Forward Mail ◆ AOL Mail Help

Read New Mail

- There are several ways to know whether you have new mail in your mailbox. If your computer has a sound card and speakers, you will hear "You've Got Mail" when you successfully connect to AOL. The 

link is replaced by the You Have Mail link, and the mailbox button on the main screen has the flag in the up position 

.

To display and read new and unread mail:

1. Click the You Have Mail button 

on the AOL main screen.

   OR

   Click the Read button 

on the main screen toolbar.

   OR

   Press Ctrl+R.

   ✔ *The New Mail list displays new and unread mail for the screen name used for this session. If you have more than one screen name, you must sign on under each name to retrieve new mail. Click Sign Off, Switch Screen Names to switch names without logging off AOL.*

   ✔ *New and Unread e-mail messages remain on the AOL mail server for approximately 27 days before being deleted by AOL. If you want to save a message to your hard disk, click File, Save As and choose a location for the message. By default the message will be saved to the Download folder.*

✔ *You can set up AOL to save read messages up to seven days by clicking the My AOL button from the toolbar. Click Preferences, and then click the Mail button . Set the number of desired days in the Keep My Old Mail Online option box.*

2. To read a message, double-click on it from the New Mail list.

Compose a New Mail Message

1. Click Mail Center, Write Mail.

   OR

   Click the Write button  on the main screen toolbar.

   OR

   Press Ctrl+M.

   ✔ *The Compose Mail screen displays.*

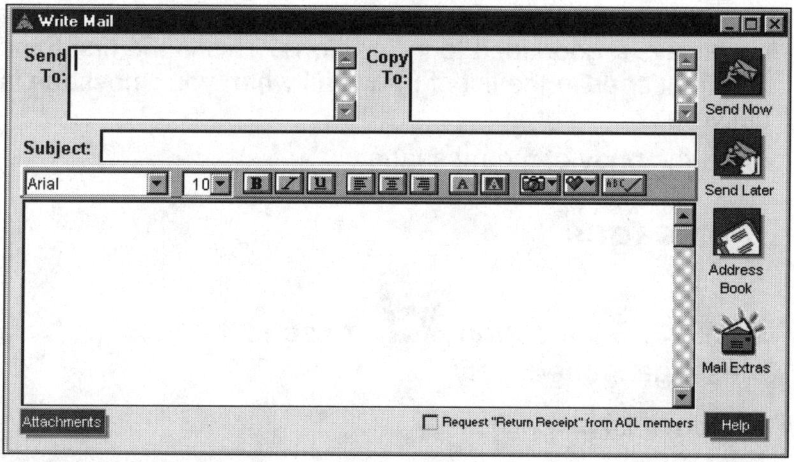

2. Fill in the e-mail address(es) in the Send To box of the Compose Mail screen.

   OR

   Click the Address Book button  on the right side of the Write Mail screen and double-click on an entry from your Address Book to insert an address automatically in the address field. (See page 91 for more information on your Address Book.)

- ♦ If you are sending the same message to multiple recipients, fill in the Copy To (Carbon Copy) box with the e-mail addresses of recipients who will receive a copy of this message. These names will display to all recipients of the message.

✔ *Multiple addresses must be separated with a comma.*

- ♦ If you want to send a Blind Copy—copies of a message sent to others but whose names are not visible to the main or other recipients, enclose the address in parenthesis, for example: (joes@ddcpub.com) or click the Blind Copy button 

when inserting addresses from the Address Book.

✔ *You can enclose multiple Blind Copy addresses in one set of parentheses, e.g., (joes@ddcpub.com, Zacz).*

3. Fill in the Subject box with a one-line summary of your message. Although AOL will now deliver mail without a heading it's always a good idea to include one. This is the first thing the recipient sees in the list of new mail when your message is delivered.
4. Fill in the body of the message.

Send Messages

- Click the Send button 

to send the message immediately.

✔ *You must be online.*

OR

Click the Send Later button 

to send a message later that you have composed offline.

Reply to Mail

- You can reply to mail messages while online or compose replies to e-mail offline to send later.

To reply to e-mail:

1. Click the Reply button 

from the displayed message screen. If the message has been sent to more than one person, you can send your response to each recipient of the message by clicking the Reply to All button 

. The addresses of the sender and, if desired, all recipients will be automatically inserted into the address fields.

   ✔ *To include part or all of the original message in your Reply, select the contents of the original message to be included in quotation marks in your message. Then click the Reply button to begin your reply.*

   ✔ *You can select mail preferences like the quotation style by clicking My AOL, Preferences, and the Mail icon.*

2. Click the Send button 

if you are online and want to send the reply immediately or click the Send Later button 

.

Forward Mail

- There are times when you may want to send mail you receive to someone else.

To forward e-mail:

1. Click the Forward button 

from the displayed message screen and fill in the address(es) of the recipients of the forwarded message. The Subject heading from the original message is automatically inserted into the subject heading box.

2. Click the Send button 

if you are online and want to send the reply immediately or click the Send Later button 

.

AOL Mail Help

- For answers to many of your basic e-mail questions, click Mail Center, Mail Center, and click on the Help button 

on the Mail Center screen.

America Online E-mail: 17

◆ Add Entries to the Address Book
◆ Enter an Address Using the Address Book
◆ Delete an Address Book Entry

Add Entries to the Address Book

- Once you start sending e-mail, you may be surprised at how many people you begin to communicate with online. An easy way to keep track of e-mail addresses is to enter them into the Address Book. Once an e-mail address entry has been created, you can automatically insert it into the address fields.

To create Address Book entries:

1. Click Mail Center, Address Book.

   ✔ *The Address Book dialog box displays.*

2. Click the New Person button 

from the Address Book screen.

   ✔ *The New Person dialog box displays.*

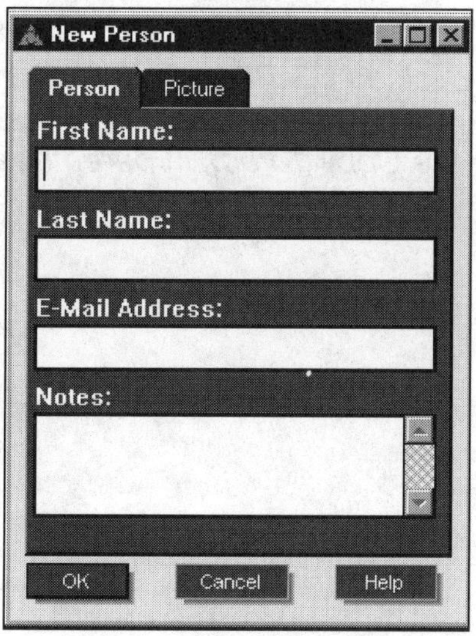

3. Enter the first and last name or a nickname (e.g., JohnV). The name(s) you enter in these boxes is how the entry will appear in the Address Book list.
4. Press the Tab key to move to the E-Mail Address box and enter the complete e-mail address of the recipient.

   ✔ *When entering the address of an AOL member, you do not need to enter the @aol.com domain information. Enter only their screen name as the e-mail address. For all other Address Book entries you must enter the entire address.*

5. Include any information you might want to remember about the person in the Notes box.
6. Click 

.

Enter an Address Using the Address Book

1. Place the cursor in the address field.
2. Click the Address Book button 

to open the Address Book.
3. Double-click the name or names from the Address Book list to insert in the Send To or Copy To address box using the appropriate buttons from the Address Book screen.

   ✔ *Unlike addresses entered in the Send To or Copy To address fields, addresses entered using the Blind Copy feature will not be visible to other recipients of the e-mail message. Clicking the Blind Copy button* 

after selecting an address from the Address Book inserts the address in the Copy To box in parentheses.

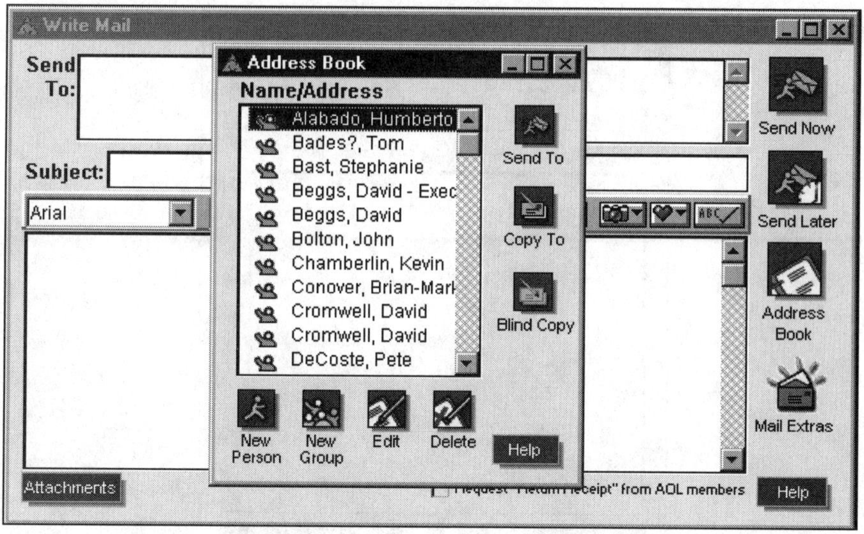

4. Click 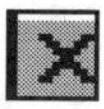 in the upper right-hand corner to close the Address Book.

To add an Address Book entry from mail received:

1. Open the e-mail message.
2. Click the Add Address button 

 from the message screen.
3. Enter the first and last name of the sender. The information entered into these fields will appear in the Address Book listing.
4. Notice that the e-mail address has been filled in for you.
5. Enter any information you may want to remember about the person in the Notes box.
6. Click 

.

To create a Group Entry:

1. To enter a Group listing (e.g., Book Club), click the New Group button 

 on the Address Book screen.
2. Enter the Group Name.

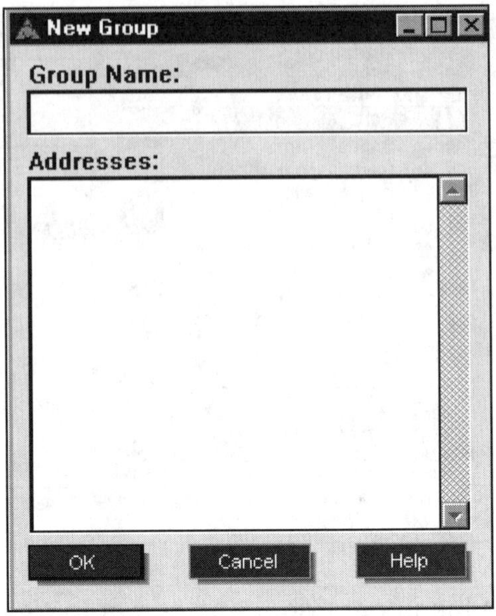

3. Enter the full e-mail addresses of each person in the group. Press Enter after typing each address.
4. Click  when done.

Delete an Address Book entry

1. Click Mail Center, Address Book to open the Address Book.
2. Select the name to delete.
3. Click the Delete button .
4. Click Yes to confirm the deletion.
5. Click 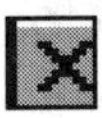 in the upper right-hand corner to close the Address Book.

America Online E-mail: 18

- ◆ Add Attachments to a Message
- ◆ Open an E-Mail Attachment

Add Attachments to a Message

- Any type of file can be sent as an attachment to an e-mail message—including text files, graphics, spreadsheets, and HTML documents.

To attach files to a message:

1. Compose the message to be sent. (See **Compose New Message** on page 87.)
2. Click the Attachments button at the bottom of the Write Mail screen.
3. Click the Attach button .
4. Select the drive and folder where the file you wish to attach is located.
5. Double-click the file to attach from the Attach File dialog box.

   ✔ *Multiple files can be sent by repeating the steps above. After you have selected the multiple attachments that will accompany the e-mail message, AOL will automatically combine these files into one compressed file called a zip file. If the recipient is not using AOL 4, he or she will need a file decompression program such as PKZIP or WINZIP to open the file.*

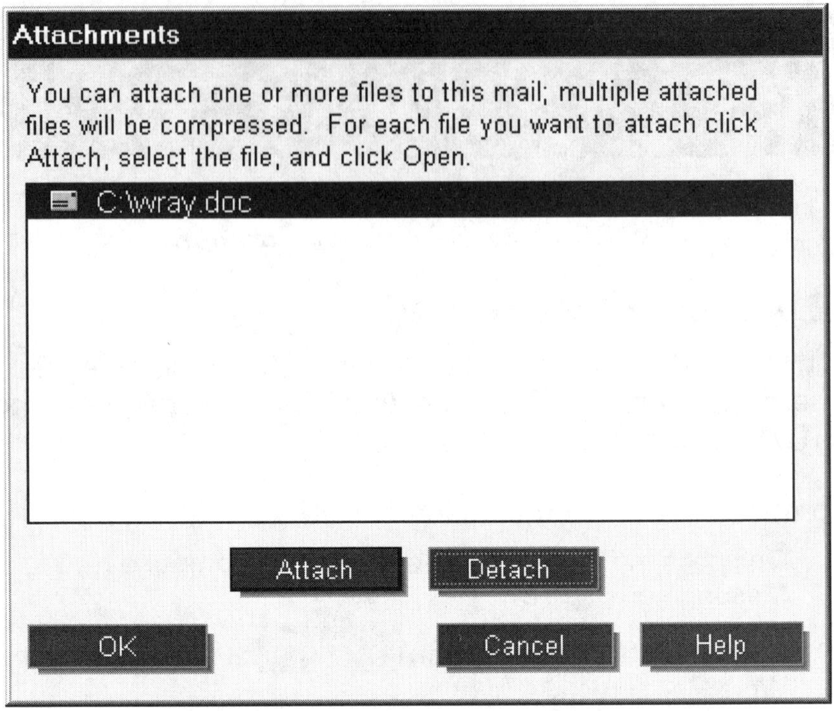

6. Click .

   ✔ *The attachment will appear at the bottom of the Write Mail screen next to the Attachments button.*

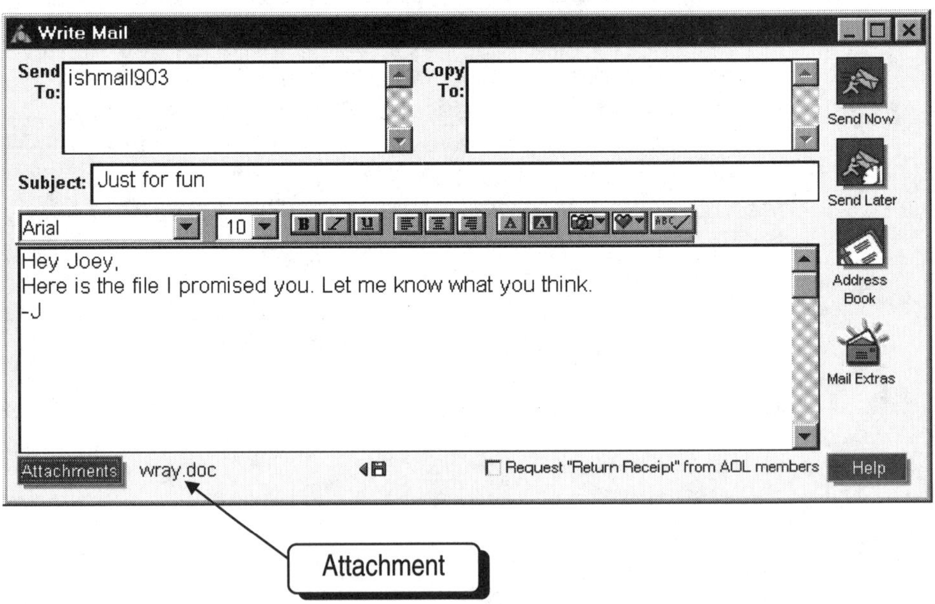

7. If you are online, click the Send button 

to send the message immediately, or click the Send Later button 

to store the message in your Outgoing Mail if you are working offline.

Open an E-mail Attachment

- An e-mail message that arrives with a file attachment is displayed in your new mail list with a small diskette icon under the message icon.

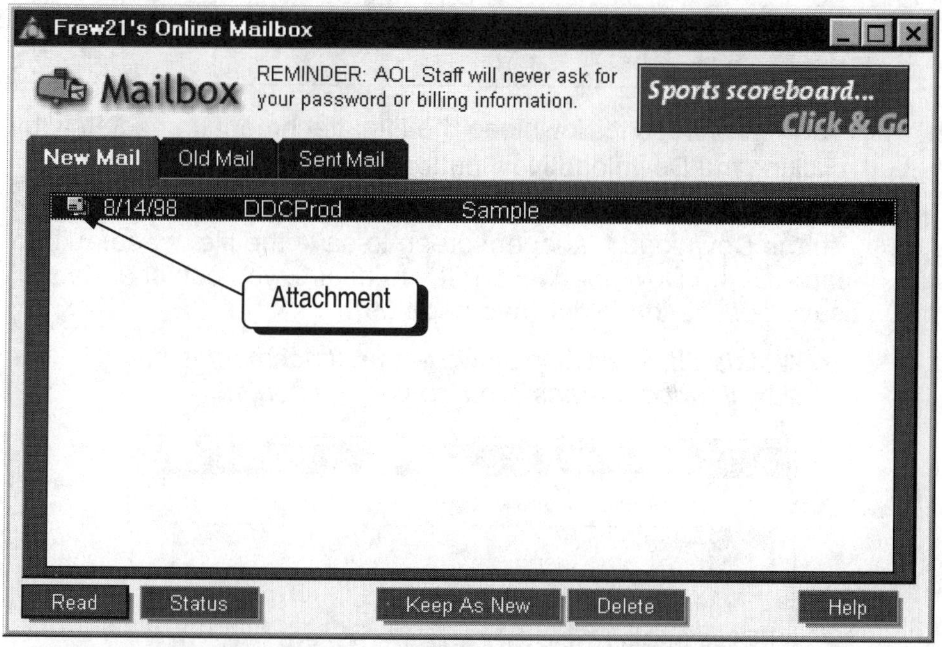

- Opening the message and viewing the attachment are two separate steps:
  1. Open the message by double-clicking on it from the New Mail list. The message will display.

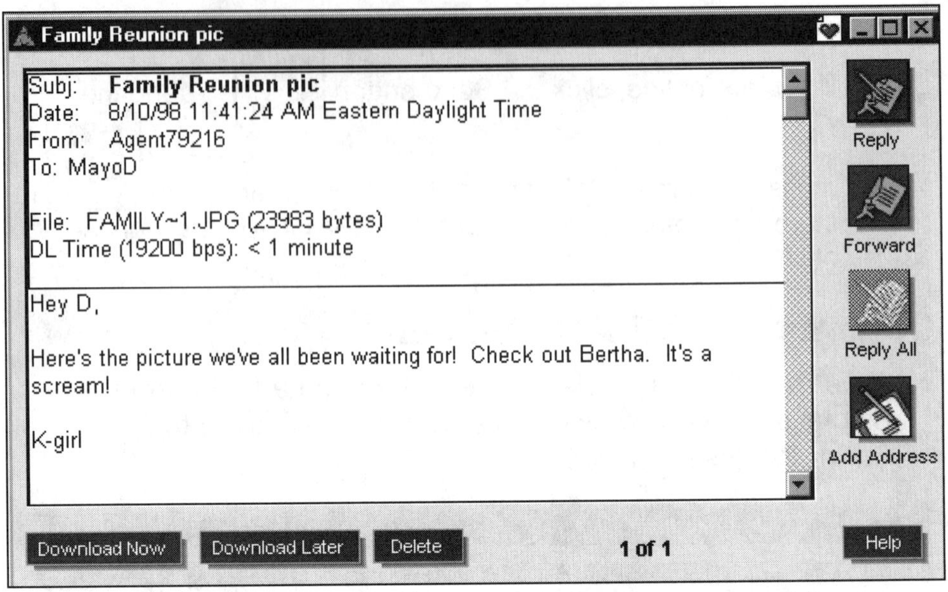

2. You can choose to download the file attachment immediately by clicking the Download Now button Download Now at the bottom of the displayed message screen. Click the Save button Save on the Download Manager screen to save the file, by default, to the AOL4.0/Download folder. If you desire, you can change the save destination folder (see page 99).

   ✔ *A status box will display while the attachment is being downloaded or transferred to your computer.*

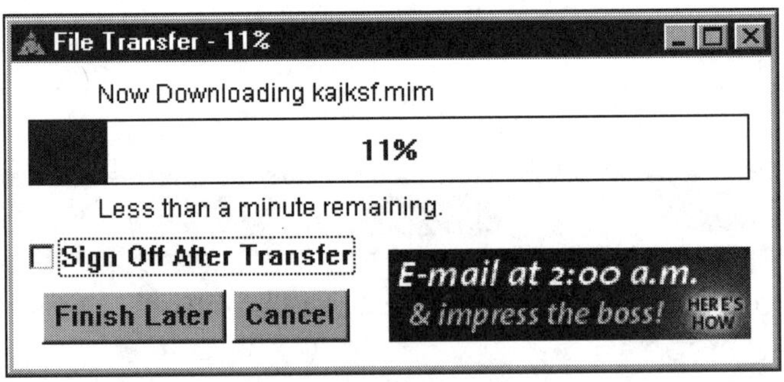

   ✔ *Click the Sign Off After Transfer checkbox if you want AOL to disconnect automatically when the transfer is complete.*

3. At the end of the download, the file transfer box will close and you will get a message confirming that the file has been transferred. Click OK.

OR

You may choose to download the file later. Click the Download Later button  to store the message in the Download Manager. When you are ready to download the file, click My Files, Download Manager, and then select the file to download. You must be online.

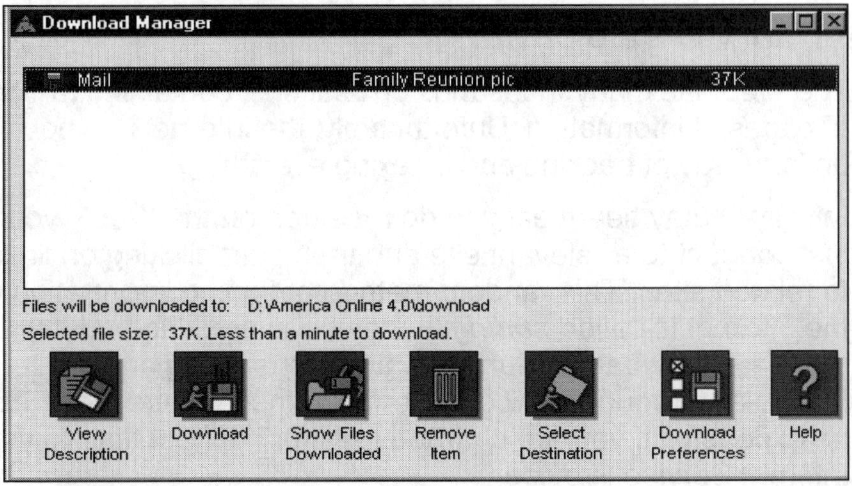

To change the default location of where files are stored:

1. Click the My Files button  from the AOL toolbar.
2. Click Download Manager and then the Select Destination button  from the Download Manager screen.
3. Select the desired destination from the Select Path dialog box.

✔ *All files will be automatically downloaded to this location.*

Search Engines: 19

◆ Surfing vs. Searching ◆ Search Sites
◆ Search Basics

Surfing vs. Searching

- The Web has many thousands of locations, containing millions of pages of information. Unfortunately, the Internet has no uniform way of tracking and indexing everything.
- Initially, it may seem easy to do research on the Web—you just connect to a relevant site and then start clicking on links to related sites. This random method of finding information on the Internet is called *surfing*. It may be interesting and fun, but there are drawbacks. Surfing is time consuming and the results are frequently inconsistent and incomplete. It can also be expensive if you are charged fees for connect time to your Internet Service Provider.
- *Searching* is a more systematic and organized way of looking for information. You can connect to one of several search sites that use *search engines* to track, catalog, and index information on the Internet.

Search Sites

- A *search site* builds its catalog using a search engine. A search engine is a software program that goes out on the Web, seeks Web sites, and catalogs them, usually by downloading their home pages.
- Search sites are classified by the way they use search engines to gather Web site data. Below and on the following page is an explanation of how the major search services assemble and index information.

Search Engines

- Search engines are sometimes called *spiders* or *crawlers* because they crawl the Web.

- Search engines constantly visit sites on the Web to create catalogs of Web pages and keep them up to date.
- Major search engines include: AltaVista, HotBot, and Open Text.

Directories

- Search *directories* are created by people who catalog information by building hierarchical indexes. Directories may be better organized than search engine sites, but may not be as complete or up-to-date as search engines that constantly check for new material on the Internet.
- Yahoo!, the oldest search service on the World Wide Web, is the best example of an Internet search directory. Other major search directories are: Infoseek, Magellan, and Lycos.

Multi-Threaded Search Engines

- Another type of search engine, called a *multi-threaded* search engine, searches other Web search sites and gathers the results of these searches for your use.
- Because they search the catalogs of other search sites, multi-threaded search sites do not maintain their own catalogs. These search sites provide more search options than subject-and-keyword search sites, and they typically return more specific information with further precision. However, multi-threaded search sites are much slower to return search results than subject-and-keyword search sites.
- Multi-threaded search sites include SavvySearch and Internet Sleuth.

■ If you are using Internet Explorer or Netscape Navigator, you can click on the Search button on the toolbar to access a number of search services.

Search Basics

- When you connect to a search site, the home page has a text box for typing the words you want to use in your search. These words are called a *text string*. The text string may be a single word or phrase.
- Once you have entered a text string, initiate the search by either pressing the Enter key or by clicking on the search button. This button may be called Search, Go Get It, Seek Now, Find, or something similar.
- For the best search results:
  - Always check for misspelled words and typing errors.
  - Use descriptive words and phrases.
  - Use synonyms and variations of words.
  - Find and follow the instructions that the search site suggests for constructing a good search.
  - Eliminate unnecessary words (the, a, an, etc.) from the search string. Concentrate on key words and phrases.
  - Test your search string on several different search sites. Search results from different sites can vary greatly.
  - Explore some of the sites that appear on your initial search and locate terms that would help you refine your search string.

Search Engines: 20

◆ Simple Searches ◆ Refine a Search ◆ Get Help

Simple Searches

- Searches can be simple or complex, depending on how you design the search string in the text box.
- A *simple search* uses a text string to search for matches in a search engine's catalog. A simple search is the broadest kind of search.
  - The text string may be specific, such as *Social Security*, *current stock quotes*, or *Macintosh computers*, or it may be general, such as *software*, *economy*, or *computer*.
  - The catalog search will return a list, typically quite large, of Web pages and URLs whose descriptions contain the text string you want to find. Frequently these searches will yield results with completely unrelated items.
- When you start a search, the Web site searches its catalog for occurrences of your text string. The results of the search are displayed in the window of your browser.
- Each search site has its own criteria for rating the matches of a catalog search and setting the order in which they are displayed.
- The catalog usually searches for matches of the text string in the URLs of Web sites. It also searches for key words, phrases, and meta-tags (key words that are part of the Web page, but are not displayed in a browser) in the cataloged Web pages.
- The information displayed on the results page will vary, depending on the search site and the search and display options you select. The most likely matches for your text string appear first in the results list, followed by other likely matches on successive pages.

✔ *There may be thousands of matches that contain your text string. The matches are displayed a page at a time. You can view the next page by clicking on the "next page" link provided at the bottom of each search results page.*

- You can scan the displayed results to see if a site contains the information you want. Site names are clickable links. After visiting a site, you can return to the search site by clicking the Back button on your browser. You can then choose a different site to visit or perform another search.

Refine a Search

- Suppose that you only want to view links that deal with Greek tragedies. Note, in the example below, the number of documents that were found when *Greek tragedies* was entered in this search. Since the search string didn't include a special *operator* to tell the search engine to look for sites that contain both Greek *and* tragedies, the results display sites that contain Greek *or* tragedies in addition to sites that contain Greek *and* tragedies.

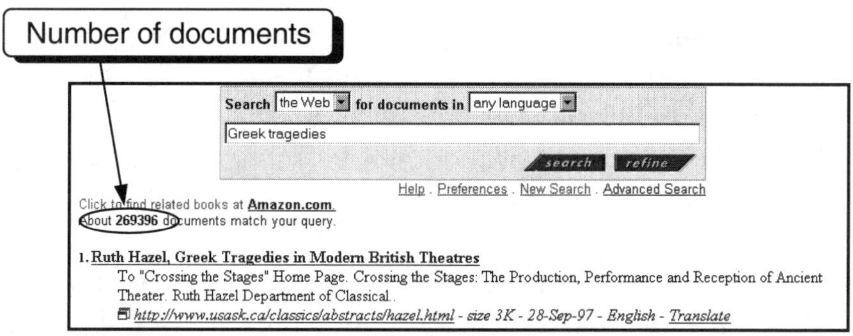

- To reduce the number of documents in this search, use operators—words or symbols that modify the text string instead of being part of it. Enter *Greek,* space once, then enter a plus sign (+) and the word *tragedies* (Greek +tragedies) then click Search. This tells AltaVista to look for articles that contain Greek *and* tragedies in the documents. Note the results that display when the plus is added to the search.

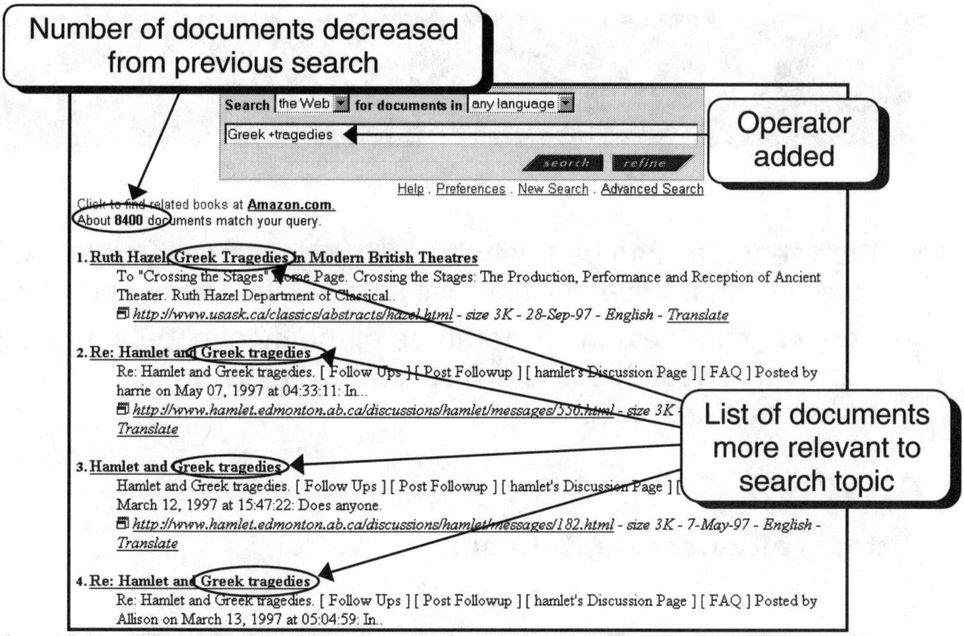

- The number of results is dramatically reduced, and the documents displayed display information that is more closely related to the topic, *Greek tragedies.*
- You can also *exclude* words by using the minus sign (-) to refine a search further and eliminate unwanted documents in the results. For example, if you wanted to find articles about Greek tragedies but not ones that deal with Hamlet, enter a search string like this: *Greek +tragedies -Hamlet.*

Get Help

- Check the Help features on the search tool that you are using to see what operators are available. Since there are no standards governing the use of operators, search sites can develop their own.

Search Engines: 21

◆ AltaVista ◆ Yahoo! ◆ excite

- Web searches can be frustrating. There are, however, a few basic tips that will almost always help you find what you want.
- Following are search tips for three of the most popular search sites. Each search site is different but some search techniques are universal.

AltaVista

http://altavista.digital.com/

- Enter your text string in the Search box. Make sure all words are spelled correctly.
- You may modify your search string with operators to narrow the search results. This will help you find more information specifically relevant to your search.
    - To modify your search string, put a (+) in front of the words that *must* be in your results and a (–) in front of the words that must *not* be in your results.

- Always use lowercase letters when searching the Web using AltaVista unless you are using proper nouns.
- You can also enter exact phrases into the search text box. If you are looking for pages that contain an exact phrase, enclose the phrase in the Search box with quotation marks.
- Search Usenets (Newsgroups) to read public opinion and postings on thousands of topics.

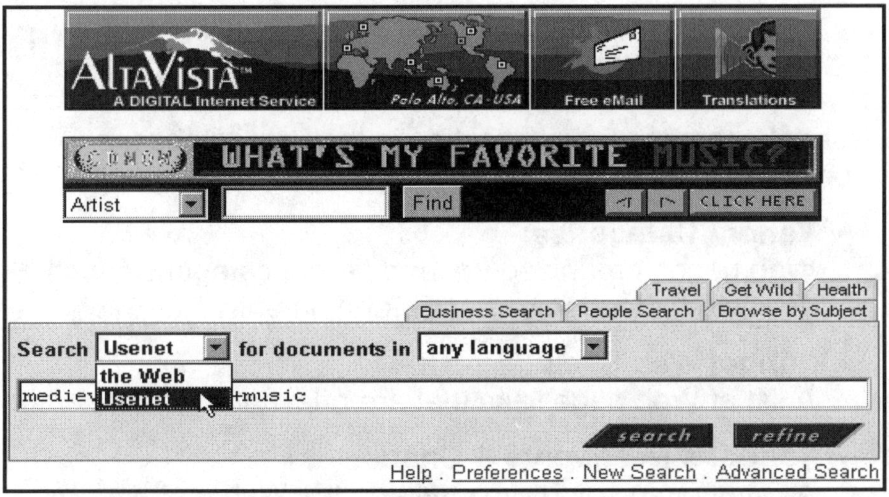

- Go to the AltaVista search areas found at the top of the search box to search a collection of Web pages and sites on everything from Travel to People.
- Click on AltaVista *Help* to get more information on searches.

Yahoo!

http://www.Yahoo.com

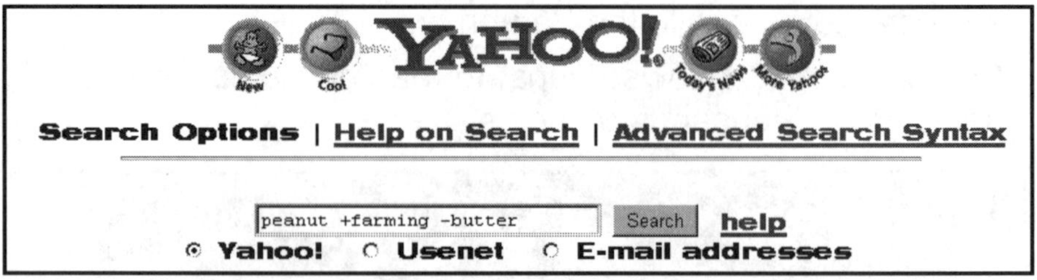

- Yahoo! searches for information in the four databases contained in its search catalog:
  - **Yahoo! Categories:**
    Web pages organized under different categories such as History, Economy, and Entertainment.
  - **Yahoo! Web Sites:**
    A list of Web page links that are relevant to your search.
  - **Yahoo!'s Net Events & Chat:**
    A list of events and live chats on the Web that are relevant based on words in your search string.
  - **Most Recent News Articles:**
    A database of over 300 online publications for articles that contain your keywords.
- Enter the keywords of your search in the search box. Make sure the words are spelled correctly.
- Be as specific as possible when entering keywords into the search box.
- Use a **(+)** in front of any keyword that must appear in the document and a **(-)** in front of words that should not.
- Yahoo! provides search syntax options to help you modify your search.
- To display search syntax options, click the *options* link next to the Search button from the home page. The following dialog box displays:

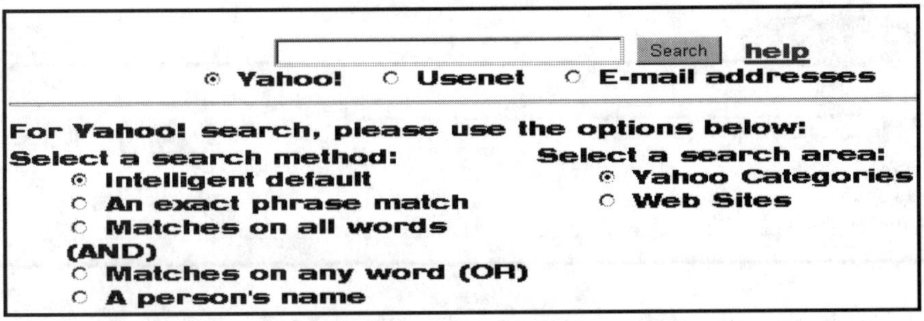

- You can also do a search by document title and URL.
- Place a *t:* in front of one or more keywords to yield Web pages with the keywords in the title of the page.
- Place a *u:* in front of keywords to yield returns with the keyword in the URL. Your search should return pages dedicated to the subject of your keywords.
- Yahoo! has specialized search areas. Click on any of the links on the Yahoo! home page to search for anything from stock quote information to buying a pet or an automobile. These links contain extensive information.

excite

http://www.excite.com/

- excite searches the Web by concept using Intelligent Concept Extraction (ICE) to find the relationships between words and ideas.
- Enter concepts and ideas rather than keywords into the search box.
- You can further modify your search by adding words supplied by excite based on the keywords or phrase you've entered.

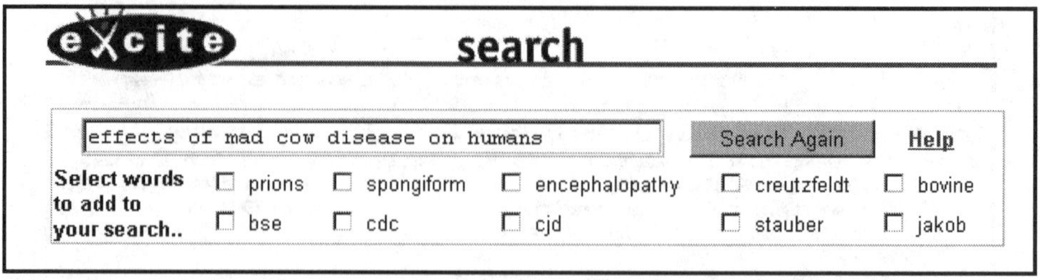

- Modify the words in your search phrase by using the (+) and (–) signs.
- Click *Help* to read more on excite search.
- You can activate a Power Search. This search uses the excite Search Wizard to help focus your search.
- Click the *Power Search* link located to the left of the search box on the excite home page. Enter the keywords or idea into the search box, as shown below.

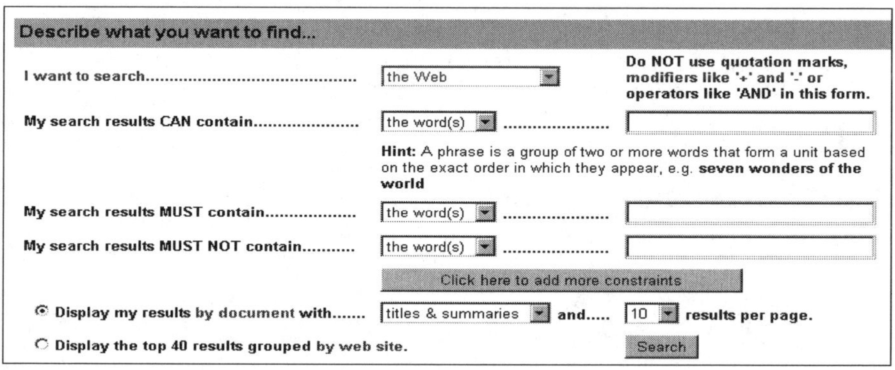

FINANCE

Getting Started

- As the Internet continues to grow and mature, one of the most rapidly expanding areas is personal finance and investing. Although this book is intended to be a guide or roadmap used to find helpful tools and resources to improve your finances, it is important not to forget some underlying principles of money management.

Principles—Financial Planning Steps

1. Set financial goals so you have something to strive for
2. Get your cash flow under control
3. Protect yourself from catastrophic risks
4. Build an emergency reserve
5. Establish and implement investment strategy
6. Minimize and manage taxes
7. Arrange assets for efficient distribution at death

The financial planning process

- Most financial planners will tell you that the best place to start is with a budget. You will never be financially independent if your expenses are greater than your income. If you are unsure how much you spend on various budget categories, pull out your checkbook register and credit card receipts for the last six months and categorize each purchase. You might be surprised how much you spend in some areas. The biggest cause of financial duress is the misuse of debt via credit cards. If credit cards are causing you problems, you might be using them to buy things you don't need, with money you don't have, and at a price you can't afford. If debt has a stranglehold on you, don't give up. We will look at various resources available on the Web to relieve the pressure and improve your life in the budgeting and debt management section.

- Once you have your cash flow under control, the next step is to build an emergency reserve. This is money you set aside for life's unforeseen needs, such as insurance deductibles resulting from an accident or major repairs on your car or home. Most planners agree that the acceptable amount of emergency reserve should be between three to six times your monthly expenses. Accumulate closer to the six-month amount if you are the only worker in your family or have an unstable job; closer to the three-month if you have multiple incomes and a stable job. Keep this money in secure, easy-to-access places like checking, savings, short-term CDs, or money market accounts. You may find that the money market rates on brokerage accounts yield more than those of banks or credit unions. Shop around some of the Web pages in the online banking and investment sections and find ways to gain a greater yield.
- While building your emergency reserve you also need to consider the financial risks or hazards in your life. Ask yourself, *What are the biggest threats to my family's financial success?* Consider things like illness, disability, premature death, fires, auto accidents, liabilities, earthquakes, etc. As you make your list, make sure you have insurance to cover the things you can't afford to have happen to you. Self-insure the little things that wouldn't cause you financial harm. For example, if you have a low deductible and a low liability on your home or auto insurance policy, consider raising the deductible (which is the small part of a claim) and use the savings to increase the maximum benefit (the part you can't afford to pay). Shop around for the best deals. This is one area of the Web that is expanding very quickly and is covered in the insurance section.
- After you have mastered your budget and built a cash reserve and cover your catastrophic risks, the next step is to look into other places to invest your surplus money. Many people like to skip the earlier steps and go straight to investing. At times this may work, but as a general rule this causes financial problems. For the purposes of this book, we have divided the investment section into three parts. The first explores places to get information and research companies in which you may

want to invest, the second and third cover sites for online brokers and mutual fund companies.

- Unfortunately, one of the privileges that comes with financial success is paying taxes. Probably no other issue unites Americans more than the dislike of taxes. For this book we have primarily looked at sites that allow the downloading of tax forms and online answers to common tax questions.
- Another area of concern, especially as your money and family grow, is how to protect and eventually distribute it to your loved ones. We call this estate planning. Everyone needs it because we all die eventually. You will want to check out the sites we have highlighted in the Estate Planning Section; however, this is a highly specialized area of the law. You may want to consult an estate planning attorney.

Finding an advisor

- As people become busier and more successful, many turn to advisors for help. In the Find an Advisor section we have pointed you to the major associations of Accountants, Attorneys, and Financial Planners. Although this does not guarantee the qualifications and integrity of the advisors, it is a starting point. And, as a general rule, most reputable advisors are members of their career-related associations.
- One final thought before you begin your journey through the maze of financial information available on the Internet. The sites we are exploring are merely tools to assist you on your journey. They will not guarantee you success. The key to financial success is discipline. All these sites provide great ideas and opportunities, but you must provide the motivation and discipline to act and stick to your goals. Happy surfing.

Financial News

To catch the latest breaking economic and financial news, tune in to any one of numerous Web pages. These sites specialize in economic, market, and business news, and also contain links to get stock quotes, charts, research reports, and more.

CNN Financial News Online

http://www.cnnfn.com

From cable TV straight to your desktop, you might want to set this up as your default page. CNNfn has one of the most complete and user-friendly financial news pages.

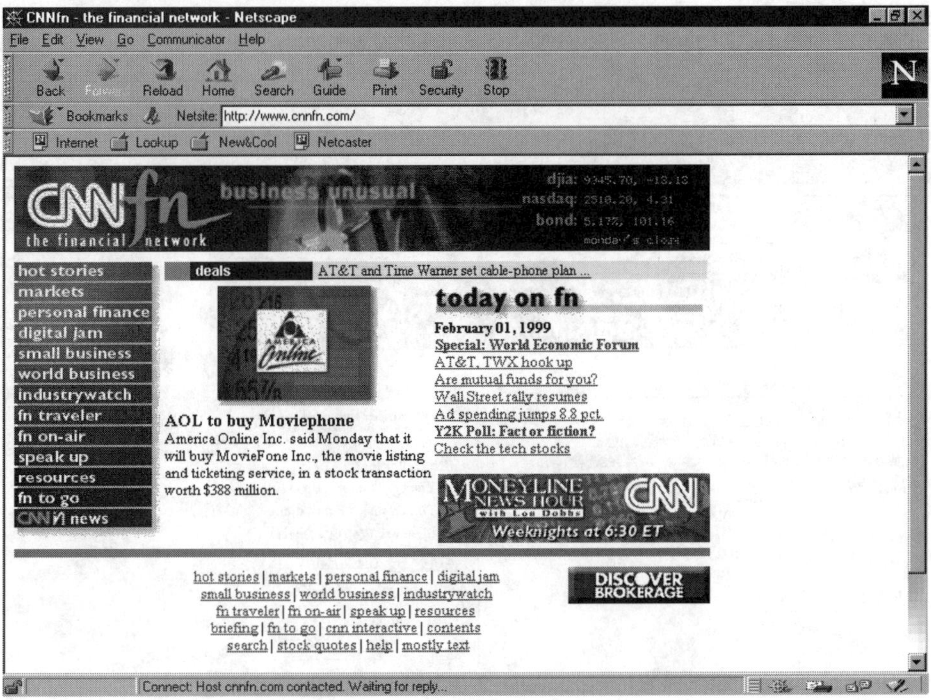

- With news from around the world and throughout the U.S., this site gives you up-to-the-minute news related to the financial markets as well as individual compaines.

- Checkout the scrolling ticker for the latest hot stories to see what's moving the market for the day. For market quotes, including international indicies, click *markets*.
- If you're a frequent traveler, click *travel center* and get currency exchange rates, travel bargains, and plane and hotel reservations.
- For the more advanced Internet user, using Windows Media Player, you can watch CNNfn news broadcasts right on your computer screen.

Wall Street Journal Interactive Edition

http://www.wsj.com

Save some trees and have the *Wall Street Journal* delivered right to your screen.

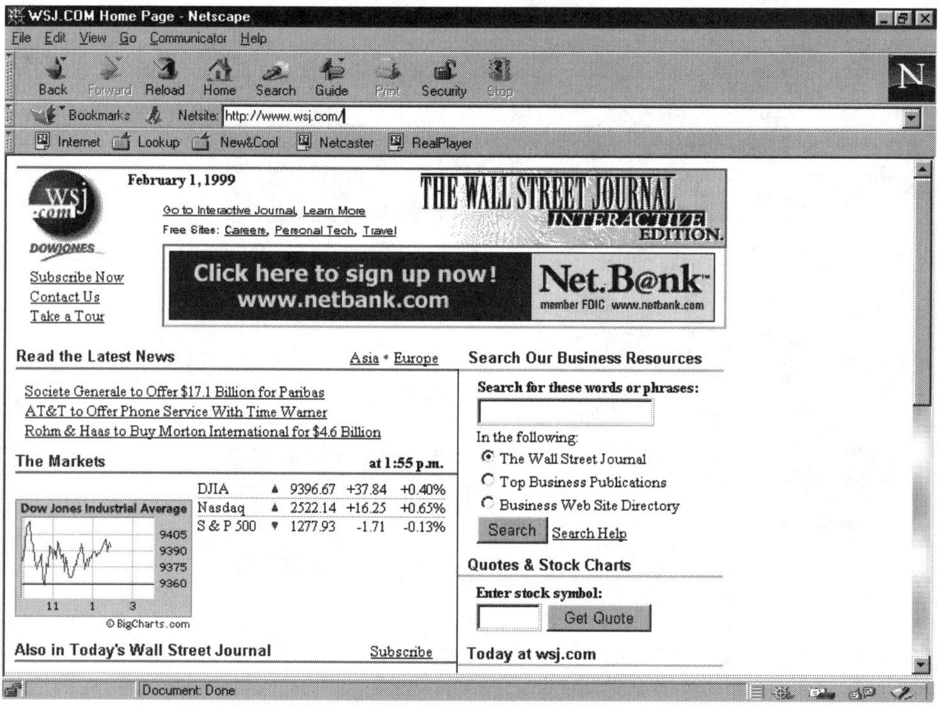

- Tired of wading through pages of meaningless stories to find the one you want? Set up your own customized version of the *Wall Street Journal* and electronically receive only the articles about companies and topics you choose daily.
- Headline stories are available at no cost. For complete access to the interactive version, you'll need to subscribe. An annual subscription is $59. A subscription also gives you access to *Barron's Online* and *Smart Money* magazine.
- From *WSJ*'s site you can also perform searches for company news among 5,500 leading business and financial publications. The headlines and recent *WSJ* articles are free to subscribers, but $2.95 each for non-subscribers.

Marketwatch

http://www.marketwatch.com

Provided by *CBS News*, Marketwatch provides tremendous amounts of market data and charts, plus many great reports on the economy and personal finance.

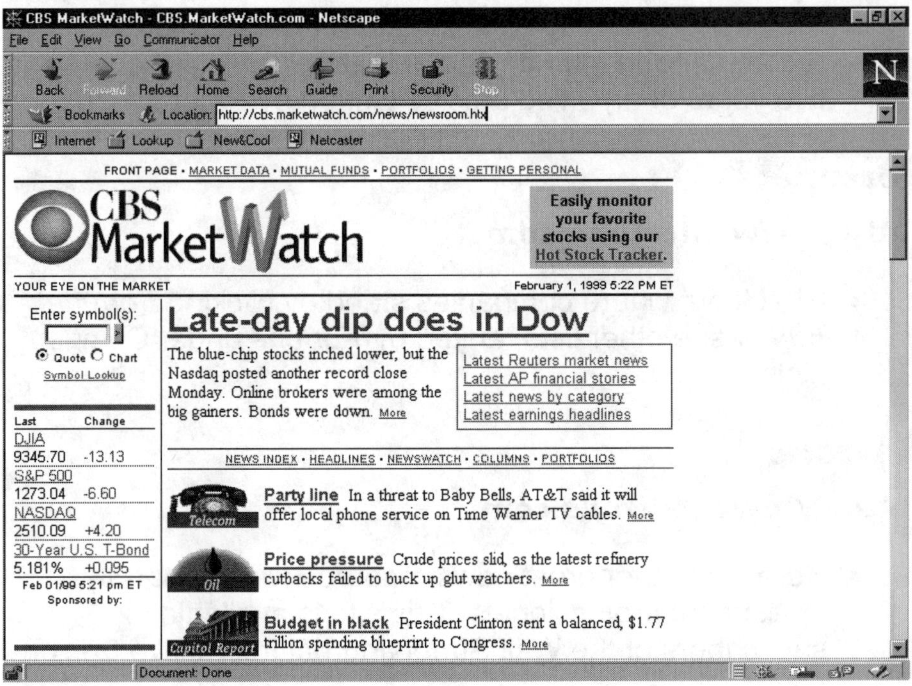

- On the main page, check out the Commentary section highlighting numerous companies and industries. IPO Coverage section provides ongoing reports on the hottest IPOs.
- From the Getting Personal section, read through the latest educational investment articles on more than just stocks. Or check out Special Reports for in-depth stories.

Other Financial News Sites

Bloomberg

http://www.bloomberg.com

- This site has complete market activity information, including currencies, commodities, and world markets. With Real Player or Windows Media Player you can watch TV and hear radio broadcasts online.

Worth Online

http://www.worth.com

- Preview *Worth* magazine's feature articles and recommended mutual fund and stock lists, and check out five years of archived articles written by Peter Lynch.

Fortune

http://www.fortune.com

- Check out where companies stand by clicking *Fortune 500* or see other lists ranked by *Fortune* under Company Lists.

Barrons

http://www.barrons.com

- Here is another great news resource widely read by investment professionals. This site is available to subscribers of the Wall Street Journal Interactive Edition.

Online Banking

The availability of electronic access to bank account information via phone and ATM is not new. The next concept is a virtual bank—a bank without tellers, drive-up windows, or branch offices—a secure Web site with access to all account information at the click of the mouse wherever you are in the world. Within these online banking sites you can transfer money among accounts, pay your bills, or check to see what transactions have cleared with a very high level of security.

Citibank

http://www.citibank.com

From one of the largest banks in the world, this site has been ranked the number one online bank by the *Wall Street Journal*'s *Smart Money* magazine.

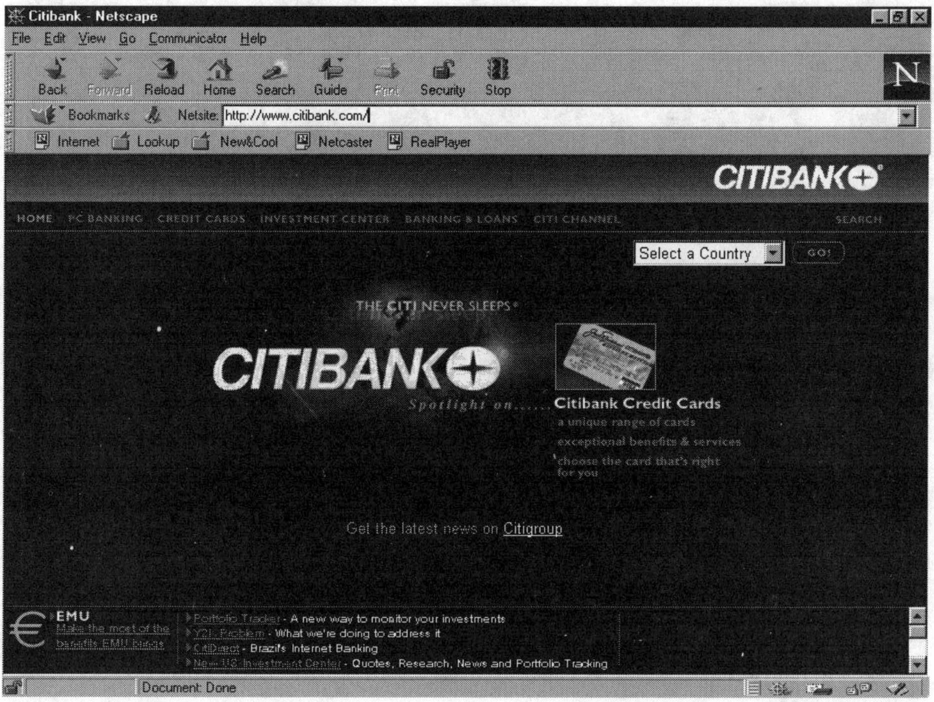

- From their homepage click *PC Banking*, then choose *Direct Access* for the U.S. Then click *Test Drive* and experience the thrill of banking online. You can pay your bills, look to see what checks have cleared, transfer between accounts, and more.
- From Citibank's Web site you can also access other services such as online investing, banking and loans, and credit card account information.

First Union

http://www.firstunion.com

One of the largest and fastest growing financial services companies in America, First Union's site provides banking and other personal finance assistance online.

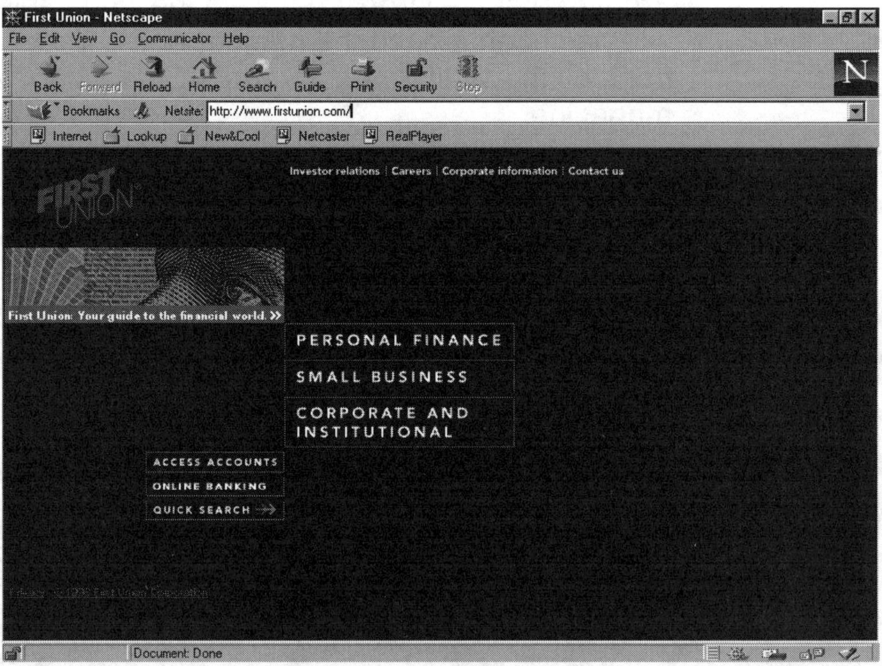

- Test drive First Union's Web access system by clicking *Online Banking* from the *Personal Finance* section. Then choose the *Online Banking demo* and see how an online account would work for you.

- Take a tour through the variety of resources and calculators in the Personal Finance section, where you'll find access to resources such as online loan applications, insurance quotes, and a retirement planning center.

Find a Bank Online

Because there are hundreds of online banking sites you might want to shorten your quest with one of the following. In addition, you may want to check with local banks or credit unions to see what services they have available online and at what cost.

Online Resources - Banks Online

http://www.orcc.com/banking.htm

Online Resources & Communications Corporation's comprehensive list allows you to search regionally by financial service company type, such as banks or credit unions.

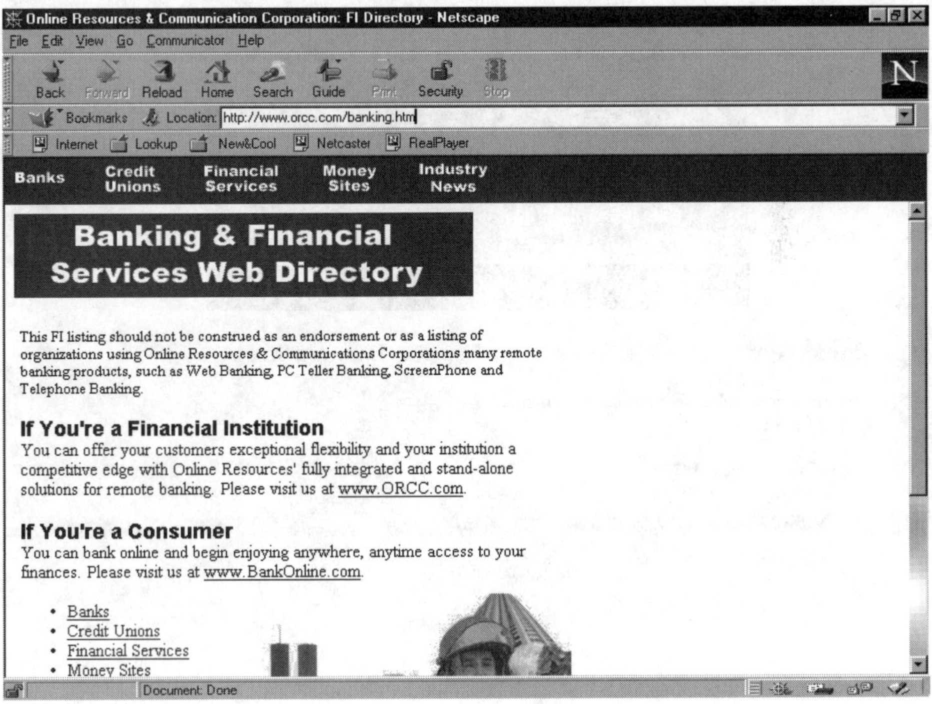

- On the homepage, click the type of financial institution for which you are looking. Next choose appropriate geographic regions to generate links to the homepages of hundreds of banks or credit unions near you.
- Click Consumer links for online brokers, government agencies, news services, money managers, loan and credit information, and more.

BankWeb

http://www.bankweb.com

Bank Web provides a directory of over 1700 U.S. banks online along with hundreds more throughout the world.

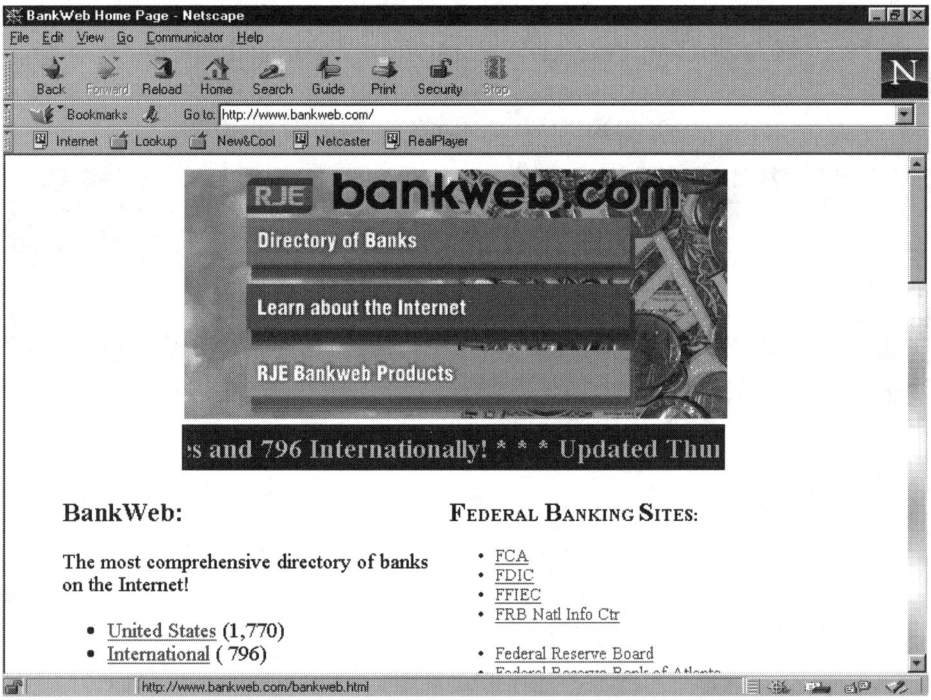

- To find a bank by location, try out BankWeb. This site offers links to banks throughout the world. To find a bank by state, click Directory of Banks or United States. A well-organized grid will appear listing each state. Choose a state to find dozens, and in some cases hundreds, of banks available online in your area.
- Listed down the right-hand side of the site are links to Federal Agencies as well as National and State Banking Associations.

Smart Cards

For those interested in the ongoing development of smart cards you may want to visit the Smart Card Forum at *http://www.smartcrd.com*. Similar to credit cards, these cards allow you to purchase merchandise without cash. Smart cards are designed, in contrast to credit cards, to replace the need for pocket change.

These cards are programmable and are electronically "filled" with money prior to their use. When purchasing, you simply insert your card into the cash register and the appropriate amount of cash is removed from the card. When it is empty, just refill it at an ATM or, eventually, your computer. Smart cards are much faster than credit cards. The merchants don't need to dial up to check the status of your account for approval. Ultimately, this shortens your time at the checkout.

Debt Management

For Americans, excessive consumer and credit card debt is the biggest roadblock to financial success. The following sites can be helpful tools for you to better manage your liabilities. One of the first steps you may want to take is to check your credit report. You can now request your credit report online for $8 in most states. Read through the report. Look for any old accounts that you've closed or paid off to ensure they are marked as such. Look at the late payment history and make sure there are no errors. If you do find errors, let the credit bureau know immediately.

Equifax Information Services

http://www.equifax.com

Make sure no one is ruining your credit history with Equifax's Credit Monitoring Service.

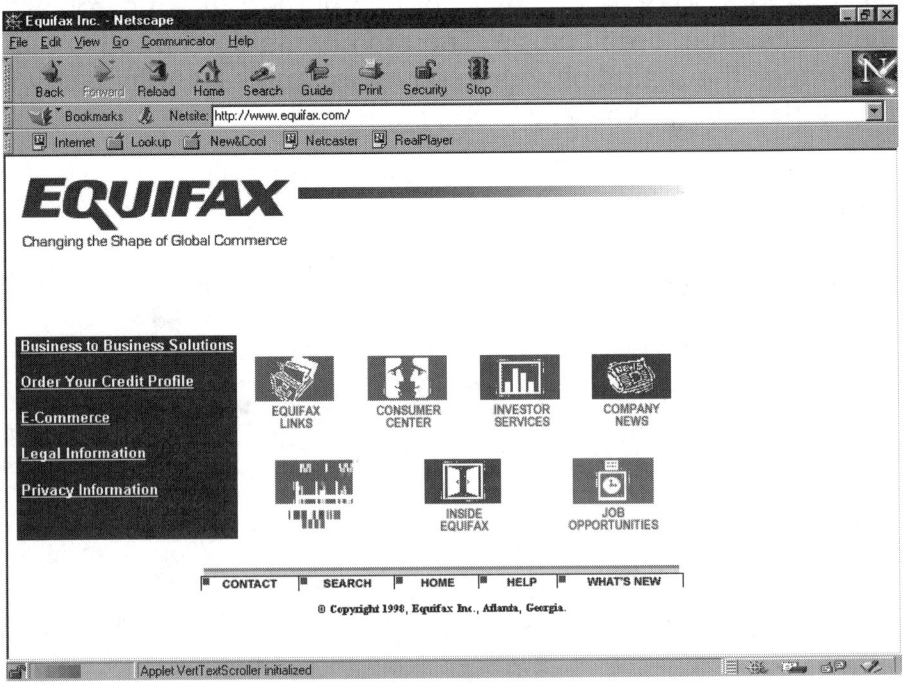

- Equifax is one of several credit bureaus available online. To obtain a credit report from this site click *Order Your Credit Profile*. Before ordering, it may be helpful to check out the *Consumer Center* and familiarize yourself with a sample profile.
- You may also want to learn about their SENTINEL® Credit Monitoring Service, which is designed to protect your identity and credit history through a quarterly report of changes and inquiries. To learn more, click *Consumer Center*, then *Products & Services*.

DEBT

Experian

http://www.experian.com

In addition to your credit report, Experian provides useful business credit and real estate property reports online.

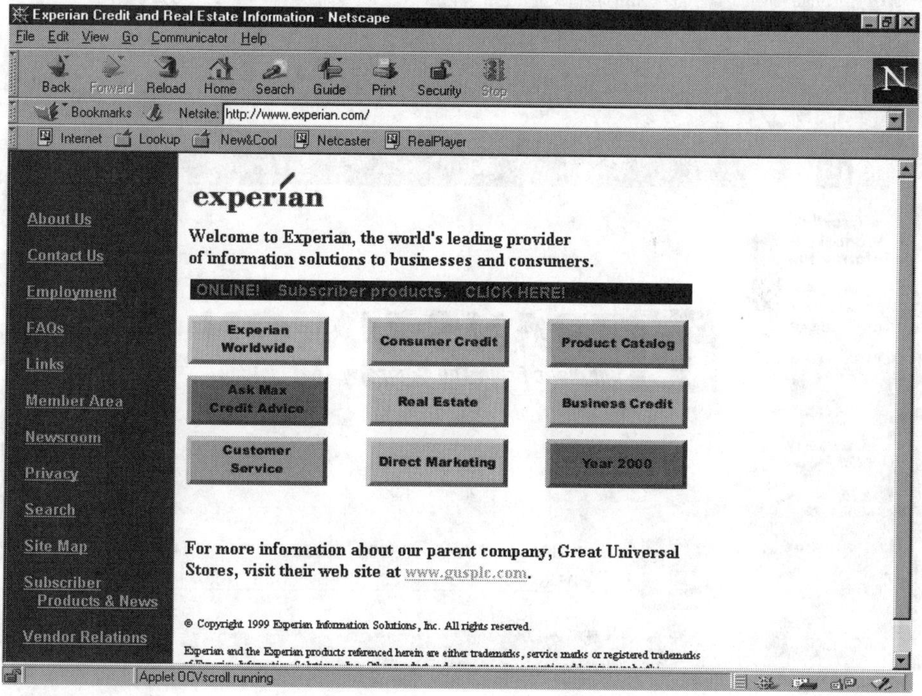

- Similar to Equifax, the Experian site also allows you to order your credit report online by clicking on Consumer Credit then Order Your Credit Report.

- This site offers a large amount of advice and recommendations for managing your credit. Check out the biweekly column under *Ask Max Credit Advice*.
- If you are self-employed or own a small business you may want to use Experian's business credit reports or Intelliscore to avoid uncollectible debts.
- Thinking of selling your house? Experian also provides several real estate property reports.

Trans Union

http://www.transunion.com

If you think you may be a victim of fraud or want to protect yourself, check out Trans Union's Fraud Victim Assistance Department.

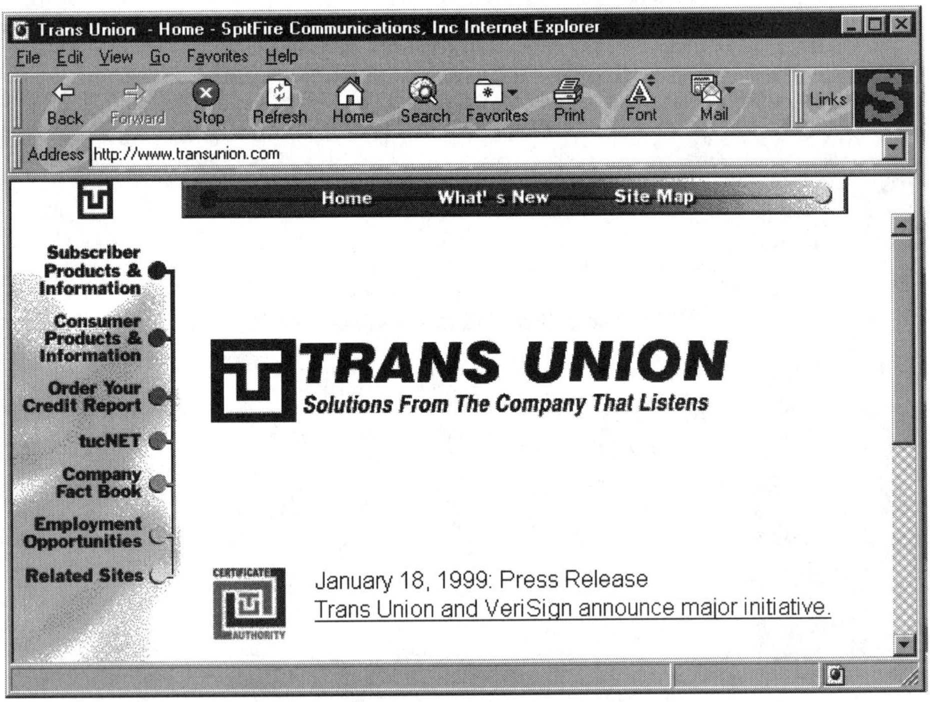

- As with the previous sites you may order your credit report online.

- The Fraud Victim Information has enlightening tips on how to solve credit problems caused by fraud or other crimes. To access this section, click *Consumer Products & Information* and then click *Fraud Victim Information.*

More Debt Management Help

Other sites can help by providing counseling through budget and debt reduction strategies. Having too much debt is not uncommon and can be embarrassing and discouraging. If debt has a stranglehold on you, don't give up. The services provided by these sites can help.

Consumer Credit Counseling Service

http://www.credit.org

Online or in person, Consumer Credit Counseling can help solve your debt problems.

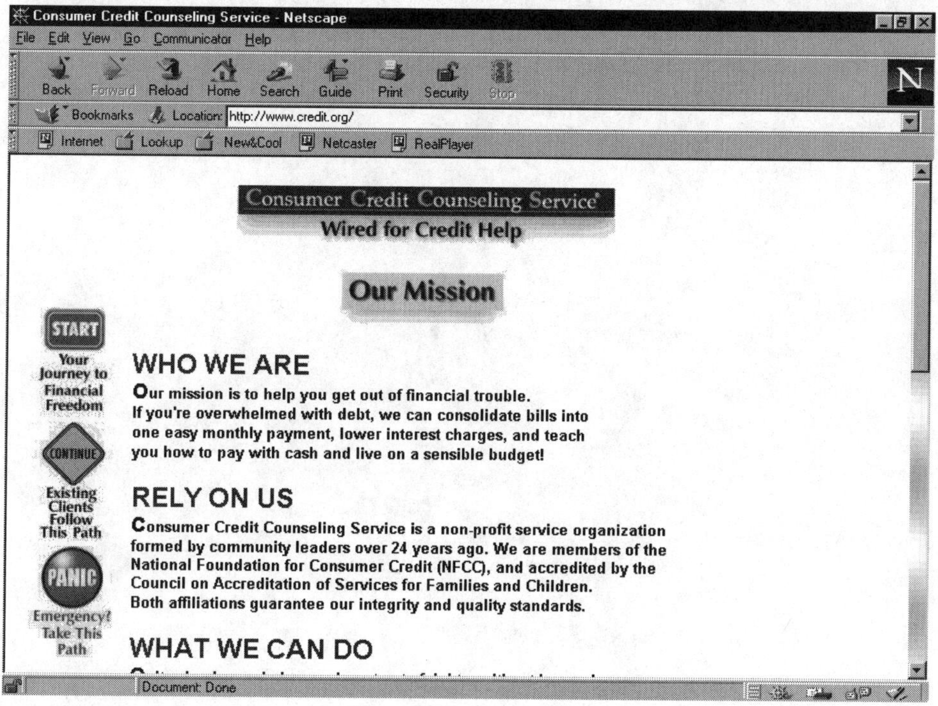

- Consumer Credit Counseling, a not-for-profit organization dedicated to helping people get out of financial trouble, is now available online.
- To get started check out their various services, including Debt Management, Credit Report Review, and Homeowner Help.
- Not sure whether you need help? Review their 10 Signs of Debt Distress.

Credit Repair Service

Another way to improve your credit rating is through credit repair services. Several are available online. Be cautious before you spend money to have someone "fix" your credit problems. In many cases you can fix the problem by contacting the credit bureaus on your own.

DirectCredit

http://www.directcredit.com

For assistance repairing your credit, you might want to download Direct Credit or Credit Pro credit repair software.

- For assistance in getting your credit report repaired, visit DirectCredit and let them walk you through their five-step process.
- To learn more about their credit repair process, browse the *Frequently Asked Questions* for a detailed explanation.

Buying & Financing Your Home

Finding Your Home

By far the biggest single purchase the majority of Americans make during their lifetime is their home. The decisions you make will have a long-lasting impact on your personal finances. A number of helpful services are available on the Web to help you make better informed and less costly decisions.

Realtor.com

http://www.realtor.com

With access to information on more than one million property listings, this site is a great place to start.

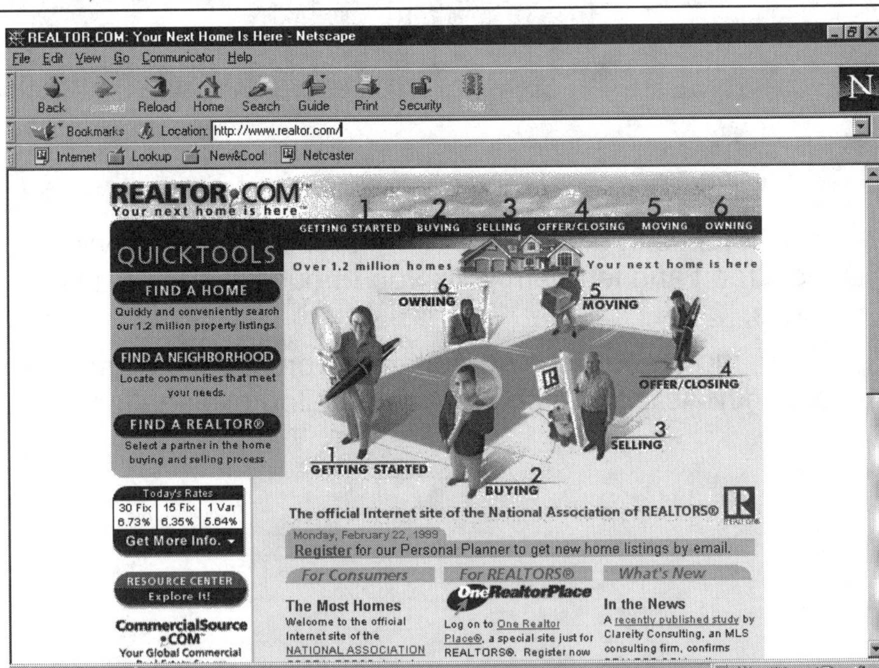

- Click *Find a Home* and follow the prompts to search by City, State, ZIP, or by MLS data. Once you find an area, fill out the survey of the features you desire, such as numbers of bedrooms and bathrooms, and size of basement and garage.
- This site also has a great Resource Center that provides links to other sites with advice on home improvements, appliances, moving services, and more.
- The Moving section of the site has helpful tips and calculators to help you estimate the cost of relocating.

Home Shark

http://www.homeshark.com

With information and resources for financing, buying, managing rental properties, choosing a real estate agent, and more, Home Shark wants to be your home-buying partner.

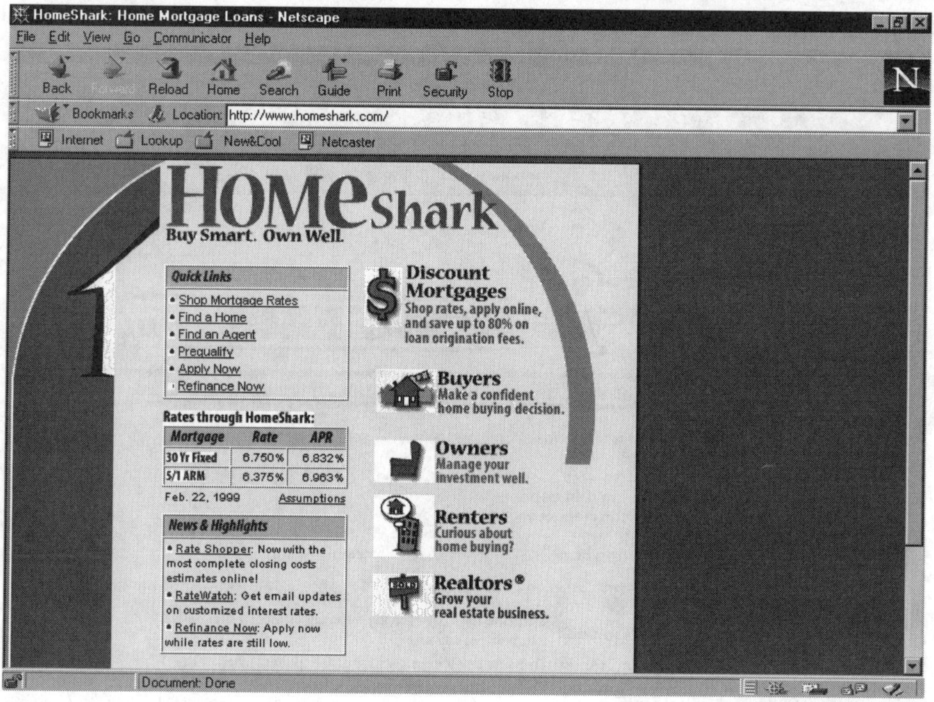

- To find a home using Home Shark's HomeScout, simply click *Find a Home* and provide your requirements, such as location, price range, and number of bedrooms.
- The Owners section of the site has resources such as a Home Valuation calculator, which helps estimate the value of your home based on comparable homes recently sold in your neighborhood.
- If you're preparing to buy your first home, the Buyer section has some helpful advice on down payment strategies and choosing the right mortgage.

Homefair

http://www.homefair.com

Thinking of moving to another area of the country? Check out Homefair.com to receive a free e-mail city report.

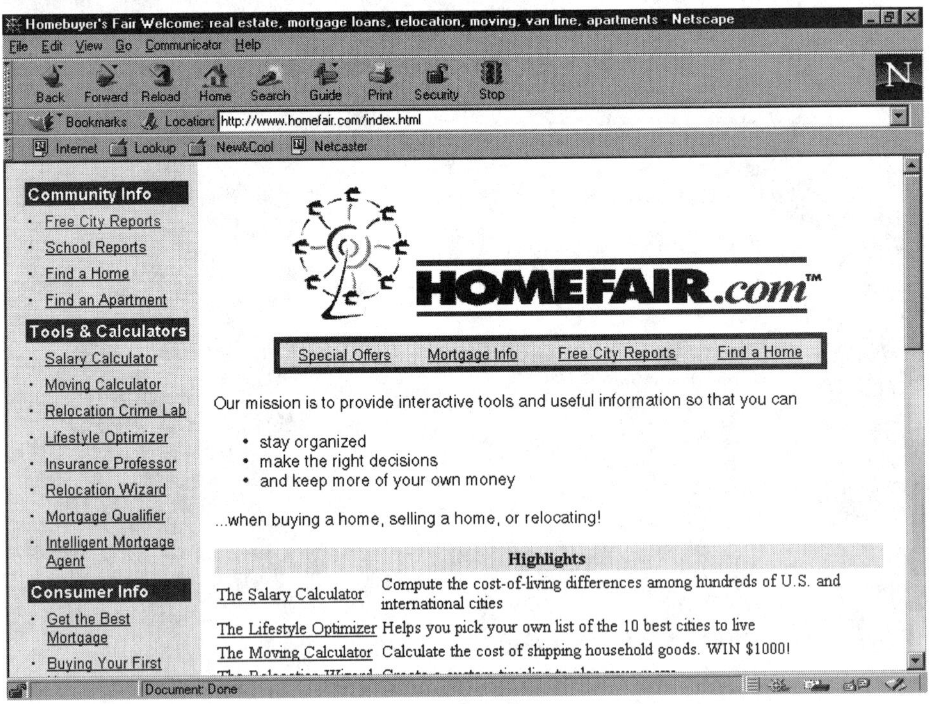

- Click *Free City Reports* and choose the nearest area you are moving from and one or two areas you are considering. Fill out the online form to have the report sent to you. This free service is offered as a marketing tool to generate leads for realtors, so expect a follow-up call.
- While at the site, use the salary calculator to see how much of a cost-of-living difference there is between your current home and another area of the country.

Mortgages & Loans

If you're considering refinancing your home or need money for another project, you'll find these mortgage and loan sites very resourceful.

Bank Rate Monitor

http://www.bankrate.com

This is a great place to find the best mortgage, loan, and savings rates available by geographic region.

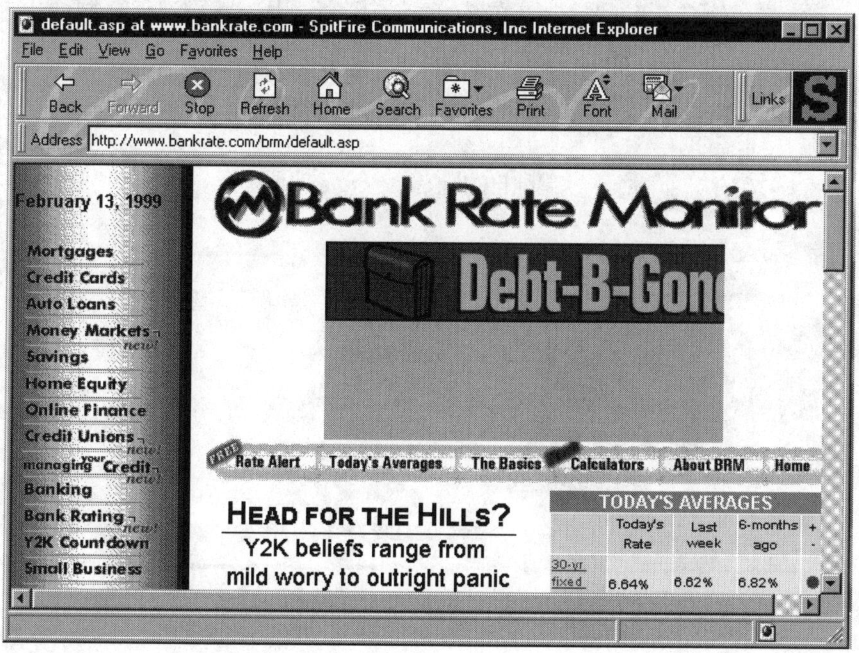

- Are you paying too much loan interest or not getting a high enough yield on your CDs? Bank Rate Monitor tracks loan, mortgage, credit card, CD, and money market rates for banks and credit unions throughout the U.S.
- To find the best rates, simply click the category of financial product you're looking for and choose a state, closest major city, and other product details. This will generate a list of vendors and their most recent rate quotes along with a link to their site.
- Down the left-hand margin of the homepage is a wide variety of topics that contain great articles on things such as when to refinance your home, leasing vs. buying a car, and more.

Quicken Mortgage

http://www.quickenmortgage.com

A colorful and easy-to-use site, visit Quicken Mortgage, not only to apply for a new mortgage, but for helpful tips and advice on buying and financing your home.

- Curious whether you would qualify for a mortgage? Under the Calculators section click *What loans do you qualify for?* and *How much house can you afford?* You will be prompted to provide information about your income, current debts, and payment history, but not your legal name or social security number.
- When you get to the end of the survey, you will be given a list of the top-ten mortgage alternatives available.

E-Loan

http://www.eloan.com

With access to over 35,000 loan products from more than 60 of the nation's top lenders, E-Loan can help you find a great rate.

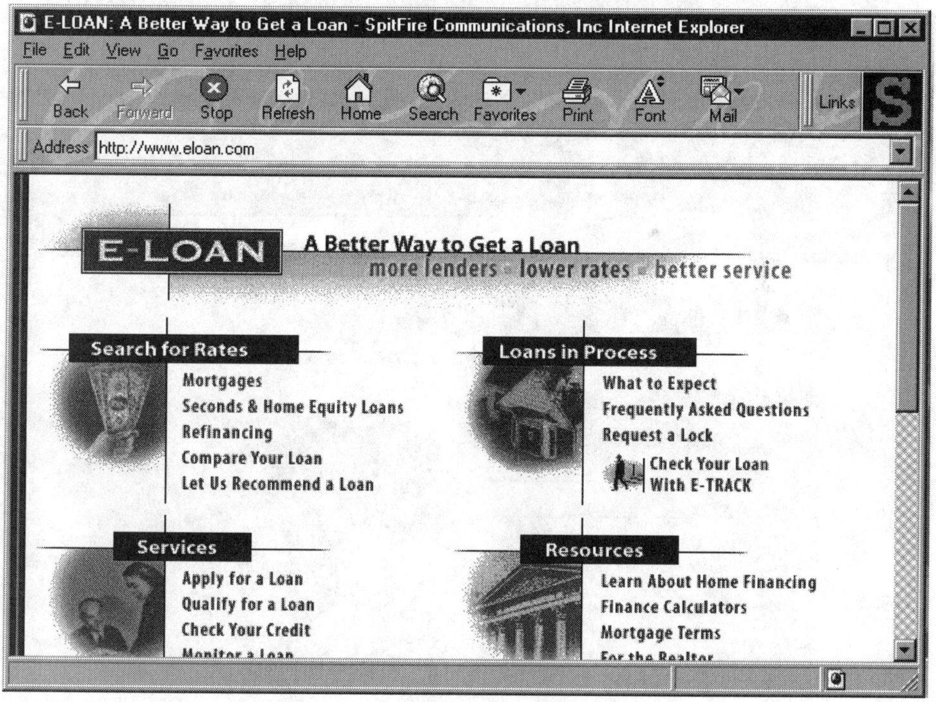

- Similar to Quicken Mortgage, E-Loan allows you to pre-qualify, apply for, and track your mortgage from their site.
- If you are waiting for a specific rate, click *Rate Watch* and provide information on the type of loan you are looking for as well as your e-mail address. When rates meet your criteria, you will be notified by e-mail.
- Want to learn more about mortgages? Click *Learn About Home Financing* under the Resources section and you'll find informative articles on types of mortgages, private mortgage insurance, points, and more.

The Money Store

http://www.themoneystore.com

The Money Store provides more than just mortgages. Check them out for online access to home equity, small business, and student loans as well.

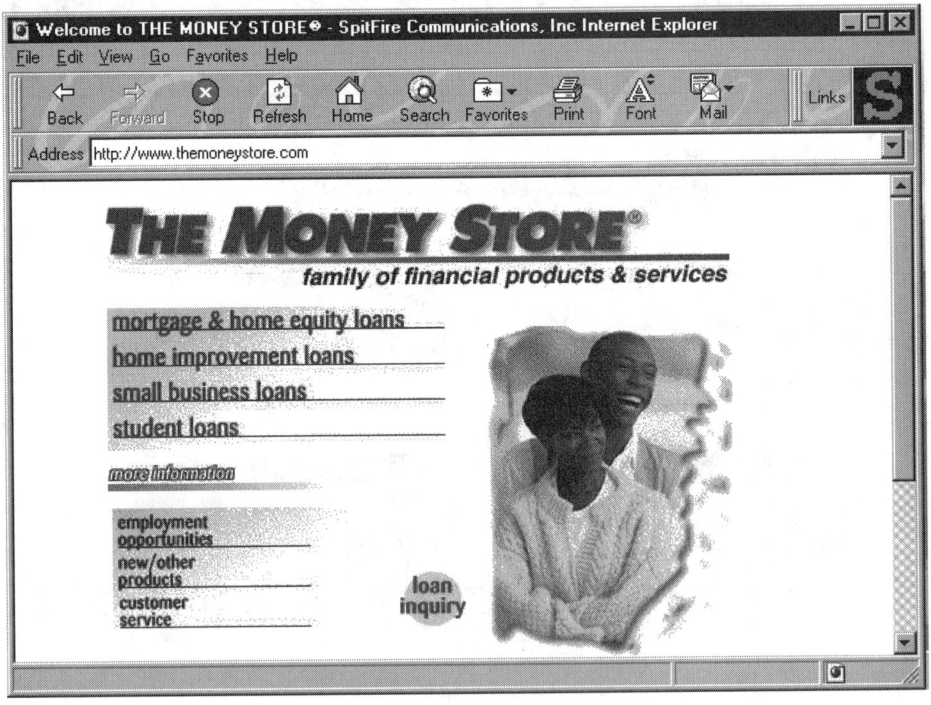

- Within the Small Business Center are informative articles to help you obtain a loan, determine whether to buy or lease, or when to consider new construction projects.
- If you are looking for a student loan, from the bottom of the student loan page, click their link to the Educaid Web site. Here you will find volumes of information about applying for student loans, grants, financial aid, scholarships, and more.

Other Mortgage & Loan Sites

MortgageQuotes

http://www.mortgagequotes.com

- MortgageQuotes provides access to 124 different loan programs from over 1,000 lenders throughout the U.S. To begin the process, click *Today's Rates* and choose the state in which the property you are borrowing against is located. Then scroll to the bottom of the next page, past all the advertising, and choose the product that interests you.

The Lending Tree

http://www.lendingtree.com

- The Lending Tree provides mortgages, home equity, personal and debt consolidation loans, as well as credit cards. The application process is completed online and forwarded to multiple vendors for approval. On their site they claim you will begin receiving real loan offers within two business days after submitting your application.

Insurance

Don't overlook the major financial risks in your life. Make sure you have adequate insurance to cover yourself and your property. Carry adequate liability insurance on each, and you may want to add additional coverage with an umbrella liability policy. When you compare policies, focus more on maximum benefits to cover the catastrophes you can't afford and avoid paying for a low deductible you may not need. There are numerous sites on the Web where you can buy insurance, but fewer that provide assistance in determining the right amount and right kinds.

Insweb

http://www.insweb.com

A better way to shop for insurance, Insweb provides access to auto, homeowners, life, and health insurance quotes online.

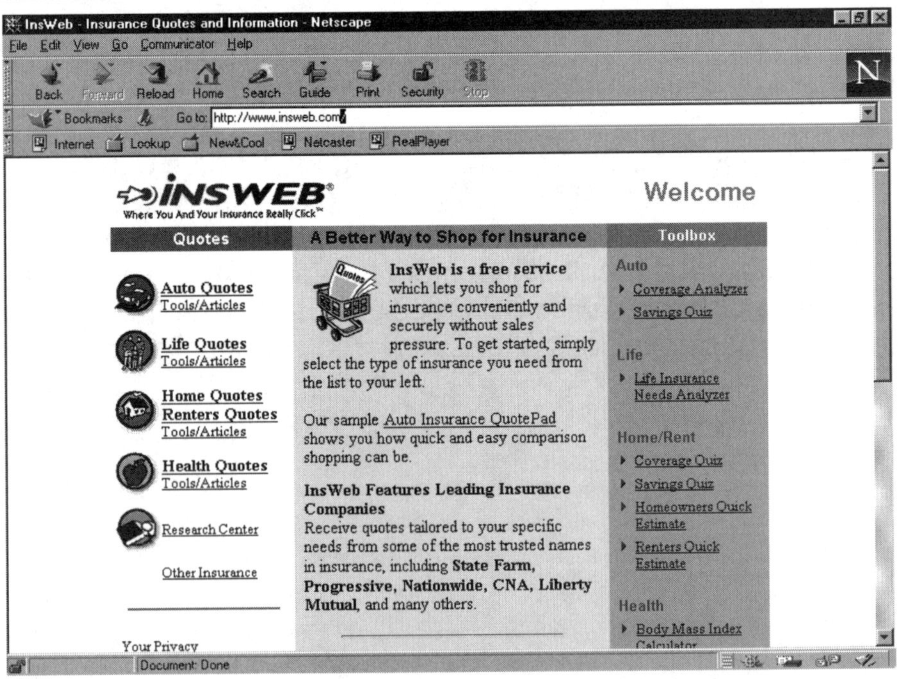

- One of the best, this site allows you to shop for nearly all of your insurance needs from 25 different companies in one place. Follow the three-step process and receive your quote either online or in the mail from the insurance company.
- Some helpful tools on the site are the coverage and need analyzers in the various categories. Use them to ensure your coverage meets your objectives.
- Having trouble understanding your policy? Check out the comprehensive glossary and frequently asked questions found on the bottom right section of the site.

InsureMarket

http://www.insuremarket.com

Quicken's Insure Market is one the most user-friendly insurance sites you'll find.

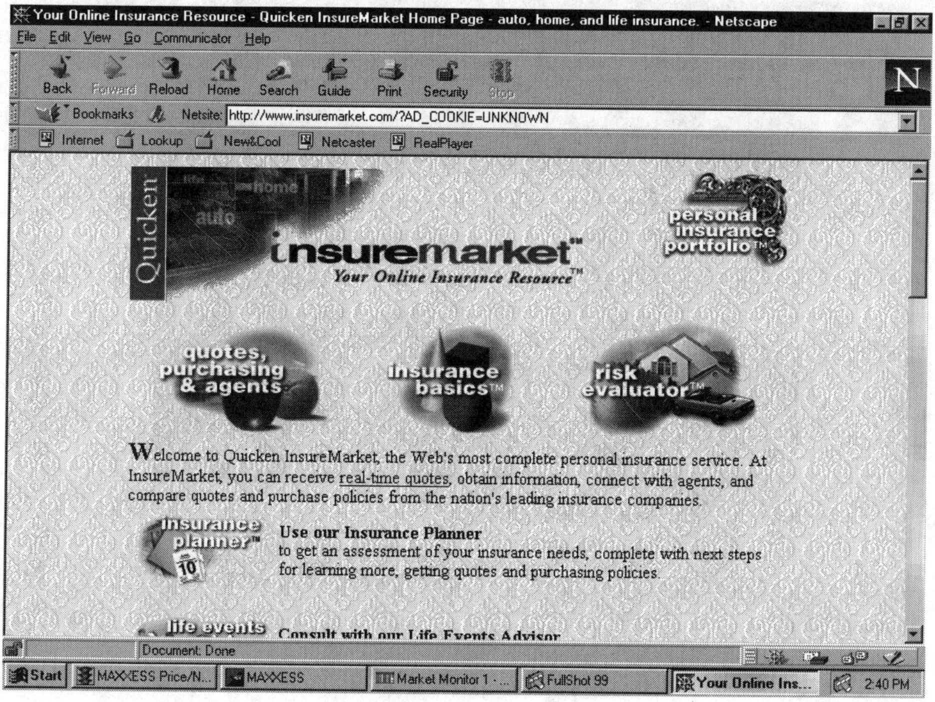

- This well laid out easy-to-use site has a very helpful Insurance Planner that requires you to register online. For other insurance advice, check out the *Life Events Advisor*, which walks you through the changing needs for insurance as a result of buying a car, getting married, buying a home, having children, retiring, and more.
- To get insurance quotes, click *real-time quotes* and select a category of insurance. This site not only provides quotes for auto, homeowners, and life, but product information on long-term care, disabilty, and small business insurance as well.

Quotesmith

http://www.quotesmith.com

Check out Quotesmith for instant quotes from hundreds of insurance companies.

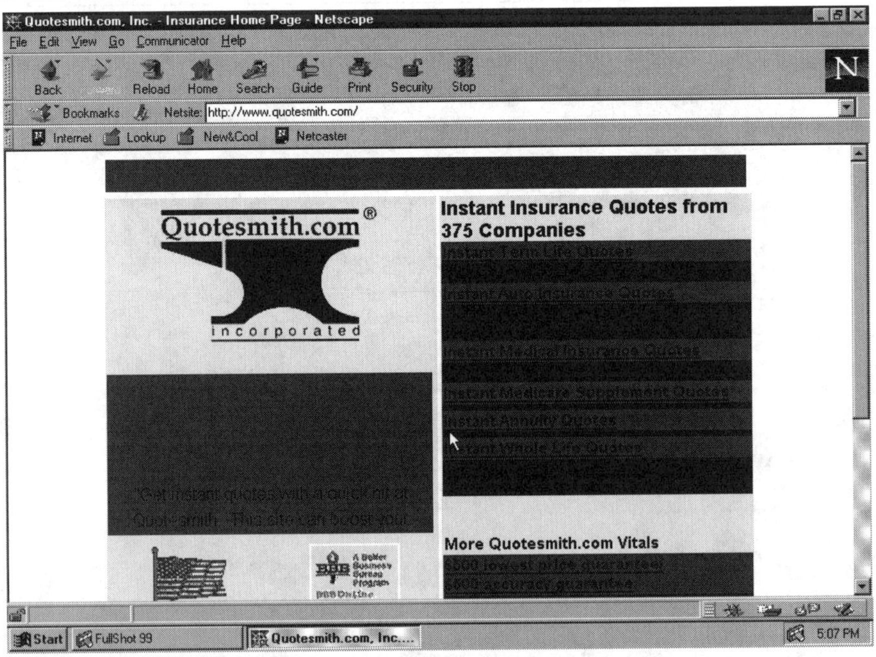

- Although not as user friendly, this site provides quotes from 375 insurance companies including term life, auto, and medical insurance.

- This site also has quotes for Medicare supplements as well as the most recent fixed annuity rates from dozens of companies.
- Want to be assured you're getting the best price? Read about Quotesmith's $500 lowest price guarantee. If you find a better deal, they'll give you a reward.

Insurance Industry Internet Network

http://www.iiin.com

Looking for an insurance company online? Visit the company boasting to be the most comprehensive site for finding one on the Web.

- This site offers links to hundreds of insurance companies' Web sites by selecting the Directory of Insurance Companies on the Web.
- You'll also find an extensive library of insurance news stories, job opportunities, insurance law firms, and other helpful resources.

Insurance News Network

http://www.insure.com

Keep up with the latest mergers and product innovations in the insurance industry with the Insurance News Network.

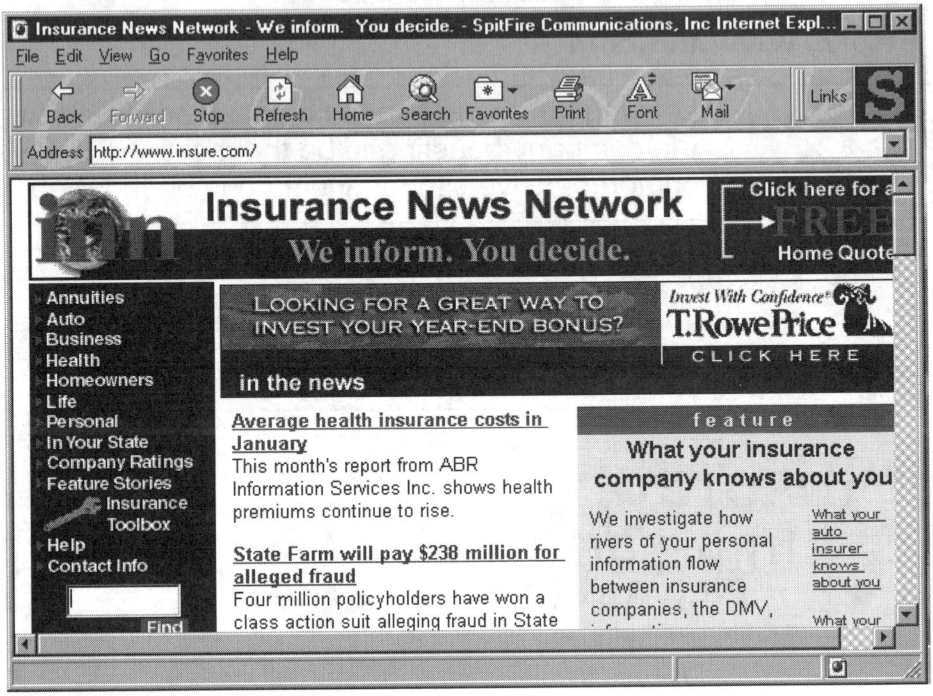

- Keep track of who's who and the latest news in the industry from the numerous articles on the main page.
- From the left side of the page click various product types to learn more about how the products work, their advantages and disadvantages, and how to select which ones best fit your needs.
- Having problems with your insurance company? Click the Help section and find articles and advice on issues like getting your claim paid and finding the new name of your insurance company.

Research Financial Strength of Insurance Companies on the Web

A.M. Best

http://www.ambest.com

A.M. Best was the first organization to rate the financial strength of insurance companies.

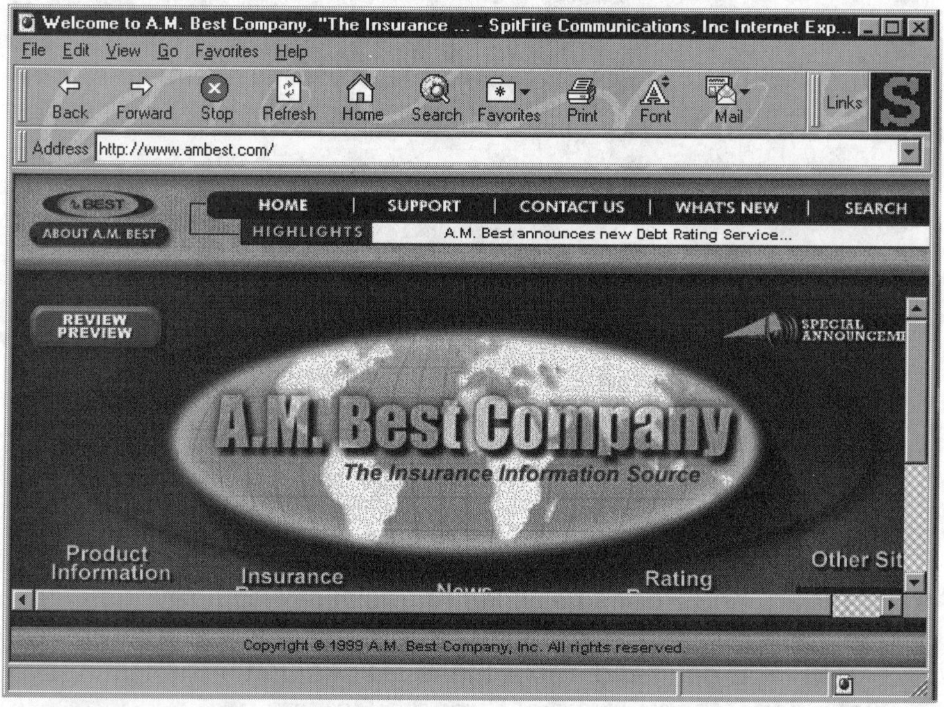

- Looking at both qualitative and quantitative criteria, A.M. Best evaluates over 5,400 insurance companies worldwide on a scale of A++ (superior) to F (in liquidation).
- To obtain a company profile and rating, click *Company Profiles* under Rating Resources and input the name of the company. You can obtain the overall rating and a snapshot of the company parent and subsidiaries as well as contact information at no charge. Comprehensive reports are available for download at a fee.

Standard & Poor's

http://www.standardandpoors.com/ratings

Standard & Poor's Rating Services are respected internationally. Check this site for timely objective credit analysis and information.

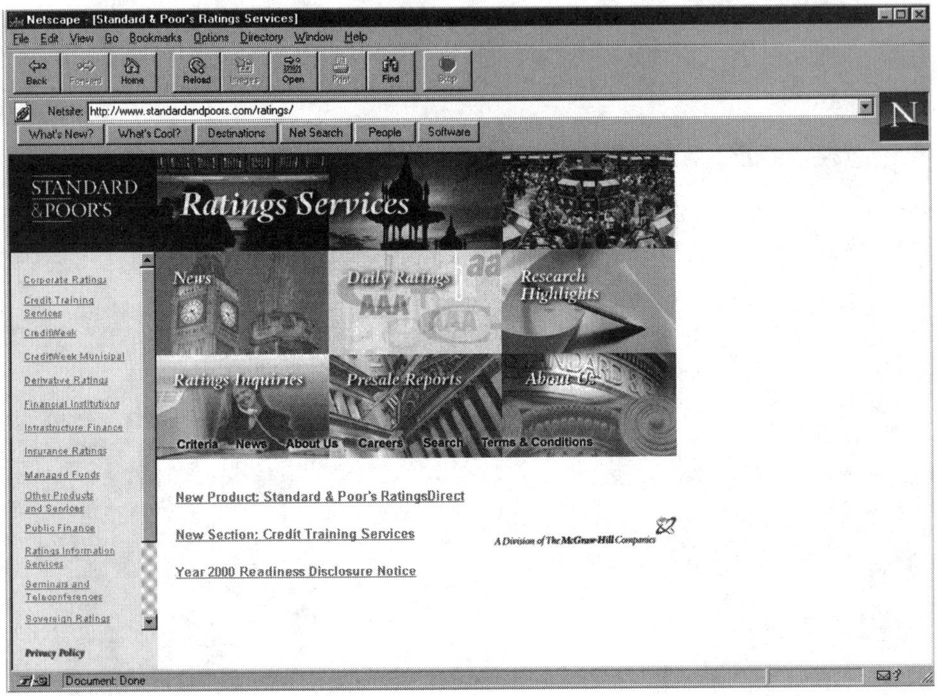

- Standard and Poor's provides financial strength ratings ranging from AAA (extremely strong) down to CC (extremely weak). You can read about these ratings under the Ratings Definitions, then Financial Strength Ratings.
- For more in depth comments on industry issues such as Y2K or the outlook for the coming year, surf through the Commentary section.

Investment Research, Tools, & Information

One of the most exciting and booming areas of the Internet is investment information and trading. A word of caution: use common sense before acting on the advice or recommendations that you find on the Internet. A good rule of thumb is not to invest in anything you don't understand. Please note: The advice and recommendations found on these sites are not an endorsement, solicitation, or recommendation by the authors of this book.

Morningstar

http://www.morningstar.net

Morningstar can help you find the top performing mutual funds and variable annuities in any investment category.

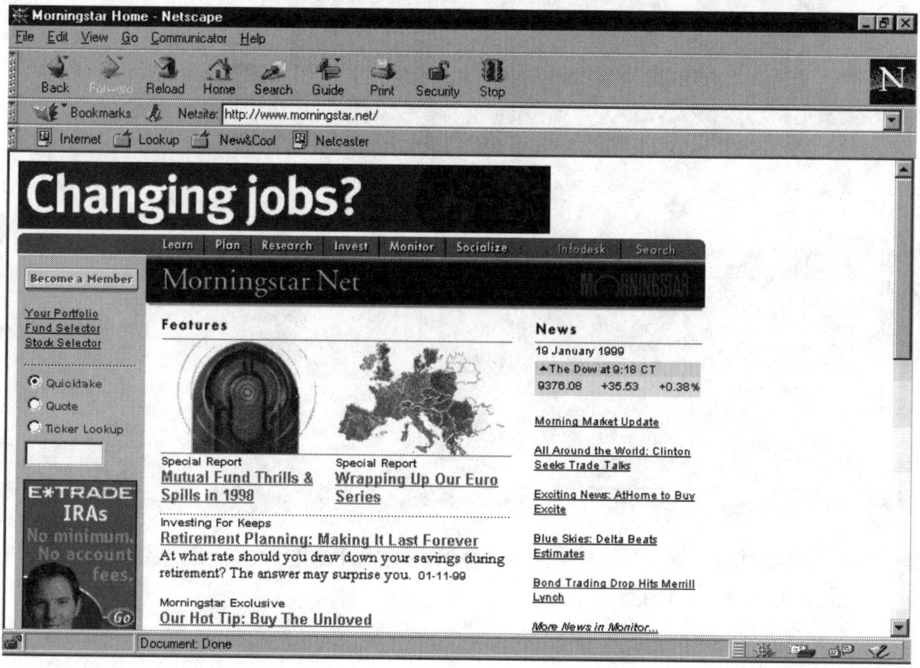

- The most trusted and quoted name for mutual fund research, Morningstar provides objective analysis and performance reporting for thousands of mutual funds.
- From the Research section use their Fund and Stock Selector databases to screen for the top-performing funds based on past performance, Morningstar ratings, or volatility.
- You might want to go to the Infodesk and read some of the definitions of terms listed under the Investment FAQ.

Standard & Poor's Personal Wealth

http://www.personalwealth.com

> For stock analysis and ratings, you might want to check out Standard & Poor's Personal Wealth site.

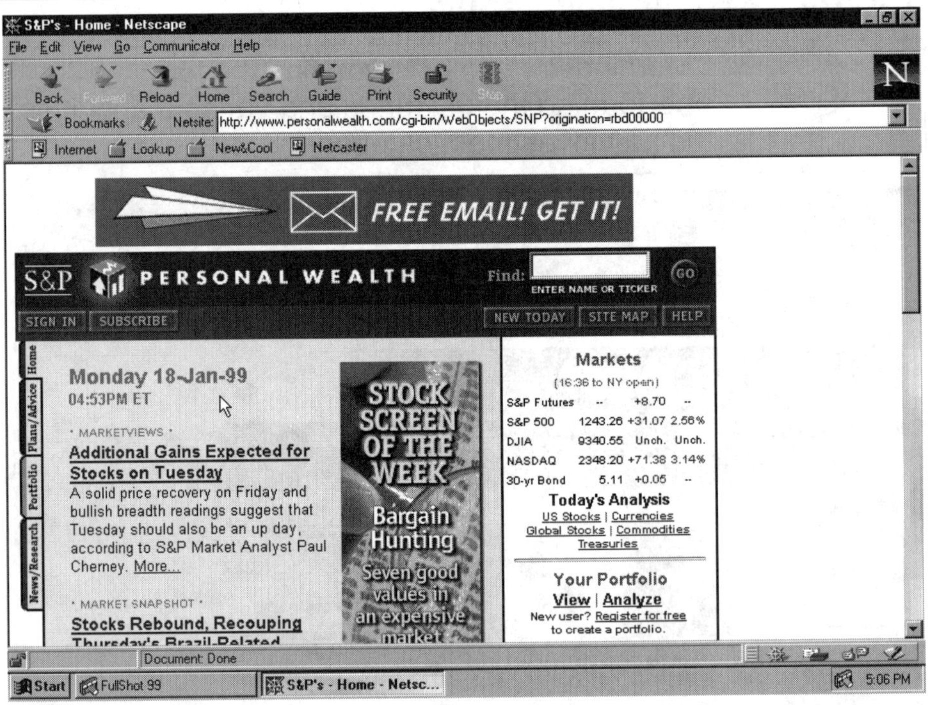

- Let Standard & Poor's research staff help you choose your individual stocks.

- From their News/Research section you can check out S & P's latest stock picks or search the S & P stock database by symbol. For more advanced financial data sorts, you must be a subscriber to S & P Personal Wealth, which costs $9.95/month.
- To buy and download individual stock reports without paying the monthly fee, go to S & P's Web site at *http://www.wsbi.com/spweb*. Complete the free online registration, then enter the site and download reports.

Investor Home

http://www.investorhome.com

> One of the best kept secrets on the Internet, this has to be the most advanced investment education site on the Web.

- This site is a must-see if you want to learn more about advanced investment concepts like Modern Portfolio Theory and Capital Asset Pricing Model.
- You'll want to check out both the Who's Who and the Anomalies sections. The Who's Who provides bios of dozens of well-known investment professionals summarizing their work and links to their sites. The Anomalies section covers historical stock market anomalies and how to identify and capitalize on them.

Briefing.com

http://www.briefing.com

> With awards from Dow Jones, *Barron's* and *Kiplinger* magazine, this site provides the basics for free, but for the real advanced analysis you'll need a subscription.

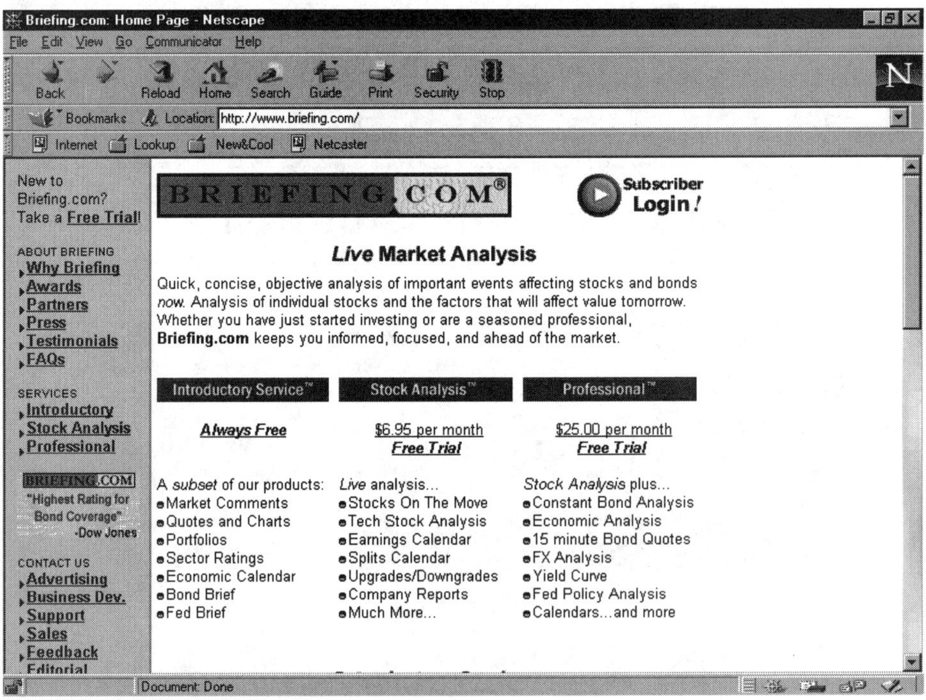

- A great site to begin your economic and market research, this site provides strong research capabilities for both stocks and bonds.
- The free section of the site provides continually updated helpful sections on Story Stocks, Upgrades & Downgrades, Split Calendar, and Fed Brief.
- For a monthly fee, Briefing provides two additional levels of service: Stock Analysis and Professional. Both are available on a free trial basis and are worthwhile if you are an active trader.

Edgar Online

http://www.edgaronline.com

Edgar Online gives you access to read the reports corporations are required to make to the SEC.

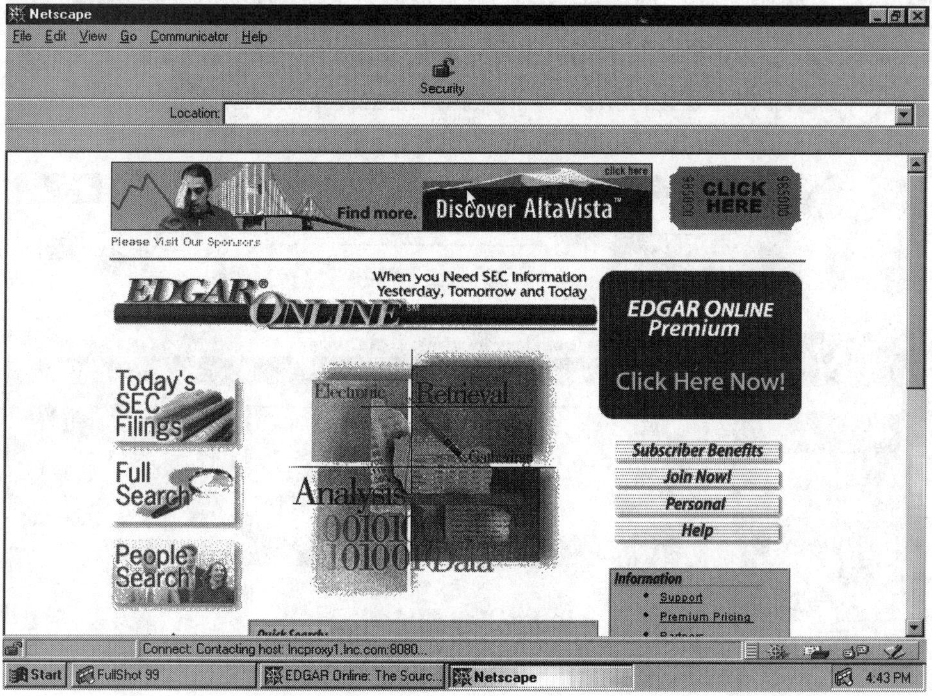

- Public companies are required to file income statements and balance sheets with the Securities Exchange Commission on a regular basis.
- Since the SEC is a government agency, these reports are a matter of public record, which can be accessed from Edgar Online. As of February 1999 the site was being rebuilt by the SEC.
- Until it is completed, you may access the database from *http://www.sec.gov/edgaux/searches.htm*.

Motley Fool

http://www.fool.com

A great educational site for the beginning to intermediate investor, Motley Fool provides a forum for investors to share investment ideas and financial information.

- One of the highlights of the site is the Stock Ideas section where various stocks are highlighted. You can read how the professionals feel about a stock, then check out the Message Board to add your comments and read others.
- As always, be careful with hot tips from this or any site. They are often considered "hot" because you can get burned easily.
- Make sure you visit *Fool School* and learn the 13 steps to investing foolishly.
- Under the News section, in addition to many other great resources, you might want to check out their listing of earning announcement conference calls available on *www.broadcast.com*.

Other Investment Research and Information Sites

TheStreet.com

http://www.thestreet.com

- The Commentary and Talk TSC sections of this site are worth the time and give you access to ongoing reports, comments, and chat opportunities from money managers, Wall Street columnists, and more. TheStreet wants to be your source for trusted, original, and timely financial news.

Value Line

http://www.valueline.com

- Some of the most widely read analysis used by investment professionals throughout the country, Value Line offers stock and mutual fund opinion articles and surveys without a subscription.

New York Stock Exchange

http://www.nyse.com

- The world's largest equities market at nearly $12 trillion, the New York Stock Exchange, through its Web site, strives to enhance your understanding of the capital formation and allocation process. More simply said, the NYSE site is designed to help you better understand how companies raise money by selling shares of ownership.

NASDAQ

http://www.nasdaq.com

- Started in 1971 after being commissioned by Congress, NASDAQ was the first electronic stock market. Among other useful resources, this site has a complex tool that allows you to screen companies based on up to 25 different financial criteria. Once you've found the company you are looking for you can read news reports, SEC filings, and basic financial information.

American Stock Exchange

http://www.amex.com

- Started more the 100 years ago, the American Stock Exchange is quickly becoming well-known for its Spiders and Webs. Visit the site to learn more about these indexed securities.

Investing Online—Mutual Funds

A mutual fund, by definition, is a collection of stocks, bonds, or other securities managed by an investment company with funds from a group of investors. Investing via mutual funds allows you to hire a professional money manager at a very low cost and still get a diversified portfolio. Following is a partial representation of some of the bigger and more popular mutual fund sites. The selection of these sites is not a solicitation or endorsement of their funds.

Fidelity

http://www.fidelity.com

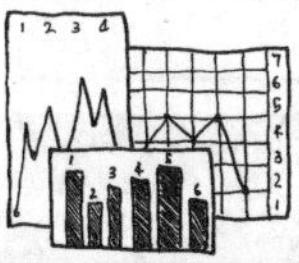

By far the largest privately held investment manager with assets under management exceeding $900 billion.

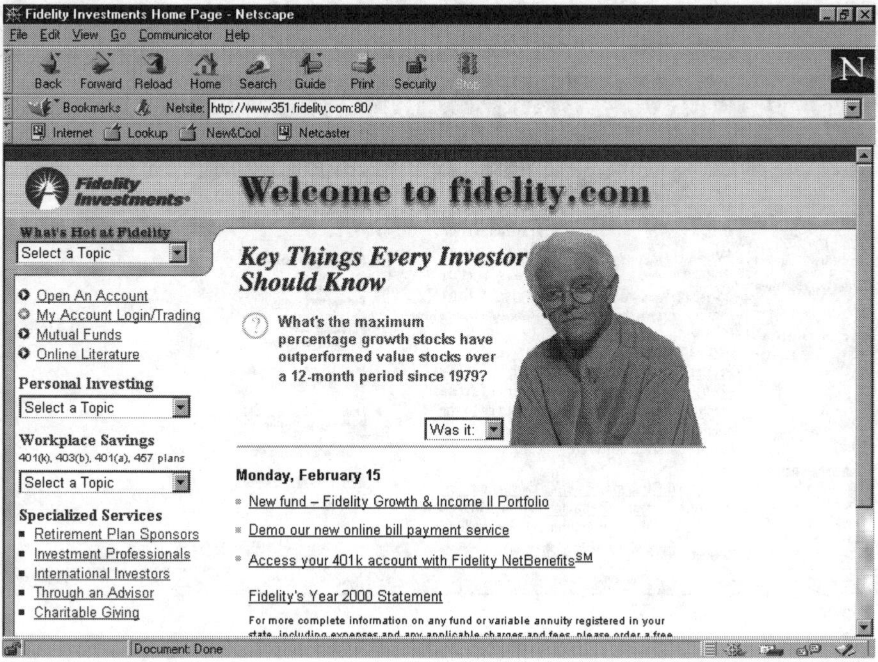

- With this much money under management, this powerhouse offers hundreds of funds to the individual investor. To look up past fund performance click *Mutual Funds*.
- Fidelity is more than a mutual fund company. Within their site, you can set up a brokerage account to buy and sell stocks, bonds, and mutual funds, and an option to enroll in their online bill payment service.
- You may want to read the latest advice from Peter Lynch in the Online Literature section. Click *Planning and Investment Guides and Services*.

Vanguard

http://www.vanguard.com

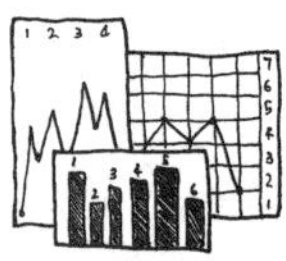

Vanguard's mission is to provide a broad range of mutual funds and financial services in accordance with the highest standards of quality at the lowest reasonable cost.

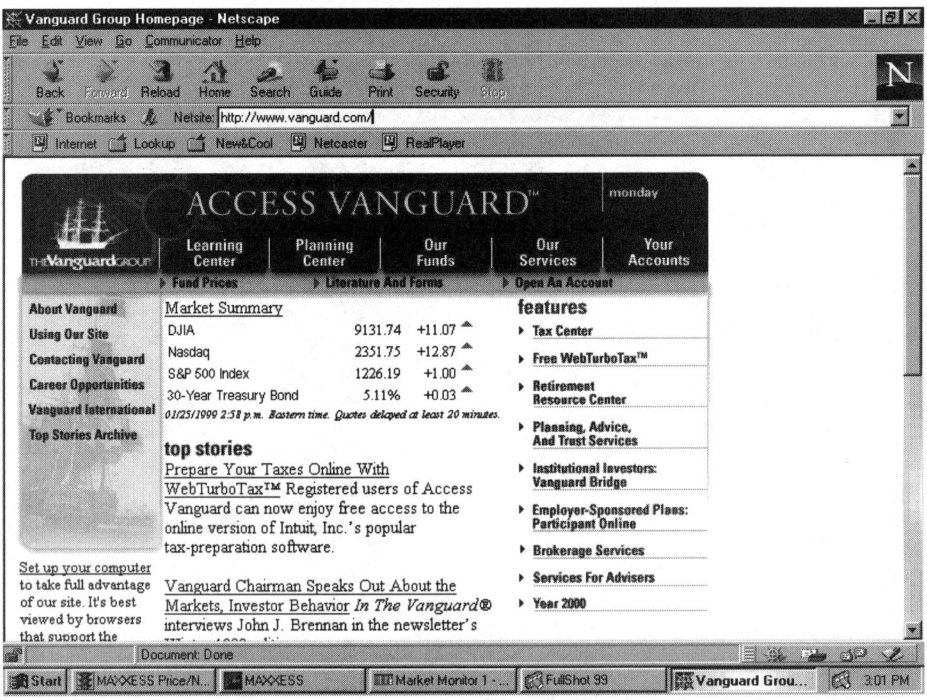

- Known for their low cost and market index funds, Vanguard has grown to be one of the largest players in the mutual fund industry.
- To look up fund performance and pricing, click *Our Funds* to find fund facts, daily pricing, and reports.
- Check out their University, which can be found by clicking *Our Services*, then *The University* in the Education section.

Putnam

http://www.putnaminvestments.com

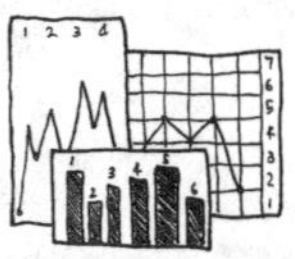

In 61 years Putnam has put $294 billion under management in nearly 11 million individual and 600 institutional accounts, making it among the largest of mutual fund companies.

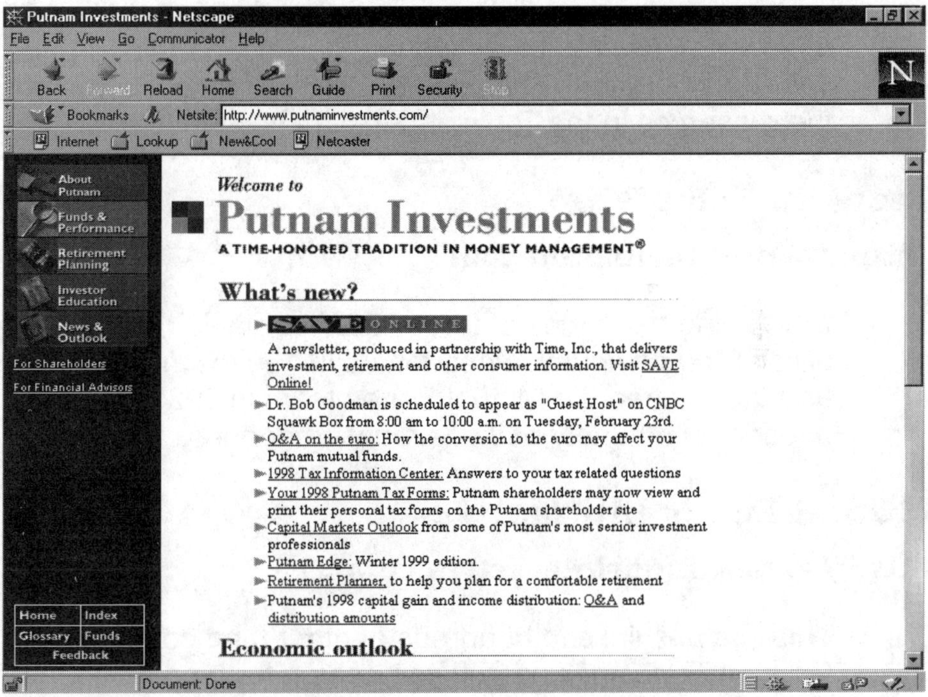

- A color-coded and easy-to-use site, the must-see section is the Economic Outlook by Putnam's Senior Economic Advisor, Dr. Robert Goodman.

- Putnam allows account holders to access their accounts in the For Shareholders section. If you have a Putnam account, you will need to get a password before entering this area.
- Another section that will give you a feel for Putnam's expectation for the future is their Capital Market Outlook in the News & Outlook Section.

Other Online Mutual Fund Sites

For more complete listings of mutual fund companies on the Internet, be sure to review the following Web sites.

T. Rowe Price

http://www.troweprice.com

- Another of the big fund companies with about $147 billion under management, T. Rowe Price provides more than 75 different funds. You might want to download their 45-page Tax Considerations of Investors Guide or try out some of the resources in the Tools and Insight section.

Franklin Templeton

http://www.templeton.com

- Combining the forces of three fund companies, this $200 billion fund company joined forces in 1992 with Templeton and then added the Mutual Series team in 1996, making it a leader in a variety of investment categories.

Mutual Funds Interactive

http://www.fundsinteractive.com

- This site has links to hundreds of other fund companies. Click on *FundLink* and you can search for fund company Web sites alphabetically by fund family name.

Investing Online—Brokers

One of the fastest growing segments of the Internet is online trading. To be an online investor you need to be confident that you can research and choose investments better than a broker or professional money manager. Another problem has been the backlog of trades, which can take several hours to execute and even longer to find out at what price. At the time this book was written the SEC was looking into ways to better regulate this industry and protect consumers.

As these sites are continually changing and improving, you may want to visit the Smart Money, Kiplinger, or Gomez sites to read about their latest reviews and ratings of online brokers. Their respective web addresses are *http://www.smartmoney.com, http://www.kiplinger.com* and *http://www.gomez.com*.

Please note that the sites reviewed are neither a specific recommendation nor a solicitation for any of these sites.

Quick&Reilly's QuickWayNet

http://www.quickwaynet.com

Voted the top-rated online broker *by Smart Money* magazine.

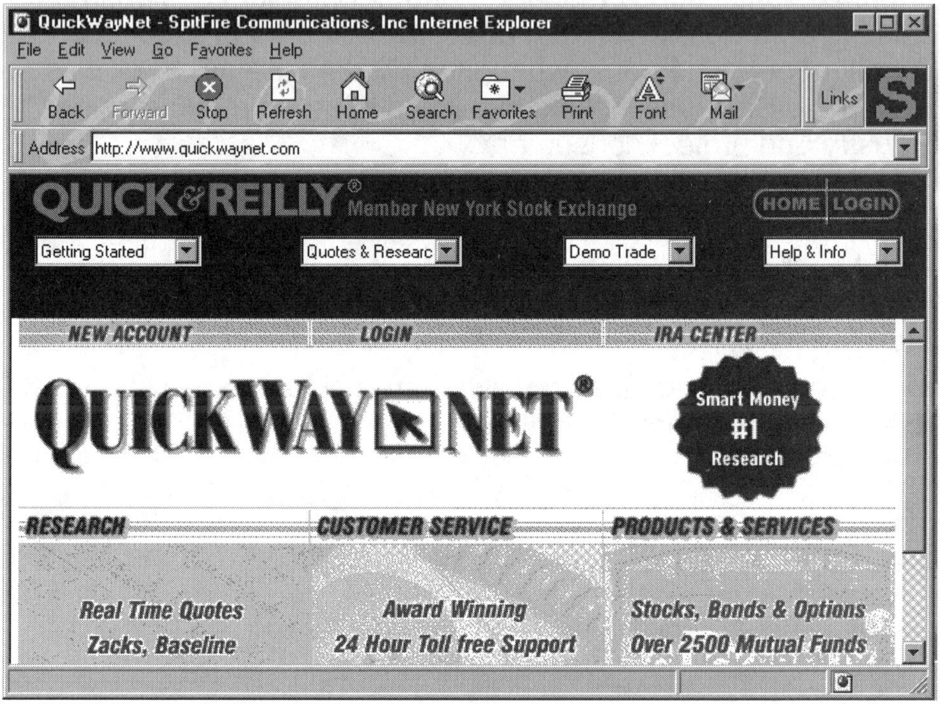

- Quick&Reilly's QuickWayNet provides 100 real-time quotes per trade you execute on their site.
- Account holders are given free or discounted access to several of the top names in market research, including Zacks, Briefing.com, and Morningstar.

Ameritrade

http://www.ameritrade.com

A very graphic and user-friendly button-pushing layout, Ameritrade claims to have one of the lowest cost market orders on the Web.

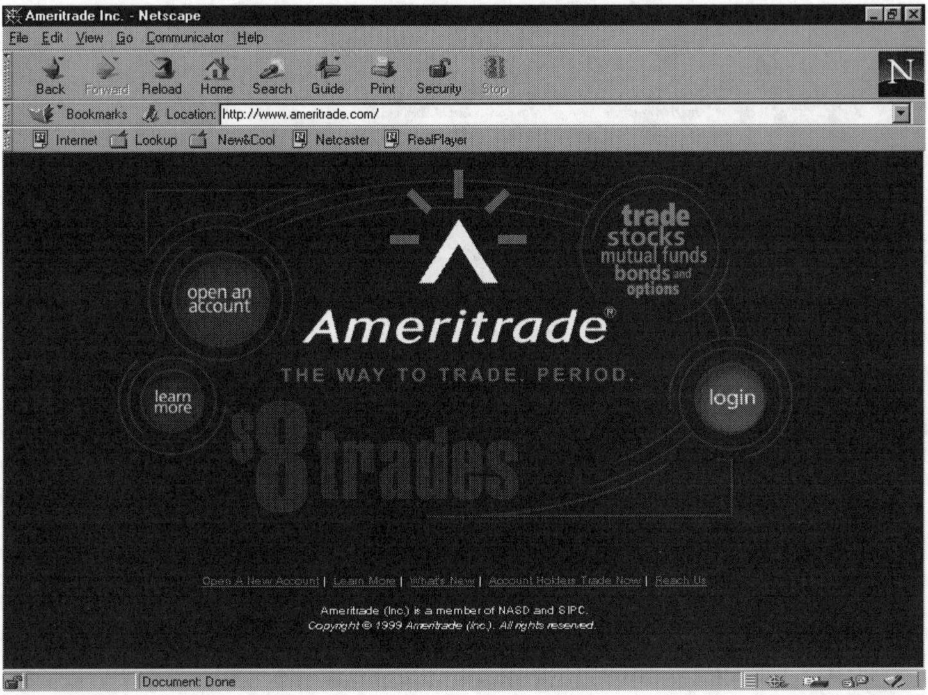

- They also offer 100 real-time quotes for each trade executed via their site.
- If you're uncomfortable with placing your trades online, Ameritrade allows you to invest by touch-tone phone or broker assisted for a higher fee.
- For faster trade confirmations, Ameritrade sends them directly to you via e-mail.

E*Trade

http://www.etrade.com

Ranked the number one online investing service by Gomez Advisors in November 1998.

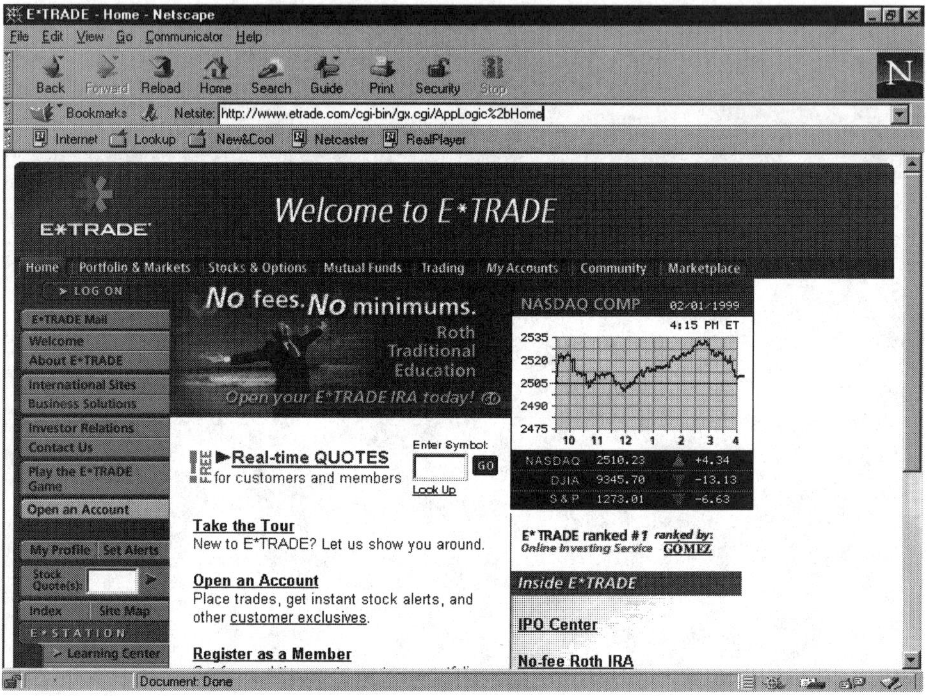

- E*Trade is one of the most popular online trading sites on the Net. The advantages they tout are more value for your money, easier access to your account, low minimum initial investments, and participation in IPOs.
- With a free membership you can join one of their many discussion groups or visit their learning center to discover the advantages of online trading.

Schwab Online

http://www.schwab.com

Claiming to be the online leader, Charles Schwab's site seems to have it all.

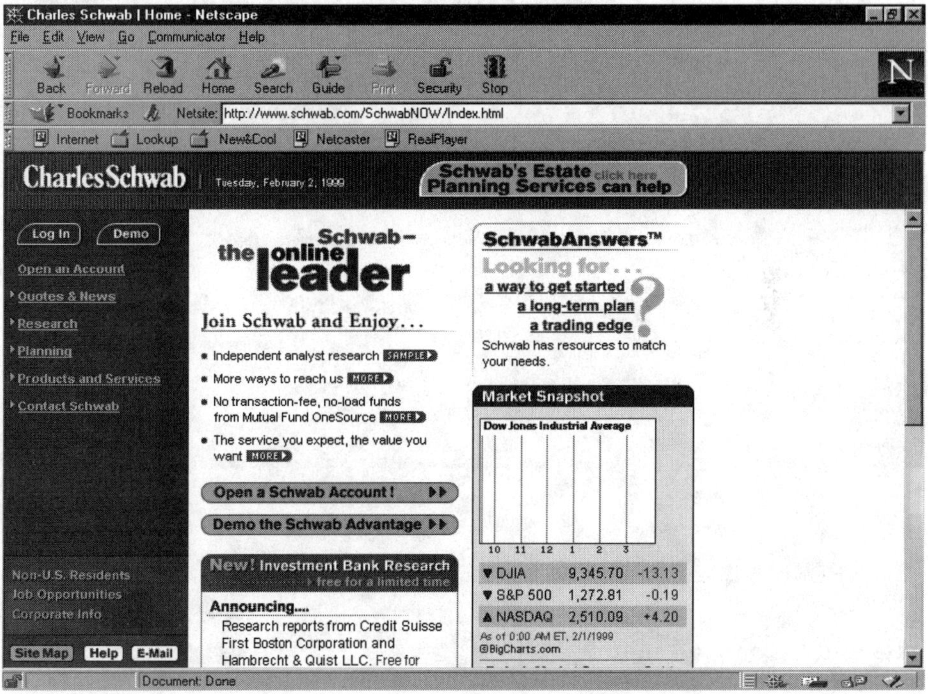

- A very complete site, Schwab Online has an easy-to-use financial planning section that covers topics such as retirement, estate, college, and tax planning.
- Another area worth review is the *Analyst Center Demo* within the Research department. Here you can get a complete overview of the type of in-depth analysis and information you can expect if you become a customer.
- For the high-end investor, Schwab also provides a variety of account sizes and levels of service.

DLJ Direct

http://www.dljdirect.com

Considered the "Cadillac of Web Brokers" by *Time* magazine.

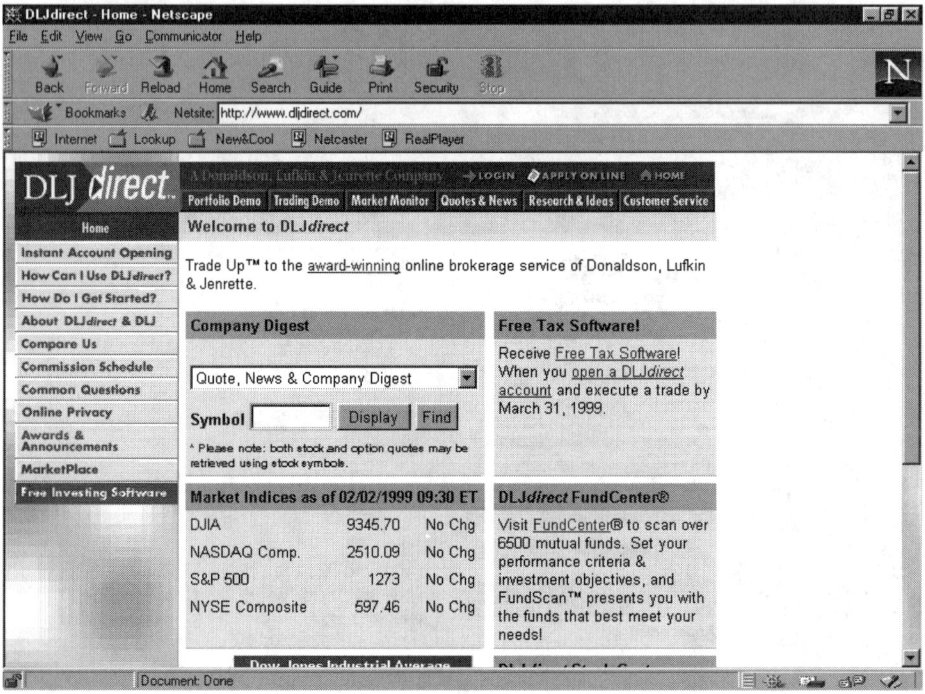

- Donaldson, Lufkin & Jenrette's DLJDirect site boasts having over 520,000 members.
- DLJ also offers instant account approval for members so they can be up and trading in a matter of seconds.
- As an account holder you can have access to their Stock Center, which allows you to research, sort, and evaluate over 4,500 stocks online using Standard & Poor's, Zacks Investment Research, and Lipper Analytical Services.

Other Brokerage Sites

Although many of these sites provide similar services at competitive pricing, choose a recognizable online broker that downloads quickly on your computer system.

Datek

http://www.datek.com

- Ranked number one by TheStreet's Online Investors and listed the fourth largest based on volume by Piper Jaffrey, Datek promises your market orders to be executed within 60 seconds or they will waive the commission. Some restrictions apply, so see their site for details.

1800DayTrade

http://www.1800daytrade.com

- 1800DayTrade offers real-time level II market quotations and point-and-click order entry. They allow the public to compete with the market makers and work their own orders by hitting the bids or taking the offers to avoid paying the market maker's spread.

Suretrade

http://www.suretrade.com

- A comprehensive Internet broker for the individual investor, Suretrade has received numerous awards from *Smart Money, Fortune,* and *Money* magazines for no frills, low-cost investing.

ScoTTrade

http://www.scottrade.com

- ScoTTrade, with 90 offices across the nation, offers online trading supported by their network of offices. As an account holder with ScoTTrade you are assigned a personal broker.

Tax Answers & Forms

As former Federal Judge Learned Hand said, "There is nothing sinister in so arranging one's affairs as to keep taxes as low as possible. Everyone does so, rich or poor; and all do right, for no one owes any public duty to pay more than the law demands." To that end, check out the following sites for helpful tax advice and reduction strategies.

IRS

http://www.irs.gov

Welcome to the most user-friendly portion of the IRS!

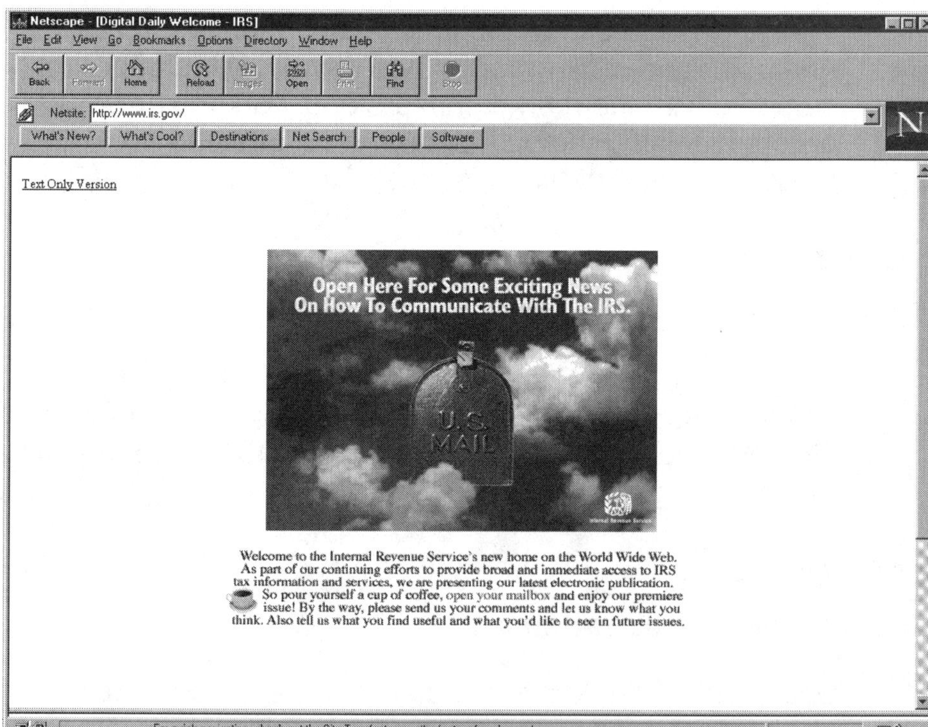

- From this site you can download IRS forms and publications or get some assistance from the Tax Payer Help & Education section accessed at the bottom.
- Once inside the Help & Education section, try the Tele-Tax Topics and Frequently Asked Tax Questions. Both provide helpful hints to expedite your tax filings and record keeping.

Ernst & Young TaxCast

http://www.taxcast.com

Provided by Ernst & Young, TaxCast provides helpful information and links to shorten your tax return preparation.

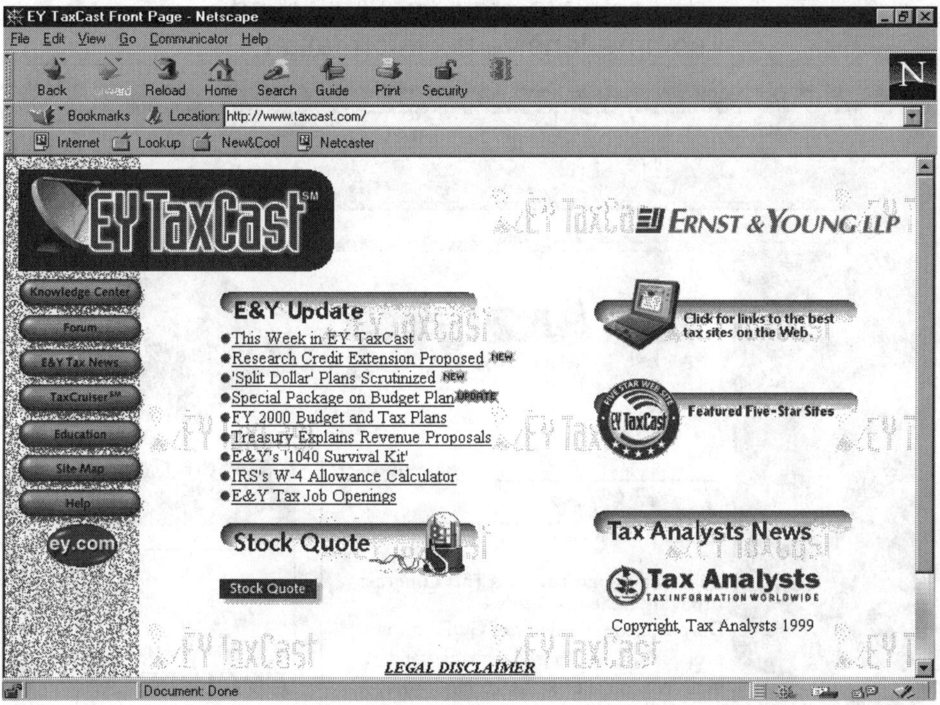

- Check out the 1040 Survival Kit. This section provides advice on tax tables, deduction, exemption, and Social Security free of charge.

- Having trouble figuring out how many exemptions to take on your W-4? Try out the Form W-4 Withholding Calculator and get a more accurate estimate of the number you should be taking. Remember, large tax refunds are not necessarily a good thing. These are interest-free loans to the IRS.
- Between the Knowledge Center, Forum, and Tax Cruiser sections, you'll find helpful articles and links covering tax law changes, commonly overlooked deductions, and more.

Tax Analysts

http://www.tax.org

Tax Analysts is a nonprofit organization dedicated to providing timely and comprehensive tax information.

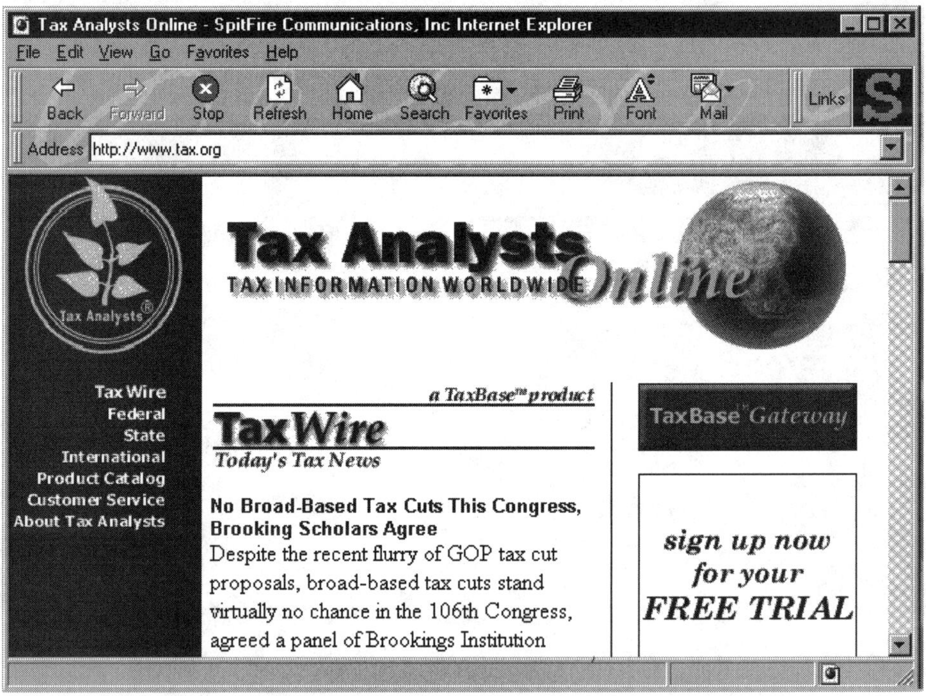

- If you prepare your own taxes, Tax Analyst is a great source for overall tax news and helpful tax links. To read the latest tax issues being considered in Congress or in the news, click *Tax Wire*.

- Be sure to review the discussion groups on a variety of tax topics. Each is an e-mail group moderated by one of the staff members. To subscribe, click *Discussion Groups*.

Now You Can File Your Taxes Online!

TurboTax

http://www.turbotax.com

Tax preparation goes to the next level. Prepare your tax returns online for a nominal fee and, in some cases, free!

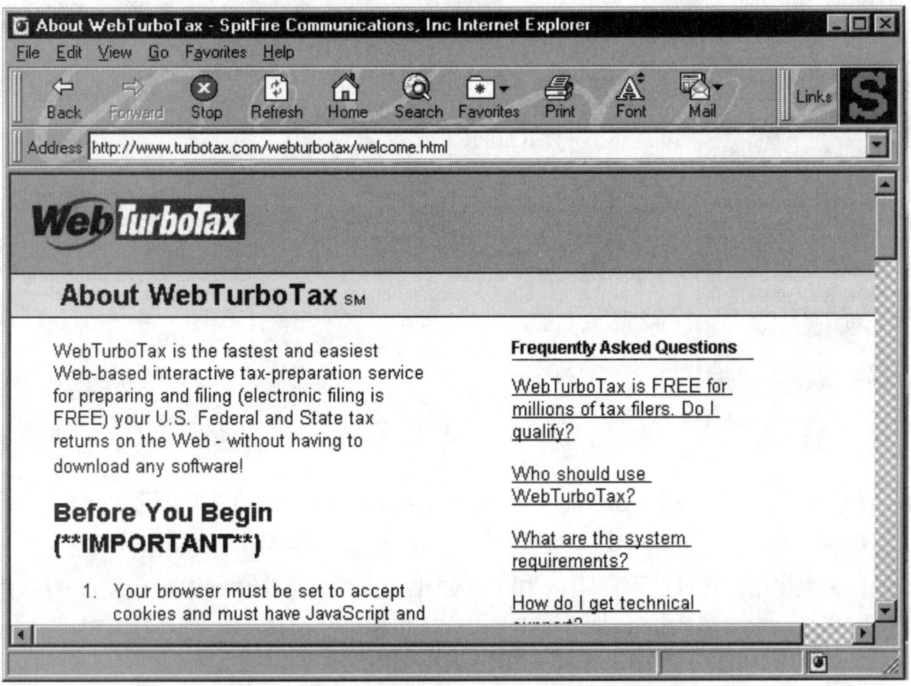

- From the TurboTax homepage, click *WebTurboTax*. In some cases the tax-preparation service is free. Click *WebTurboTax is FREE* to see if you qualify.
- If you don't qualify, there will be a service fee charged when you finish and choose to file your return. WebTurboTax supports most schedules and most returns, including 1040EZ, 1040A, and 1040.

Kiplinger's TaxCut

http://www.taxcut.com

Are you one of over 24 million people who qualify to use 1040EZ to file your taxes? Now you can file online at Kiplinger.

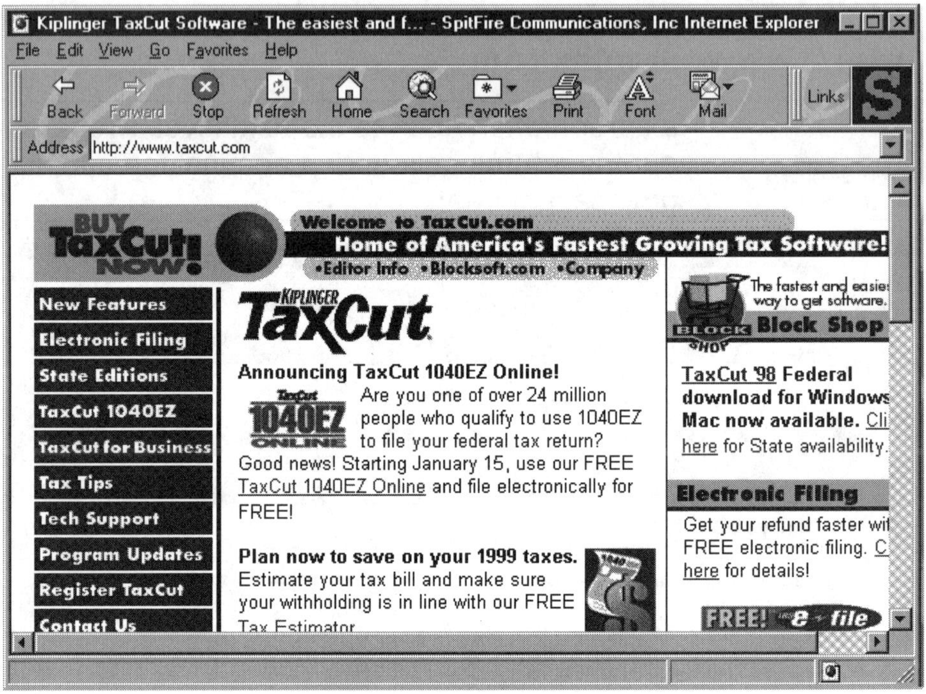

- If you have a simple tax return and file form 1040EZ, you might want to use Kiplinger's TaxCut online filing for free.
- In addition to online tax filing capabilities, this site has a great section on tax tips broken down line by line for the most common tax forms and schedules.
- Want to estimate your tax bill for next year? Try their easy-to-use calculator by clicking Tax Estimator.

Joint Committee on Taxation

http://www.house.gov/jct/

Want to stay abreast of the tax proposals in Congress? Bookmark this site for the Joint Committee on Taxation.

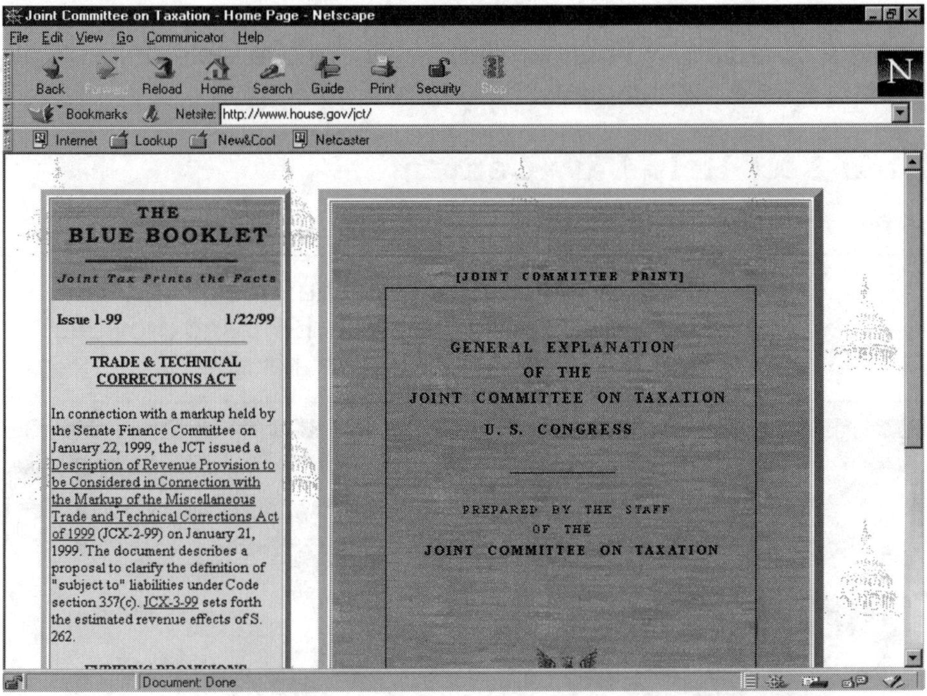

- From this site read the latest findings and thoughts coming out of Washington on taxes. When you are finished reviewing the proposals, simply return to *http://www.house.gov*, find your congressional representative, and let them know what you think.

TAXES

Planning Your Estate

Throughout your lifetime you will accumulate and manage assets. At some point, however, you must decide how to give them away. Take action and make a plan. If you have young children make sure you have a will, if for no other reason than to name a guardian. Numerous resources are available online that explain estate planning laws and concepts.

Nolo Self-Help Law Center

http://www.nolo.com

Nolo is the leading publisher of self-help law books and software since 1971 and provides an online encyclopedia on this site.

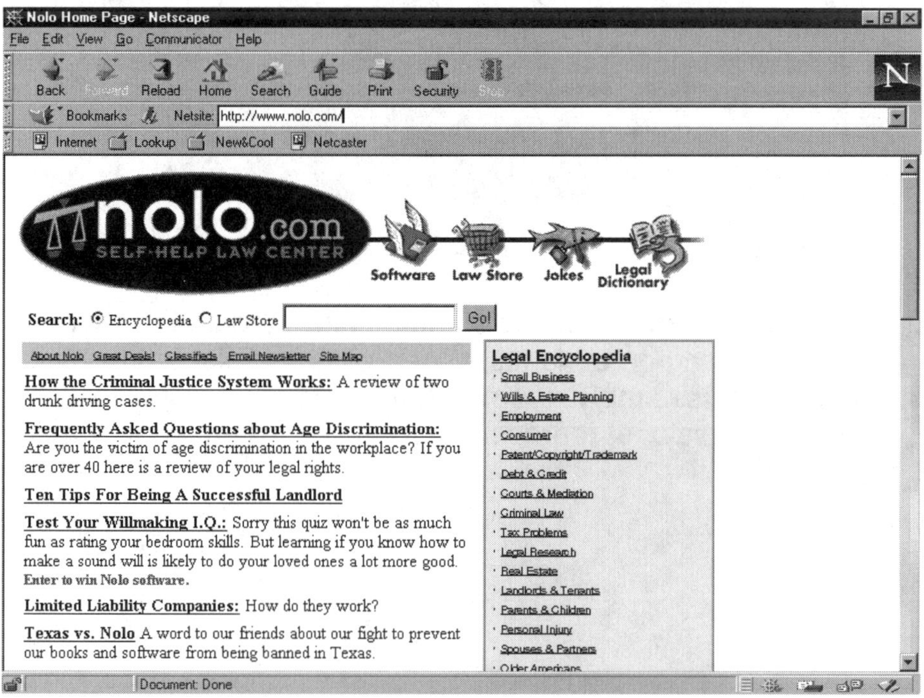

- Not only does this online encyclopedia provide information on estate planning, but on numerous other legal topics as well.
- To enter the encyclopedia's estate planning section, click *Wills and Estate Planning*. You can choose among subtopics ranging from *Wills* to *Living Trusts* to *Estate and Gift Taxes* to *Funeral Planning*.
- Also from the homepage you will find a dictionary where you can look up any legal terminology or lingo and find an understandable explanation.

Deloitte & Touche Online

http://www.dtonline.com

This site provides plenty of helpful information in both the estate and tax planning categories.

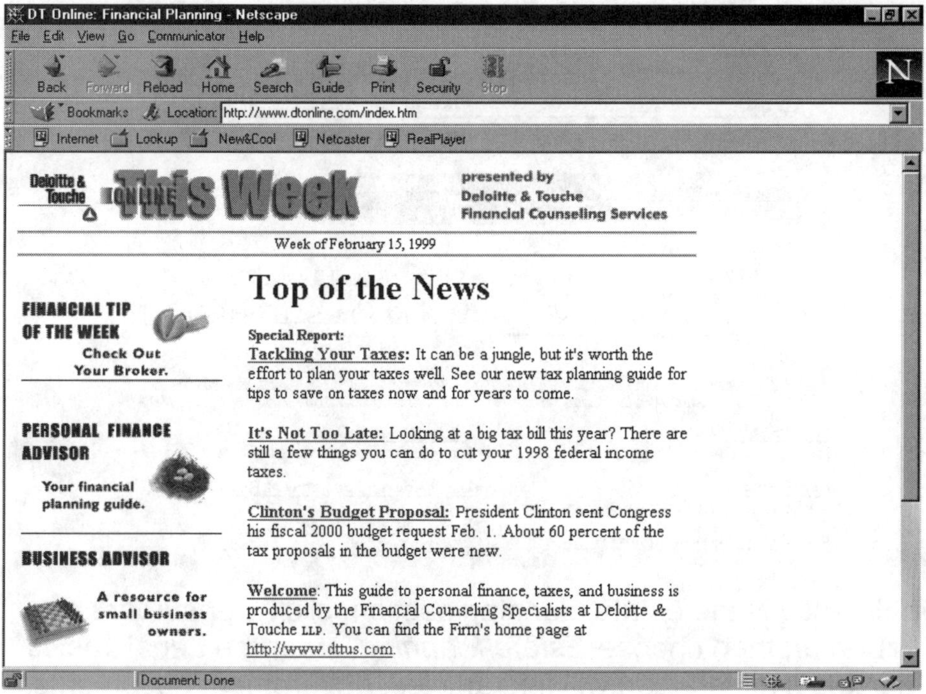

- To get to the estate planning section from the main page, click *Personal Finance Advisor*, then *Estate Planning Guide*.

- The site contains educational articles on a broad variety of estate planning issues, including estate taxes, record keeping, and coping with death.
- For less technical advice, you might find the *How to discuss estate planning with your parents* and *How to discuss a will with your attorney* links helpful.

Find Law

http://www.findlaw.com

For comprehensive technical guidance, check out Find Law's resources, including specific laws and cases.

- To access the estate planning section, click *Consumer Law Center*, then choose *Estate Planning* under the Legal Topics category. Here you will find articles, government documents, and links to other estate planning resources on the Web.

- This site provides a tremendous amount of information, resources, and links on nearly every legal topic, so you may want to bookmark it for future reference.

WWW Virtual Law Library

http://www.law.indiana.edu/law/v-lib

Need a complete law library at your fingertips? This one is worth typing the URL.

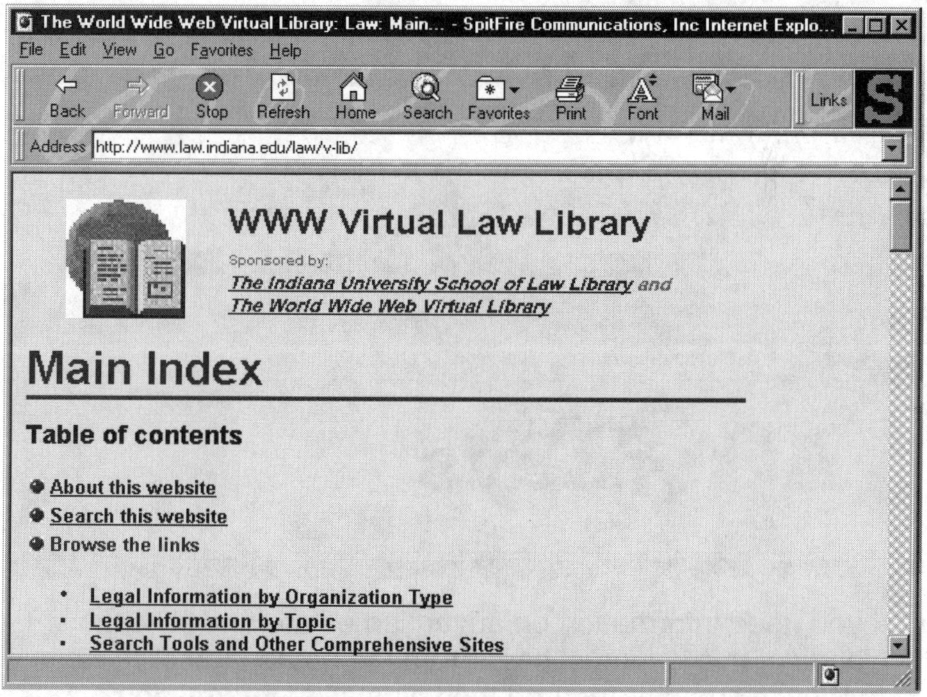

- Sponsored by the Indiana University School of Law, this site allows you to search by topic or organization type, as well as other comprehensive law sites. To begin a search within the library, simply click *The World Wide Web Virtual Library*.
- Numerous other legal resources are available by clicking *The Indiana University School of Law Library*, then *Internet Resources*. Within this site you will find law encyclopedias, fact books, legal dictionaries, and more.

National Network of Estate Planning Attorneys

http://www.netplanning.com

Check out the National Network of Estate Planning Attorneys for explanations and information on advanced estate planning strategies.

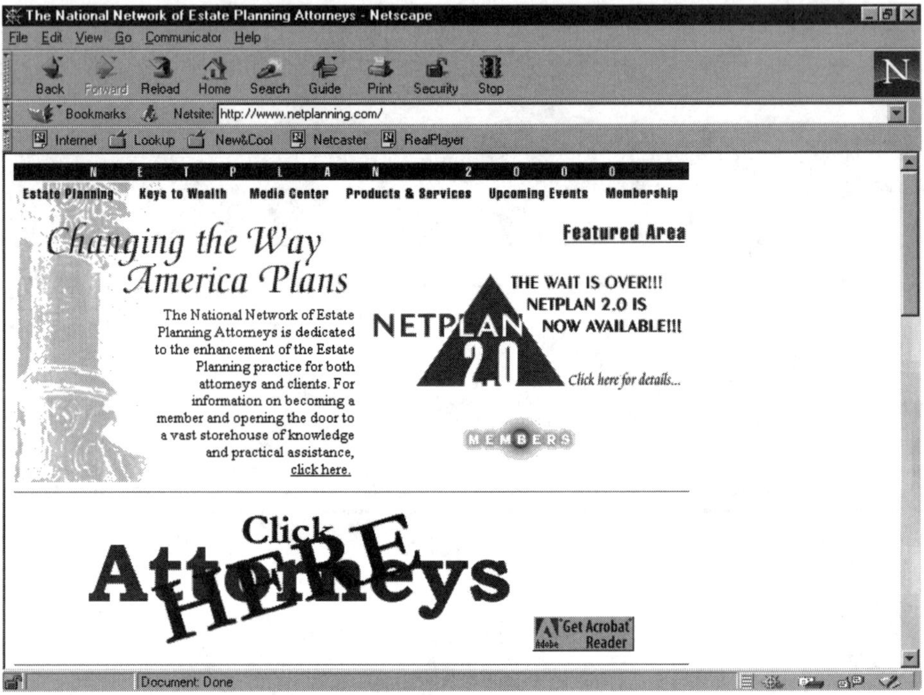

- If you need information on advanced estate and charitable planning, this is a must see. From the homepage click *Keys to Wealth* and sort through the volumes of information on Business Continuation, Retirement and Charitable Planning, and more.
- If these are important issues to you, you'll need several hours to appreciate the resources on this site.

Finding an Advisor

As you become busier and more successful, you may want to seek out accountants, attorneys, financial planners, investment advisors, or insurance sales people to help you better manage your affairs.

A number of sites are available on the Internet to help you find advisors in your area. Note: none of these sites guarantee the competency of the advisors on the list. Before you commit to a relationship you will want to meet to find out their areas of specialty, methods of compensation, and types of clientele they serve. Most advisors offer free "get acquainted" meetings, so don't be afraid to ask.

American Institute of Certified Public Accountants

http://www.aicpa.org

The American Institute of Certified Public Accountants is the premiere national professional association of CPAs in the U.S.

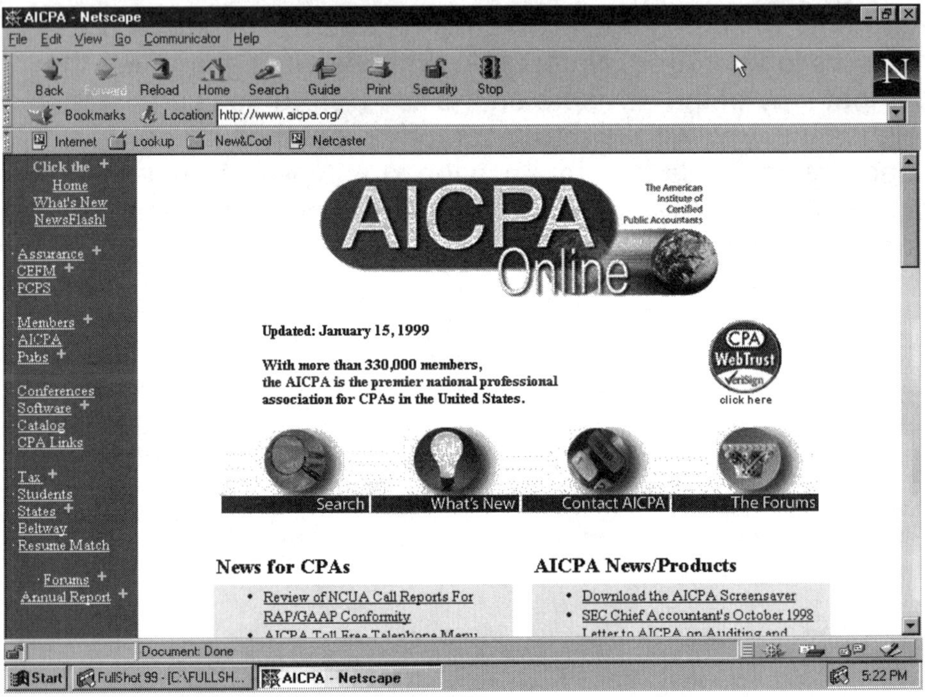

- Currently the AICPA does not provide a locator service within their Web site.
- A roundabout way to find a CPA through their site is by clicking *State Information* and then *USA Map*. Choose a state and you will be linked to its local CPA Society. Many of the state CPA Society pages have directories of CPAs and, in some cases, a quick biographical sketch.
- In order for CPAs to join this association, they must agree to a Code of Professional Conduct, which is in the Upholding the Profession section—found by clicking *AICPA* on the left side of the page.

- Having problems with a CPA? Let the association know by clicking *Contact AICPA* and use the General Feedback Form.

Association of Practicing CPAs

http://www.ap-cpa.org

This association for CPAs, designed to help CPAs network with one another, provides a national online directory.

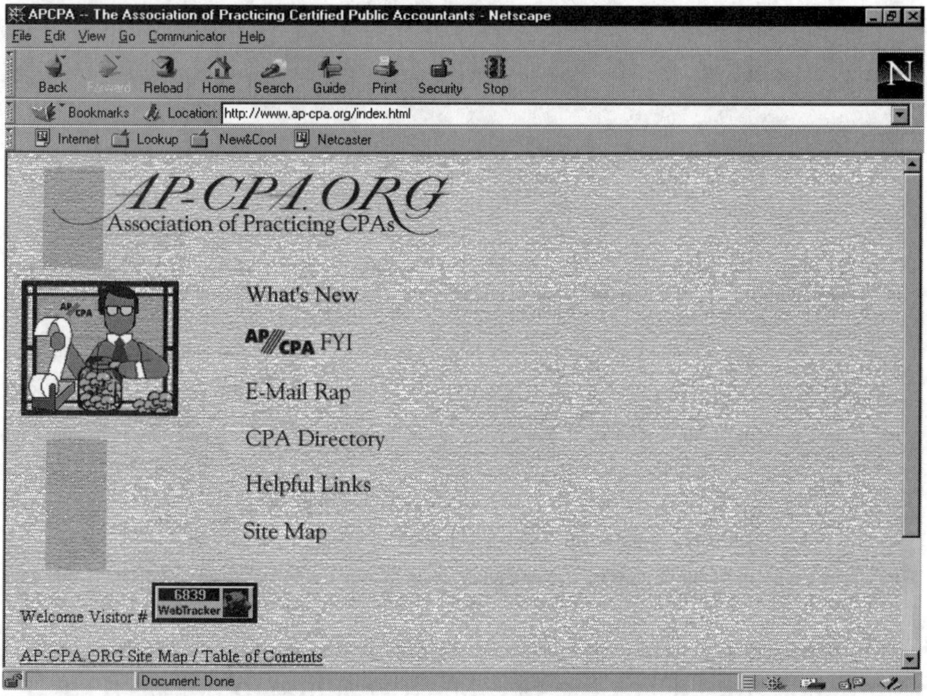

- Although not a complete listing of CPAs, this site does give you a start. To find a CPA, simply click *CPA Directory* to search by name, location, or area of specialty.
- If you are searching by state, make sure to use the two letter abbreviation.

West Legal Directory

http://www.wld.com

West Legal Directory provides profiles of more than 800,000 lawyers and law firms throughout the U.S.

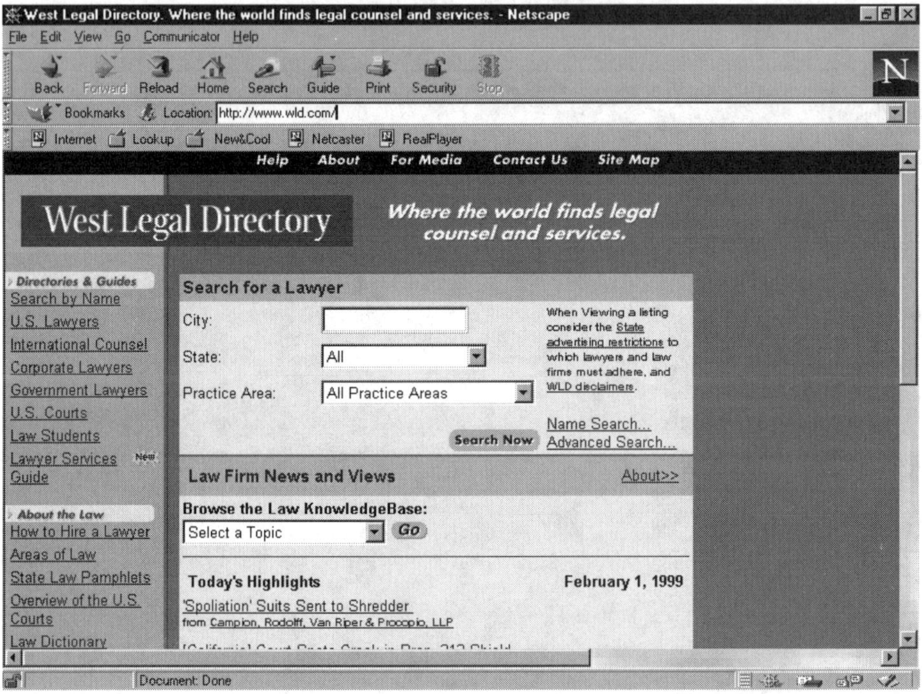

- To find an attorney in your area, choose a city, state, and a practice area. Click the *Search Now* button to pull up a list of attorneys that meets your criteria.
- Click an attorney's name to read their bio. It contains the date they were admitted into the bar, the schools they attended, their areas of specialty, and more.
- As with all sites, you will want to decide if you are comfortable with the level of expertise of these advisors. For guidance on what to ask or how the process should flow, click *How to Hire an Attorney*.

National Network of Estate Planning Attorneys

http://www.netplanning.com

Check out the National Association of Estate Planning Attorneys locator service if you are in search of this specialty.

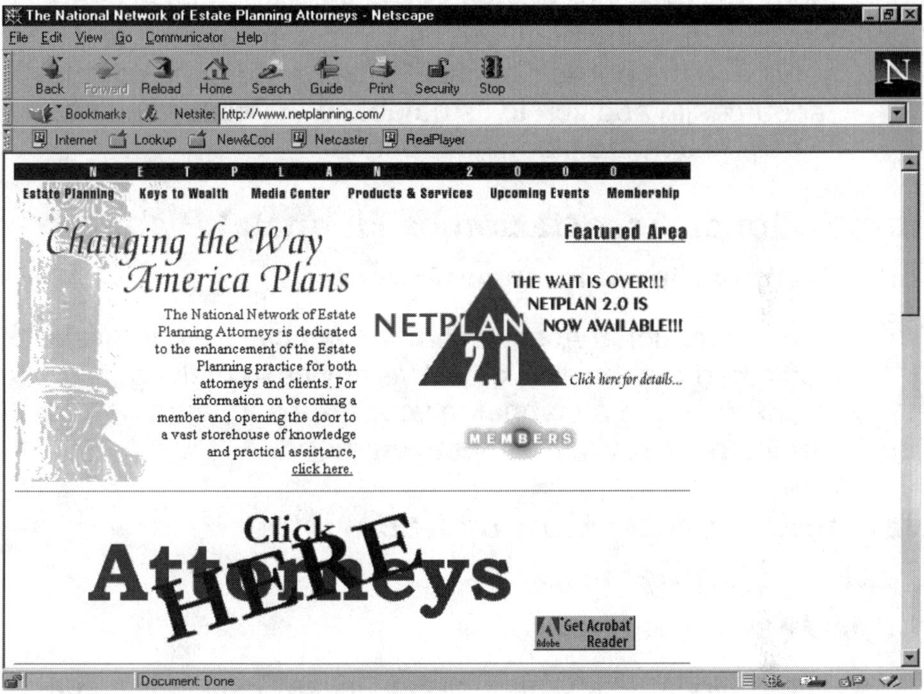

- To begin, scroll about halfway down the page and click *Search Our Online Database…*, then *Find a Network Attorney in Your Area*. You will able to search by location, calling up a list of members of the Network of Estate Planning Attorneys in that area.
- This organization provides volumes of continuing education for its members, but does not guarantee the competency level or sophistication of services.

Other Sites

Institute of Certified Financial Planners

http://www.icfp.org

- The Institute of Certified Financial Planners is the association of CFP professionals, which calls on its members to aspire to the highest levels of ethical conduct, personal development, professional competence and service to the public. The ICFP site provides numerous resources in addition to its database of financial planners to help you in the planning process.

International Association of Financial Planners

http://www.planningpaysoff.org

- The International Association of Financial Planners is dedicated to providing objective advice in making financial decisions. Find a planner in your area and learn how to get the best advisor to meet your needs.

National Association of Securities Dealers Regulation

http://www.nasdr.com

- The National Association of Securities Dealers is a self-regulatory organization that develops rules and regulations for the benefit and protection of the individual investor.

Investor Protection Trust

http://www.investorprotection.org

- The Investor Protection Trust is a nonprofit organization providing education and protection to the noncommercial investor. It was formed as part of a multi-state settlement to resolve charges of misconduct.

Buying a Car or Truck

America's love affair with cars has lead to one of the largest, but sometimes least enjoyable, industries. With all the price haggling, financing alternatives, and special incentives, the process of buying a car doesn't have to be so complicated. Highlighted here are both informational sites that provide pricing and process tips, and sites where you can find the specific car you want without stepping into a showroom.

Kelley Blue Book

http://www.kbb.com

Want to know the value of your used car? Check out Kelley Blue Book's used-car pricing guide.

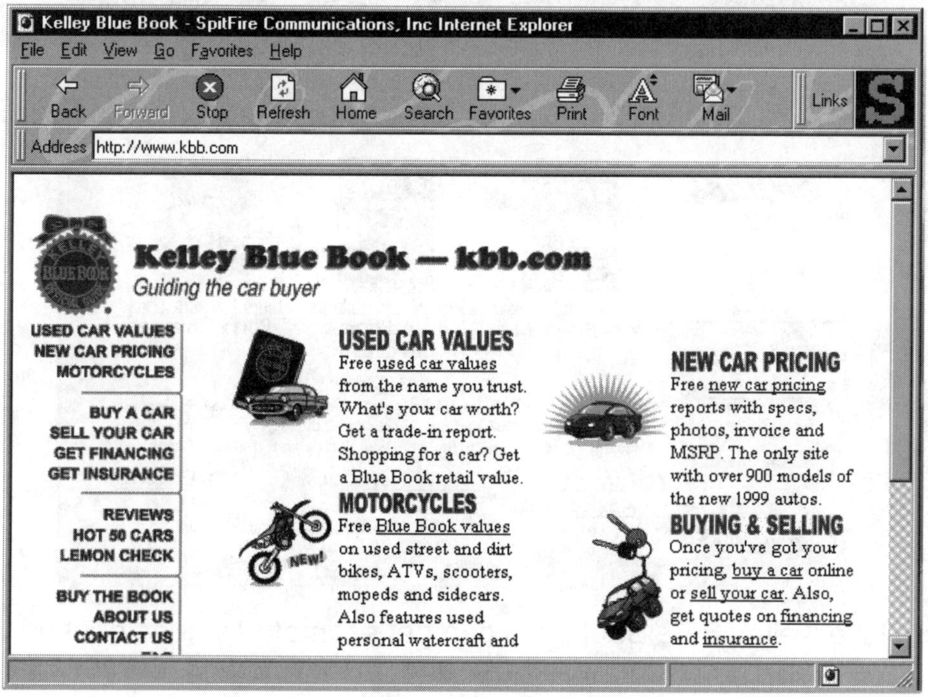

- To find the value of your used car, click *Used Car Values* from the main page. Check both Trade-In and Retail values to get a range, but don't expect to get retail value if you intend to trade in your vehicle.
- You can also look up the sticker price as well as dealer invoice information on new vehicles by clicking *New Car Pricing*.
- For advice on what to buy, try out the Reviews section to see what the pros think.

Edmund's Car and Truck Prices & Reviews

http://www.edmunds.com

Find out the dealer invoice of a new car or see the best manufacturers' incentives from Edmund's, a company with over 30 years experience.

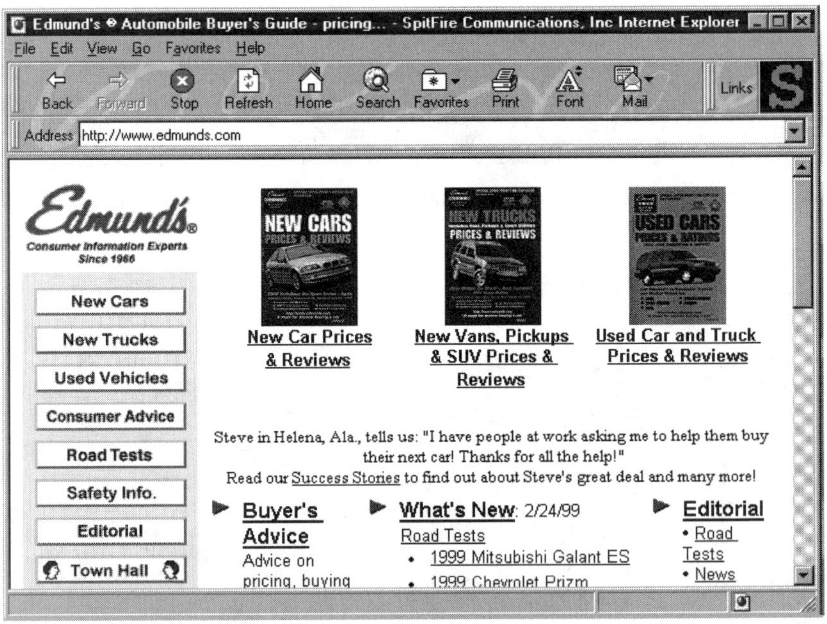

- Like Kelley Blue Book, you can get estimated values of used vehicles by clicking *Used Car and Truck Prices & Reviews*. Some different features: the What's New for This Model Year, Equipment and Mileage Adjustments, and Edmund's Ratings.

- Another section worth nothing is Consumer Advice. The articles intend to help you choose the best car at the best price.
- Click *Incentive, Rebates & Subsidized Leases* to see which manufacturers are offering the greatest deals.

Car and Driver Online

http://www.caranddriver.com

From one of the most trusted names in auto publishing, let *Car and Driver* guide you through the buying process.

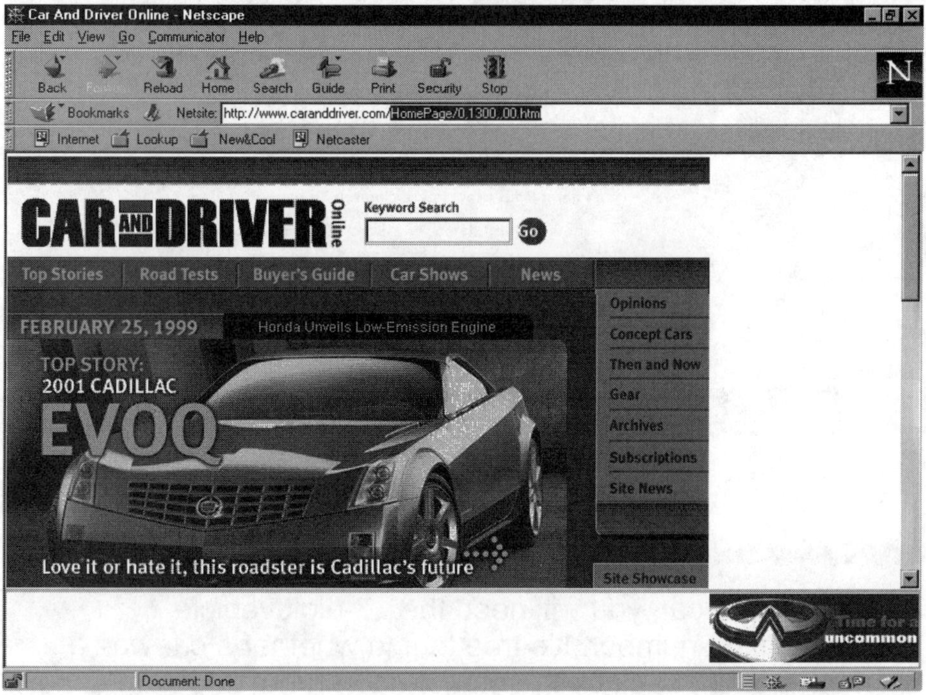

- From the main page, click *Buyer's Guide* to use their database to screen vehicles based on manufacturer, vehicle type, price range, or model year. The reports available on nearly every vehicle are informative and helpful.
- Also provided are several of the features found in the magazine, such as Concept Cars, Then and Now, and Gear.

- The Archives section provides past articles online for the past four years.

Carfax Vehicle History Service

http://www.carfax.com

Are you about to buy a lemon? Carfax's Vehicle History Database has over 850 million records.

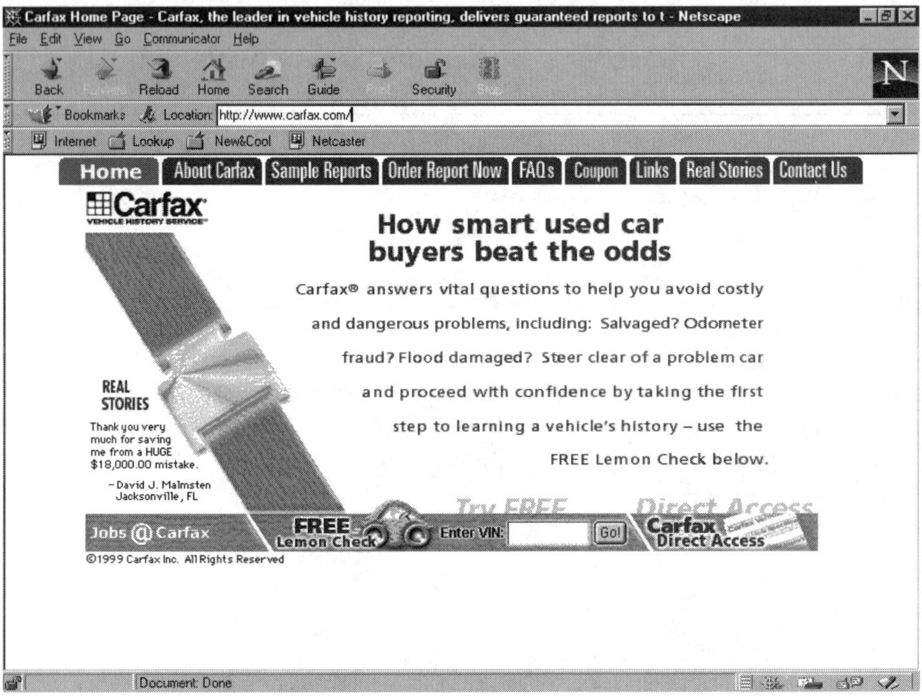

- To look up a car, you will need the 17-digit vehicle identification number. It's free to find whether a car was a lemon bought back by the manufacturer; but to obtain a more complete report looking into issues like odometer fraud, flood damage, or salvaged status, you will be charged a fee.

AutoVantage

http://www.autovantage.com

Let AutoVantage help you buy your next car.

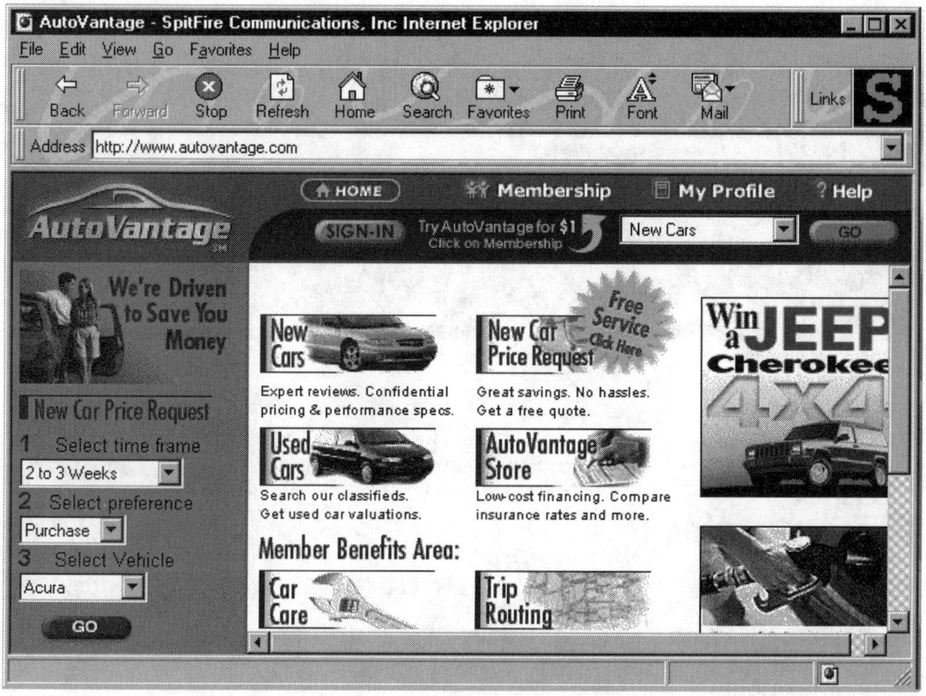

- To find and ultimately buy a new car, select *New Cars* or *New Car Request*. After you provide information about the type you're looking for, AutoVantage will send you an e-mail report with the price information and the participating dealer near you.
- By clicking Used Cars, you will be able to search their nationwide database of vehicles for the one matching your criteria. To sell a car, add your car to their database at no cost.
- For full access to the site's services, you'll need to become a member.

Autobytel

http://www.autobytel.com

Now processing more than 100,000 purchase requests per month, Autobytel helps make the car-buying process painless.

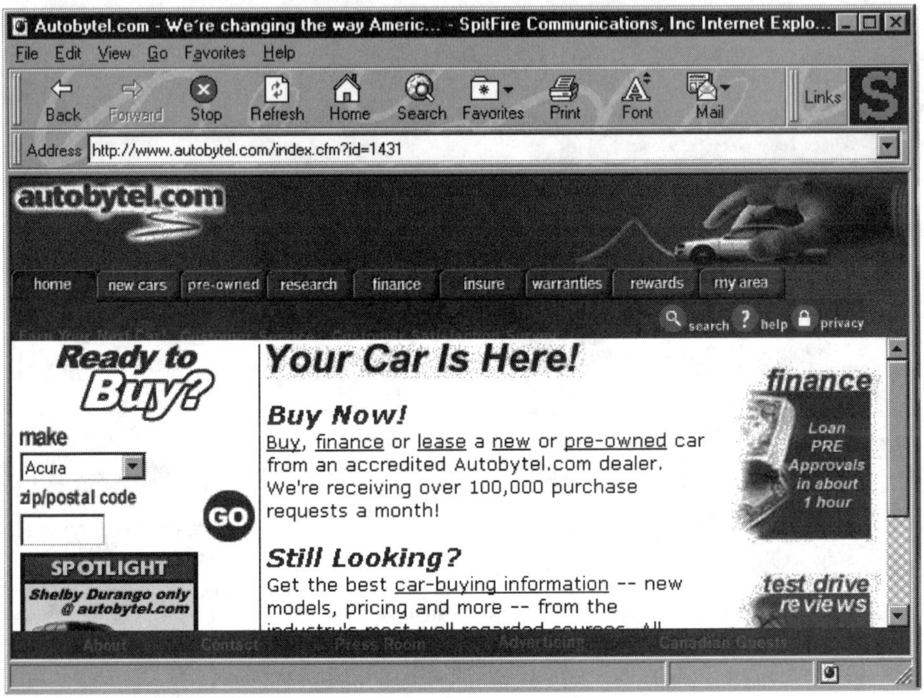

- Like other car-shopping services, Autobytel allows you to search their database for both new and used vehicles based on your criteria.
- Some additional features that might help are the *Purchase or lease?* and *What can I afford?* calculators.

Planning for Retirement

For those of us who work, it seems every Monday morning that we think to ourselves, I can't wait until I'm financially independent and don't have to do this anymore. While having enough money for retirement is a primary concern, there are other issues—healthcare, traveling, hobbies, volunteering, working part-time, children, and grandchildren. This section is designed to point you toward resources to meet these needs.

American Association of Retired Persons

http://www.aarp.org

The AARP Web site is a comprehensive resource every retired person can use.

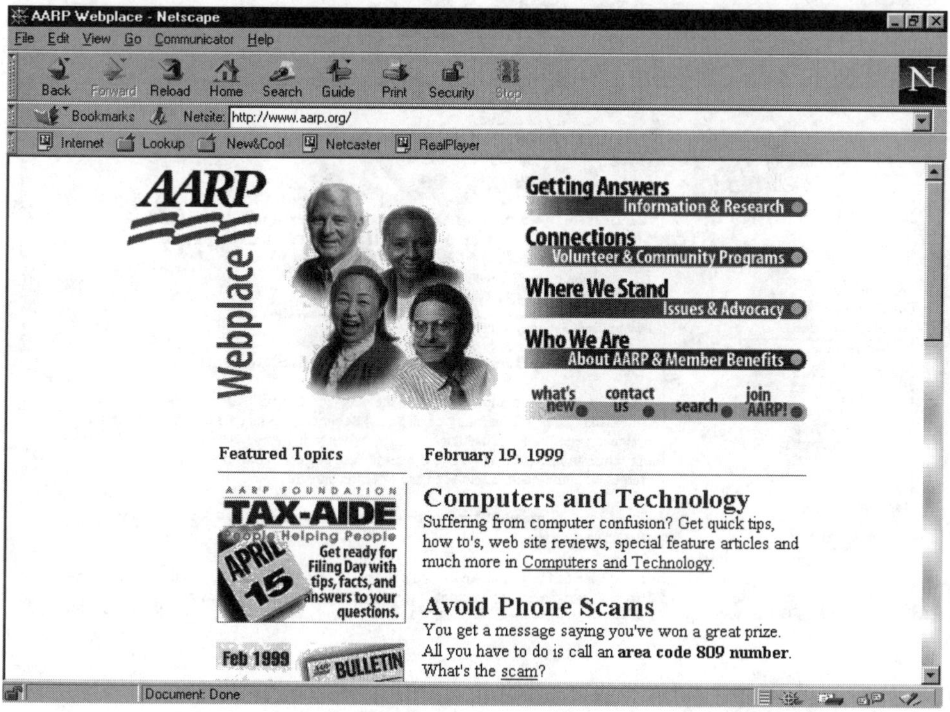

- The AARP is a nonprofit, nonpartisan organization dedicated to helping older Americans achieve lives of independence, dignity, and purpose.
- Visit the Getting Answers section to get volumes of information about healthcare, work, economic security, independent living, consumer issues, and technology.
- Not only are the articles helpful and educational to retired persons, they are also a great resource for those caring for their parents.

Social Security Online

http://www.ssa.gov

Visit the official Web site of the Social Security Administration to find out how much benefit you will receive.

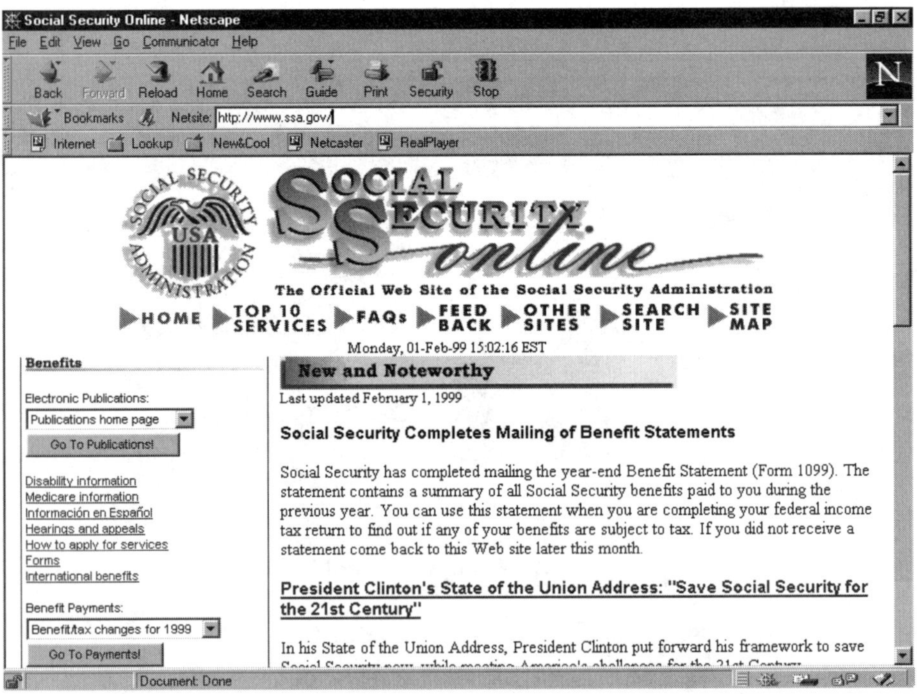

- One of the highlights here is getting an estimate of your retirement benefit from Social Security with their Personal Earnings Benefit Statement.
- To get an estimate click *Top 10 Services* then *PEBES*. After reading the instructions, scroll to the bottom and click *PEBES* and fill out the request form. Most financial planners recommend you request a statement every few years to ensure that you are being credited for the taxes being sent in.
- Another alternative is to download the SSA's Benefit Estimate Program and run your own calculations. To get this service, click *Top 10 Services*, then *Compute Your Own Benefit Estimate*.
- There's more helpful information on this site, such as cost-of-living adjustments, replacing a lost card, and applying for benefits.

MoneyCentral Retirement

http://www.moneycentral.msn.com/retire/home.asp

Huge volumes of retirement information, advice and resources can be found on the Money Central site.

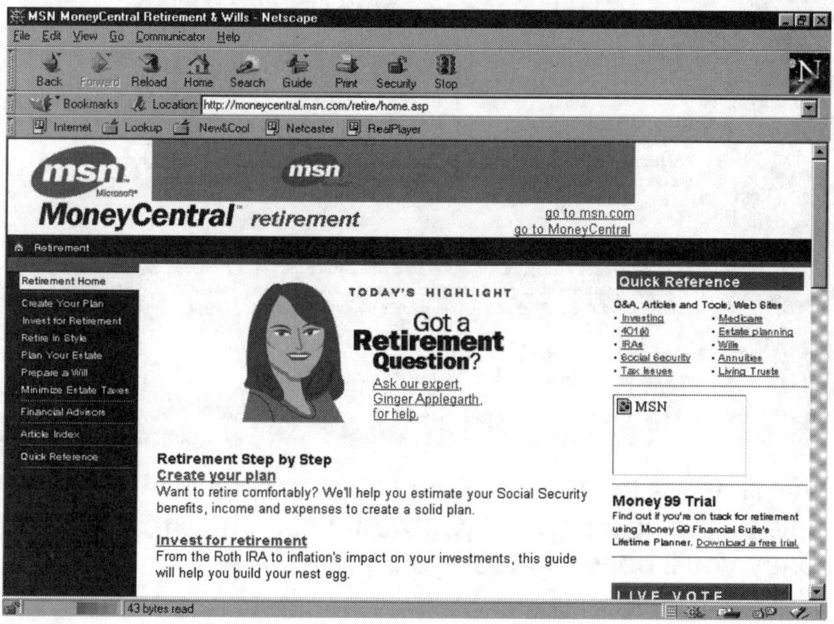

- To get started on planning for your retirement, click *Create Your Plan* and work your way through, step-by-step.
- Have a specific question you'd like answered? You can post questions in the Ask our expert help section.
- By scrolling down you'll find calculators to help you quantify some of your retirement goals and needs.

Retirement.com

http://www.retirement.com

This is a great resource provided by Strong Funds to help you plan for retirement.

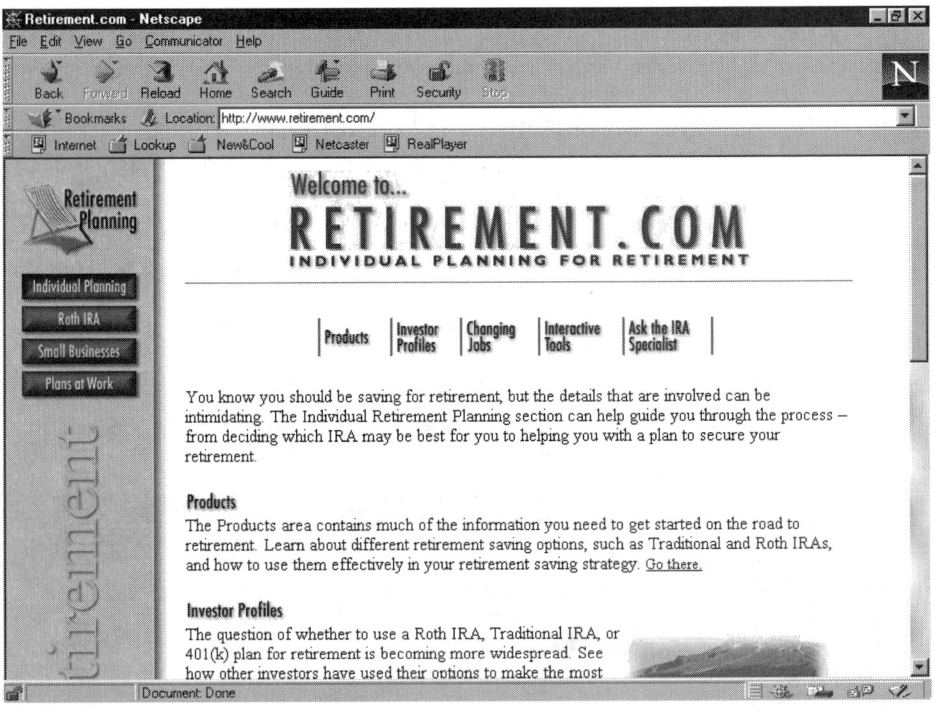

- Overall, this site provides helpful tips and advice on retiring early, changing jobs, or if you want to see how much more money you'll need to reach your goal.

- To learn more about various kinds of retirement accounts and how they work, go to the Products section. To help you decide where to invest money at various stages of your life, check out Investor Profiles.
- Within the Interactive Tools you'll find a number of helpful calculators; for things such as converting to a Roth IRA or deductibility of an IRA deposit.

Other Sites

Access America for Seniors

http://www.seniors.gov

- This site provides endless information on a wide variety of helpful topics, such as Health & Nutrition, Taxes, Travel & Leisure, and Education and Training.

Administration on Aging

http://www.aoa.dhhs.gov

- You'll find helpful, nonfinancial retirement information and resources on this federal agency's Web site.

Planning for College

The second most common savings goal after retirement for parents is college for their children. College costs in America have been increasing considerably faster than the inflation rate, causing many to wonder how they'll ever afford it. We hear reports of scholarships going unclaimed or Washington bureaucrats promising new incentives. To help you make heads and tails of the dilemma, numerous Web sites are now available to help.

Petersons

http://www.petersons.com

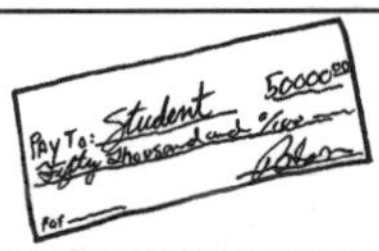

Claiming to be the most comprehensive education resource on the Web, this site is a complete college guide.

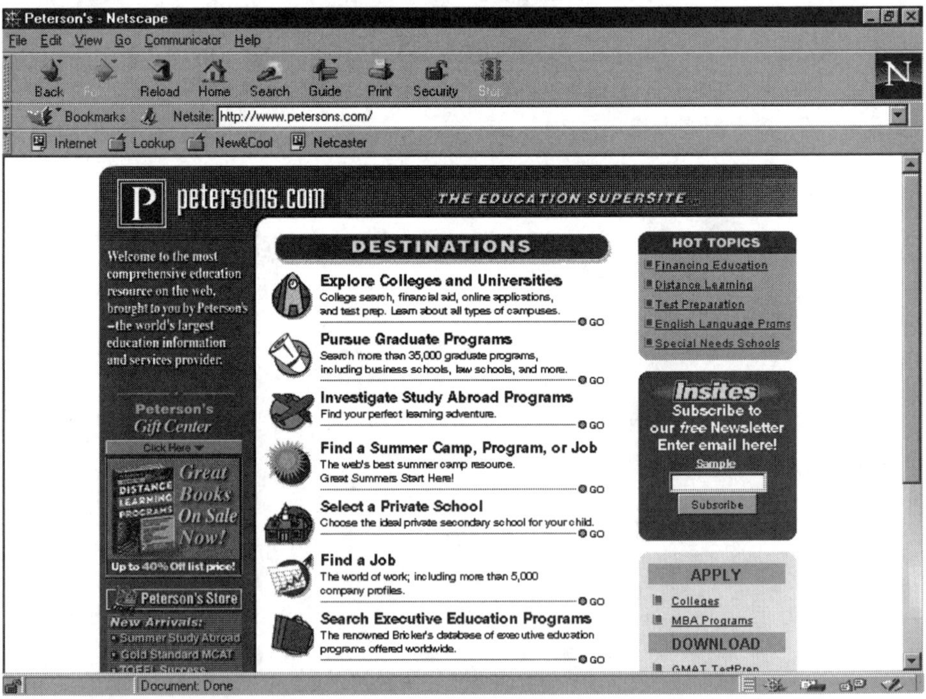

- Here is everything you can imagine to find a college, financial aid, online applications, and much more.
- In addition to a comprehensive list of schools, this site also has a great source of summer opportunities, including jobs, travel programs, and summer camps.
- This site also contains helpful articles on how colleges review applications, planning college visits, and what to expect the first month of college.

CollegeView

http://www.collegeview.com

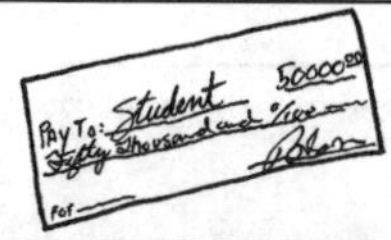

You'll shorten your search for a college with CollegeView's database of profiles of every accredited university in the U.S. and Canada.

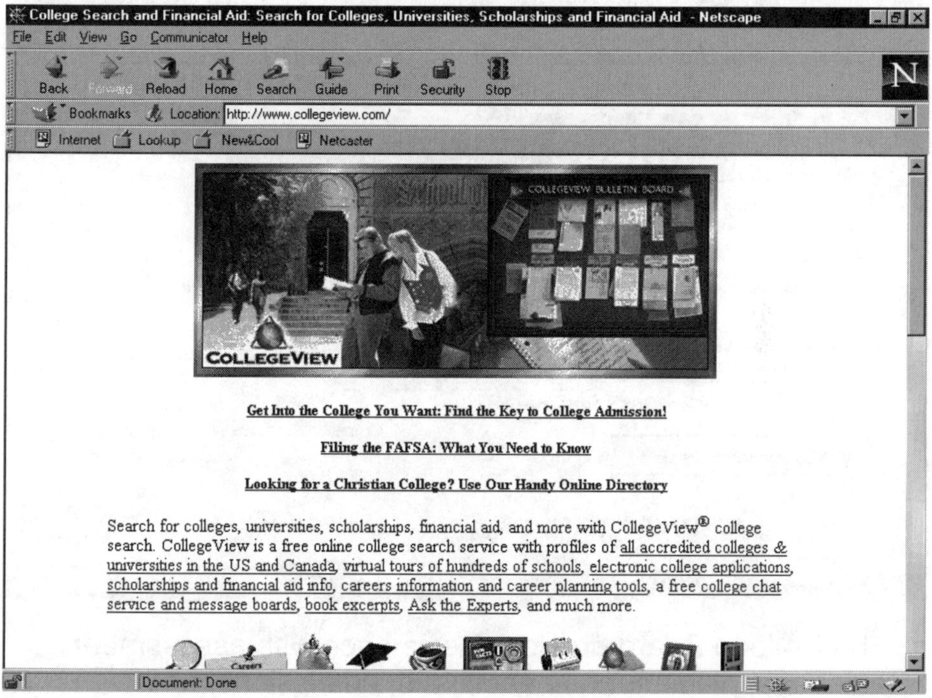

- This site provides electronic applications, career information and planning tools, and virtual tours that contain video, audio, key facts, and links to the Web sites for hundreds of schools.

- To search for a particular college profile, click *All Accredited Colleges and Universities in the U.S. and Canada*. Search by school name.
- For slower computers and modems, you'll need some patience during downloading.

College Board Online

http://www.collegeboard.org

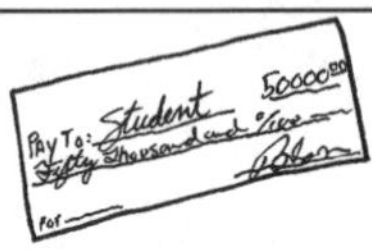

The College Board is an association of schools, colleges, universities, and other educational organizations dedicated to putting college within reach of all students.

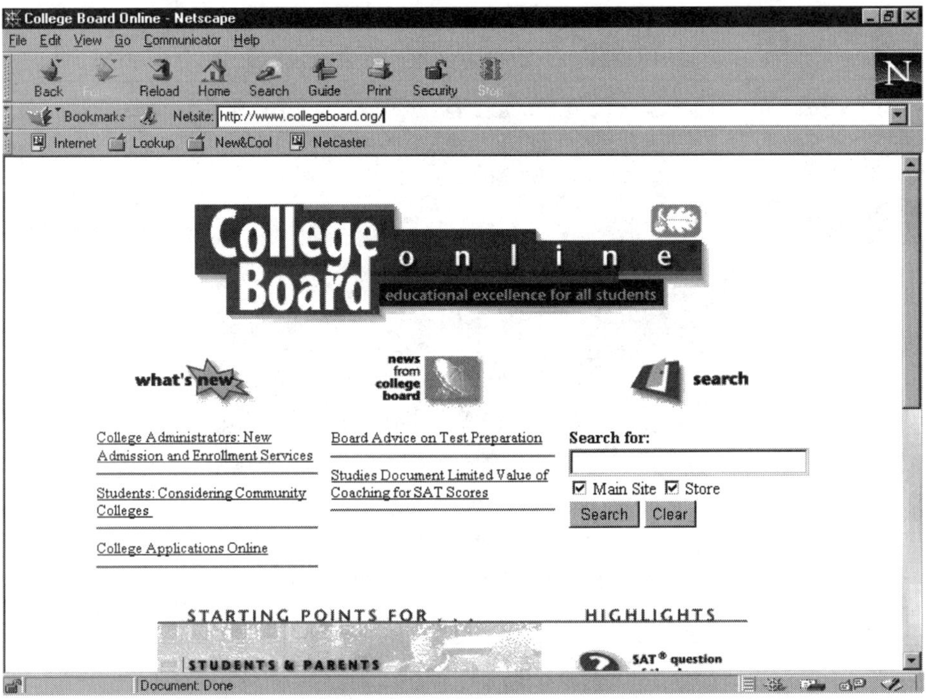

- The College Board provides assistance with assessment, guidance, placement, financial aid, admissions, and enrollment at different levels, and has sections for Students and Parents, Counselors, Financial Aid, and Admission Staff.

- The Students and Parents section, includes SAT exam preparation tips and sample questions, as well as a Library containing informative newsletters, articles, and resources.

eStudent Loan

http://www.estudentloan.com

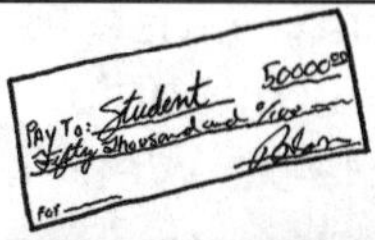

For easy one-stop shopping for college financing, check out eStudent Loan's Loan Finder.

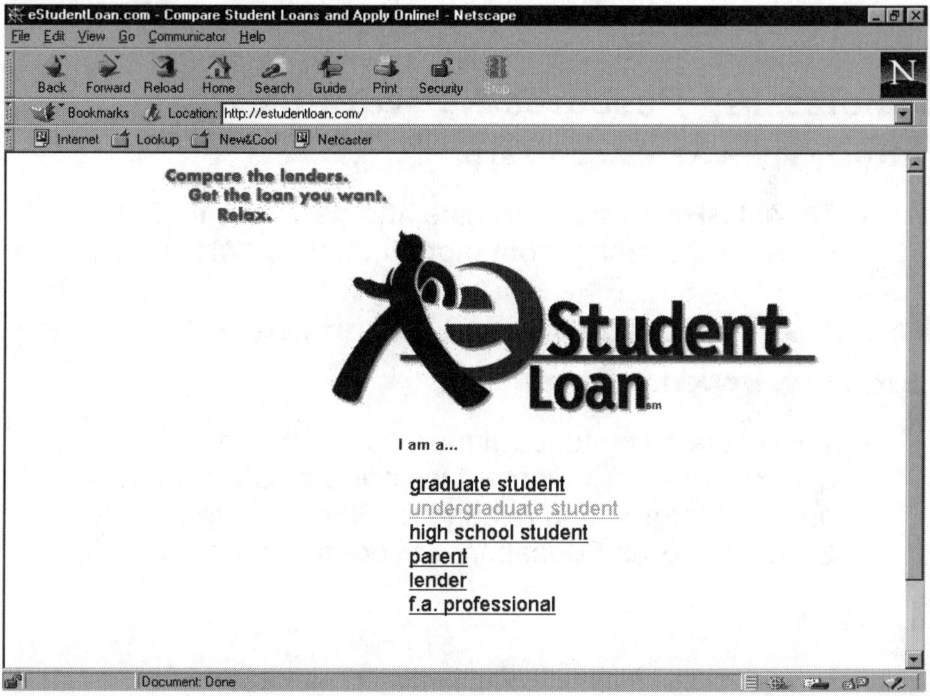

- After signing in and providing some basic information, you will be taken through the loan interview process to help determine the best program for your situation.
- Choose the criteria that is most important, such as lowest payment, lowest interest rate, lowest fees, and deferment options. The outcome of the interview will be a list financial institutions, rates, and product types.
- Not to be overlooked, this site also provides helpful advice and tips.

Other Sites

Sallie Mae: Student Loan Marketing Association

http://www.salliemae.com

- This financial service corporation currently funds close to 40% of all insured student loans. As one of the nation's largest financial services companies, Sallie Mae's Web site provides volumes of information on financing a college education.

Scholarship Resource Network Express

http://www.rams.com/srn

- Try out SRN's search engine and database to find a private scholarship from more than 8,000 programs.

The U.S. Department of Education

http://www.ed.gov

- This is the place to learn more about the federal government's involvement in your education. Find program information relating to Gifted & Talented Students, Adult Education, Childcare, and more.

Other Tools & Resources

The following chapter contains other sites that can be useful resources: some you may want to see now; others you may want to archive for future use. The last site of this section should bring some hope and enjoyment as you work through the financial planning process. Finance has its share of smiles, too. Happy surfing!

FedStats

http://www.fedstats.gov

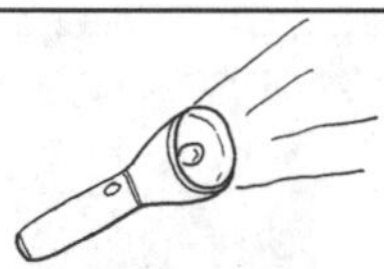

FedStats provides links to more than 70 different U.S. Government Agencies with statistics that may be of use (or at least interest) in managing your money.

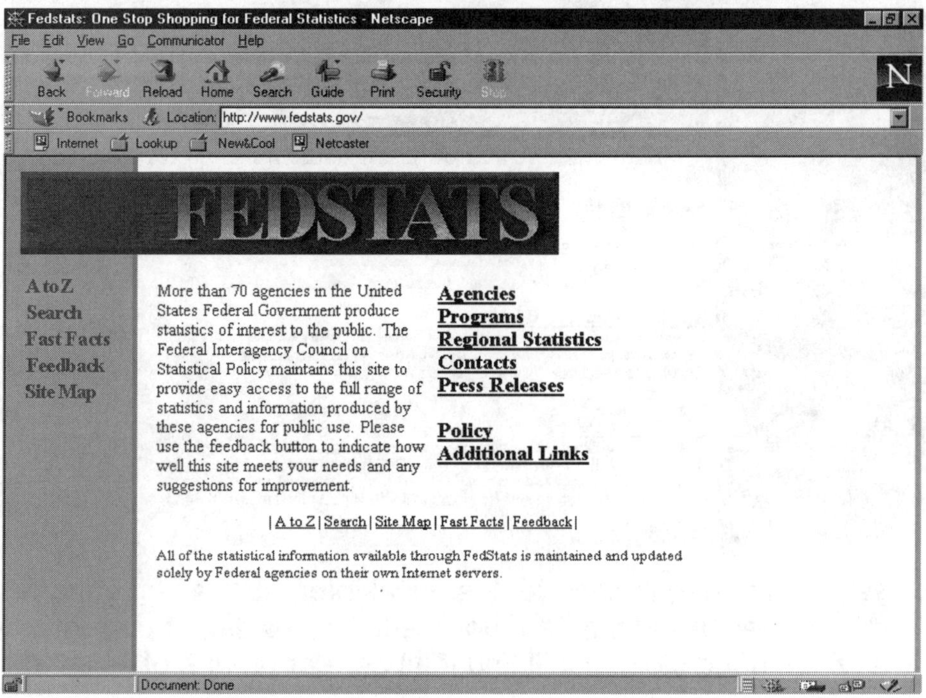

- If information equals money, then this site might come close to paying off the national debt. Including all of its links, this site is huge.
- The site is conveniently divided into three parts—Agencies, Programs, and Regional Statistics. Click on the name of an agency to find out what statistics it tracks and makes accessible. This is quite educational.

U.S. Treasury

http://www.publicdebt.treas.gov

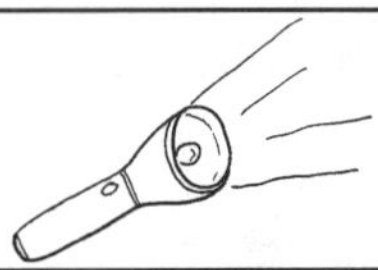

Here you'll find the national debt to the penny, along with volumes of other financial data.

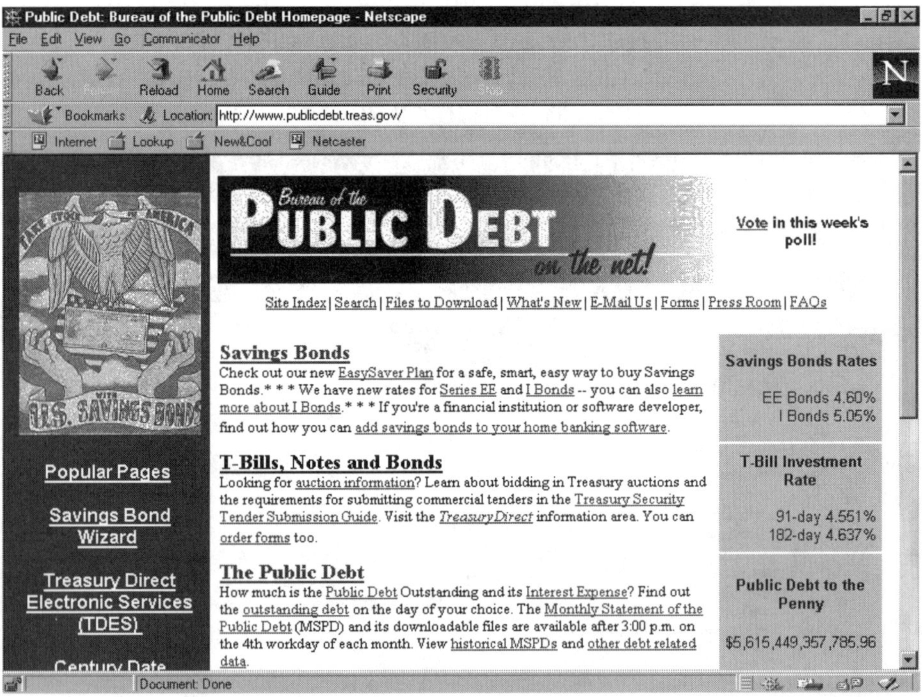

- Whether you're looking for historical interest rates on various government bonds, recent bond auction results, or current savings bond yield, you'll find it all here or on one of its links.

- If you own savings bonds, download the latest version of Savings Bond Wizard, which will help you manage your inventory of bonds and determine the current redemption values and interest earned.

Consumer Reports Online

http://www.consumerreports.com

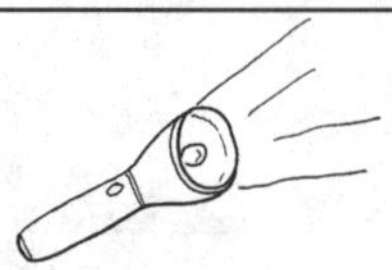

From one of the biggest and most trusted names in consumer product testing and research, let *Consumer Reports* help you make your purchase decisions.

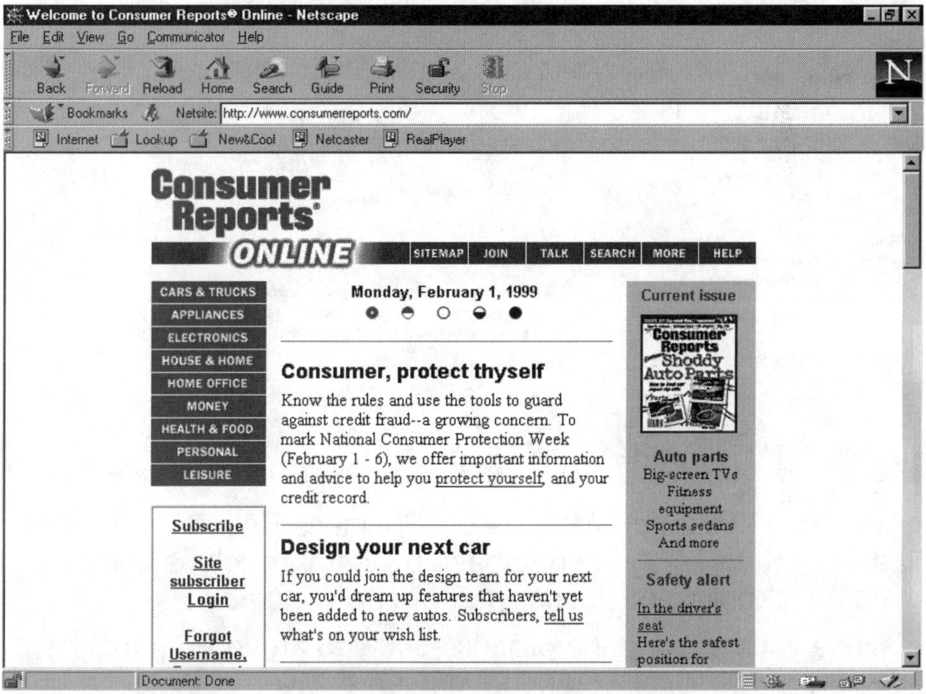

- From the free area of the site you can obtain information (safety issues, late-breaking consumer news) and advice (how to shop) about products and services.
- For a fee, enter the subscriber area to access ratings, test results, and recommendations on hundreds of products and services from *Consumer Reports* magazine.

TOOLS

The Better Business Bureau

http://www.bbb.org

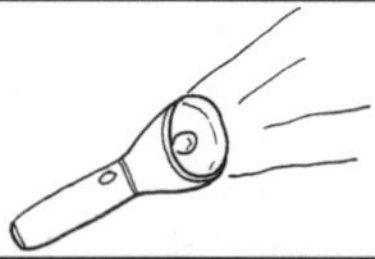

Before you do business with a company or send money to a charity, find out how they've treated past customers.

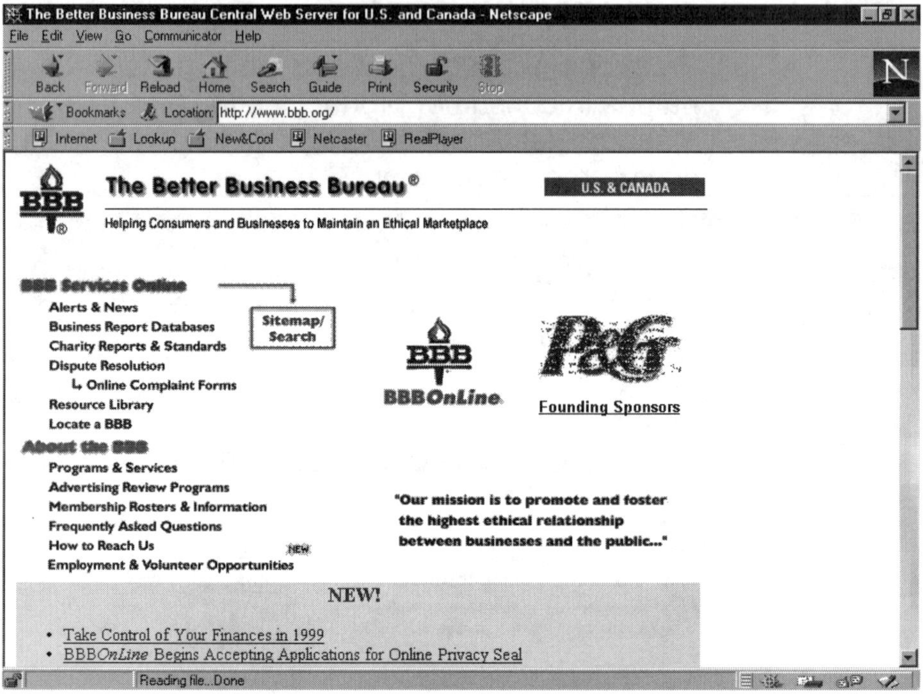

- To search for a company, select Business Report areas. You are able to search the database by factors such as company name, address, business type, or phone number.
- Once you've found the organization you are looking for, the BBB report will tell you about any unresolved complaints against them, as well as some tips on how to select that type of firm.
- Before you send a donation, check out the Charity Reports & Standards section for helpful data on many large national charities.

The Universal Currency Converter

http://www.xe.net/currency

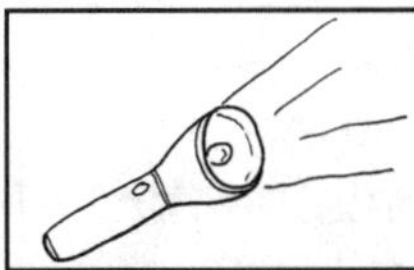

Traveling overseas? The Universal Currency Converter can provide up-to-the-minute currency exchange rates.

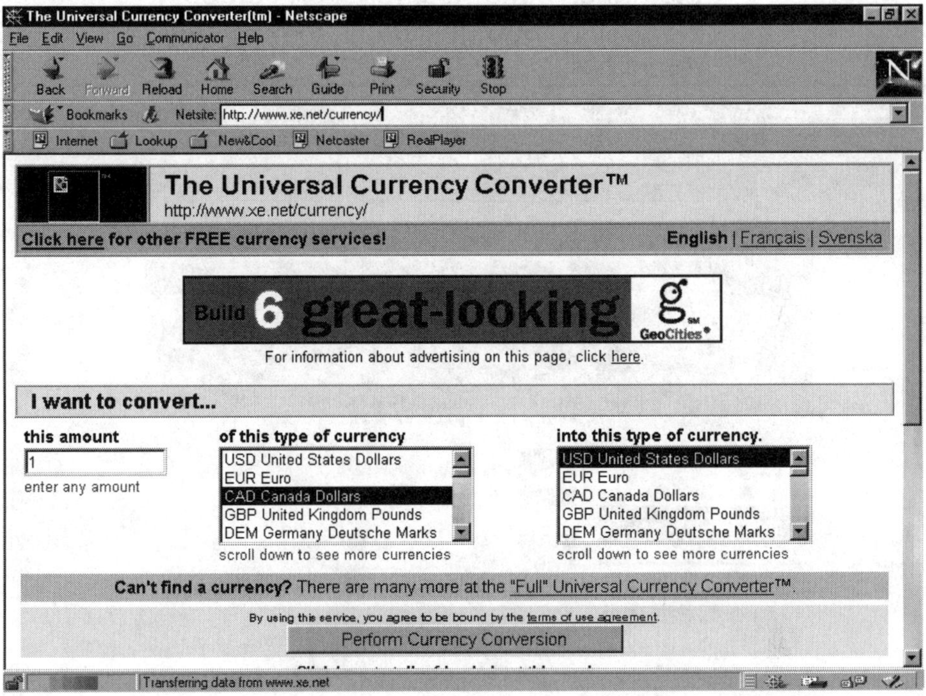

- This site provides an easy-to-use currency exchange calculator to convert a specific amount of one currency to another. The exchange rates are updated regularly and are based on actual market data. For more information on the source of their data, read the frequently asked questions.

Federal Trade Commission

http://www.ftc.gov

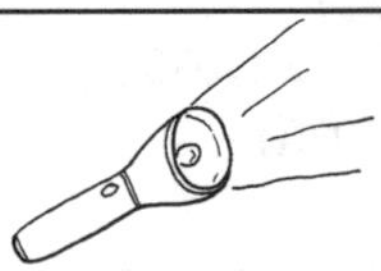

The Federal Trade Commission enforces a variety of federal antitrust and consumer protection laws. The FTC seeks to ensure that the nation's markets function competitively, vigorously, and efficiently and are free of undue restrictions.

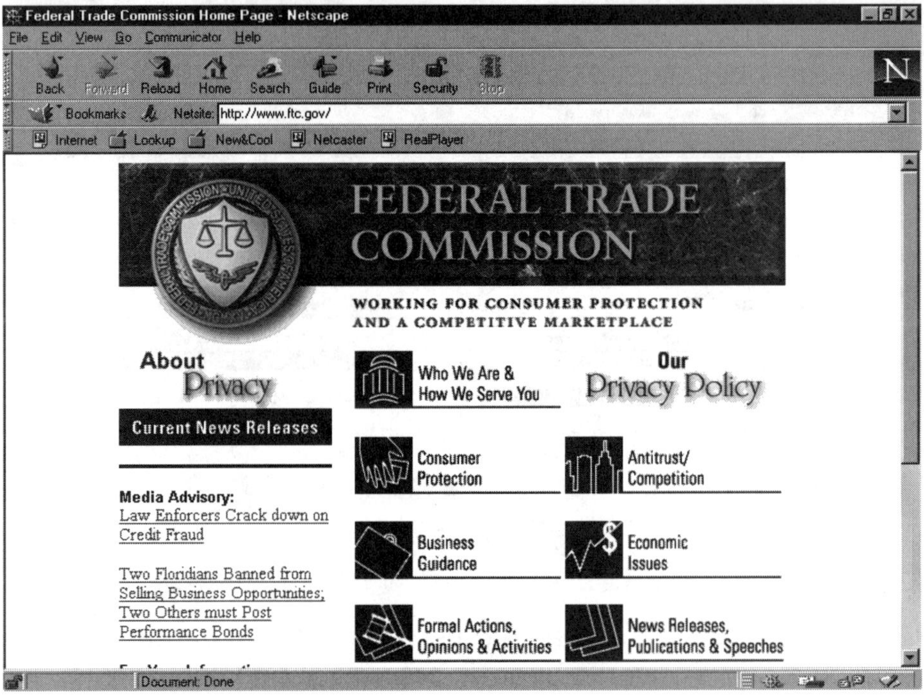

- To simplify the mission statement above, the FTC serves as the watchdog of the free enterprise system.
- Read about rules and procedures and access dozens of consumer and business publications, covering topics such as Doing Business on the Internet, Fair Credit Reporting, and Automatic Debit Scams.
- You'll find many helpful publications under News Releases, Publications & Speeches.

Dilbert Zone Financial Pages

http://www.dilbert.com/comics/dilbert/financial/

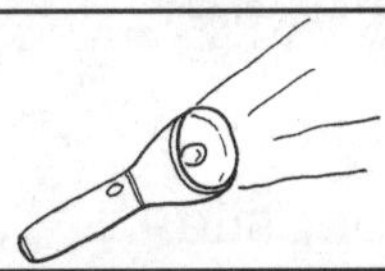

On the lighter side...

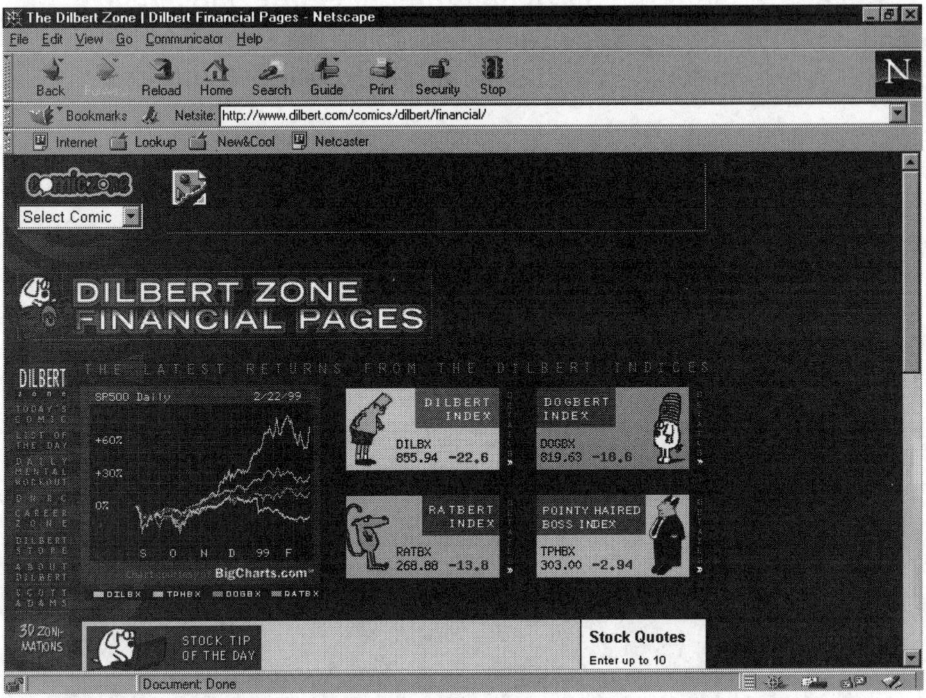

- Need a good laugh? You'll get a kick out the business and financial cartoons found in the Dilbert Zone.
- Have fun tracking the performance of their four portfolios, named for some of the characters in the series. You may also enjoy checking out the stock tip of the day.
- If nothing else, click *Today's Comic* for a laugh!

TOOLS

Financial Super Sites

Several sites on the Internet offer such a wide variety of financial information, analysis, and products that the term super site seems appropriate. A lot like department stores, they have a little bit of everything and are a great place to start. For more depth, move on to sites that specialize in their own areas.

Quicken

http://www.quicken.com

From one of the most trusted names in financial planing software, this site provides more financial planning resources than you could ever use.

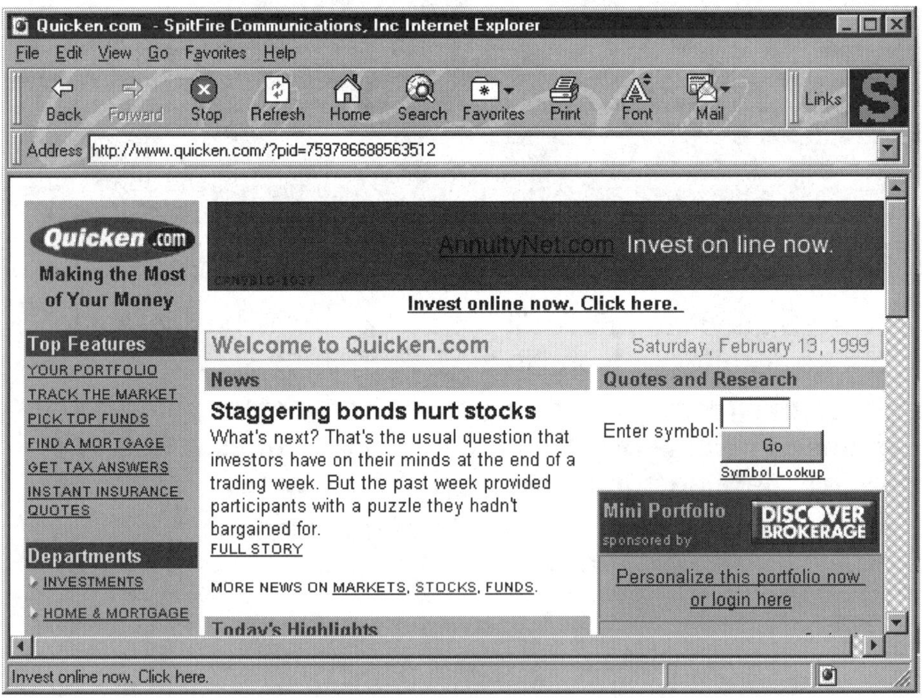

- Covering everything from investments to insurance to taxes to banking, this is one of the most comprehensive personal finance resources there is. If you're following a group of stocks or mutual funds, click *Your Portfolio* and set up your own list that can be refreshed with current prices. For financial advice on things such as college and weddings, click *Life Events* to find numerous articles and helpful tips.
- Plan on taking plenty of time on this site. The abundant information and advice offered is well worth the time.

Smart Money

http://www.smartmoney.com

From the folks that bring you the *Wall Street Journal*, you need to see *Smart Money* magazine's investment resources and answer center.

- More technical and investment oriented, this site provides helpful resources, such as an asset allocator, broker ratings, and economic news.
- Make sure you scroll down toward the bottom of the homepage and check out the Answer Center. Topics covered include Autos, Best Buys, and Home Ownership. Articles here discuss the pros and cons and appropriate steps to take based on your scenario.
- Also check out Our Latest Picks in the Tools section to see what stocks, mutual funds, and bonds they recommend.

Money Central

http://www.moneycentral.msn.com

This high-tech financial site provided by Microsoft has great information and resources to help you plan your future, manage your money, and find bargains on the Internet.

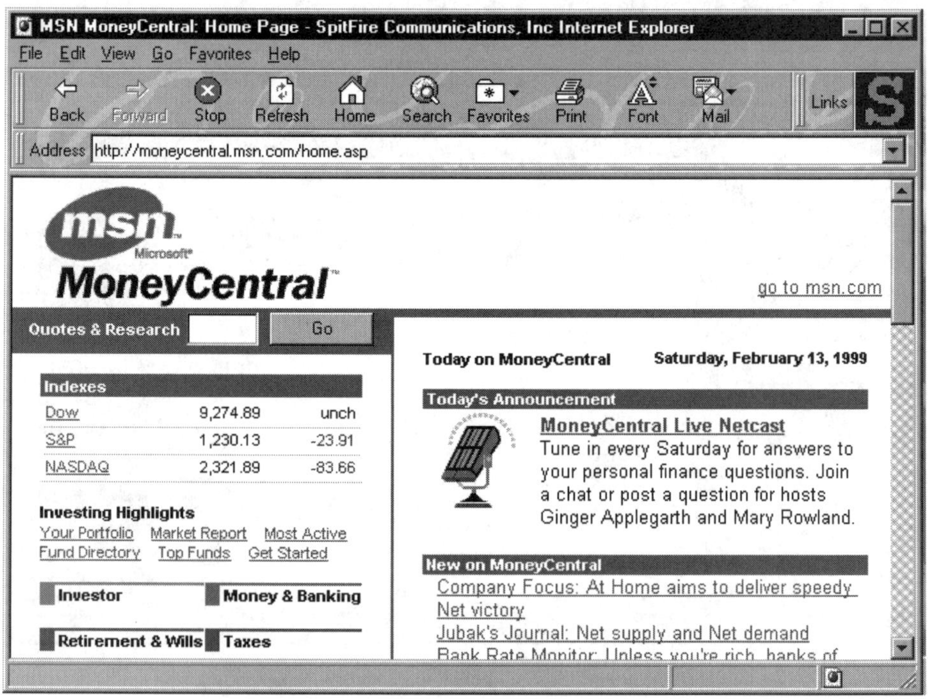

- Part of the Microsoft Network, Money Central is well laid out, downloads quickly, and provides helpful advice and tips on planning for retirement, buying a home, managing your debt, buying insurance, and more.
- For great money-saving tips, click *Smart Buying* to find articles and links to great resources to save money on travel, cars, and more.
- Also worth a look is the Family Finance section. You'll find informative advice, strategies, and Q&A on topics such as College Financial Aid, Divorce, and Death.

Kiplinger Personal Finance Magazine

http://www.kiplinger.com

One of the most widely read financial magazines in America, visit *Kiplinger's* site to get personal finance advice on nearly every topic.

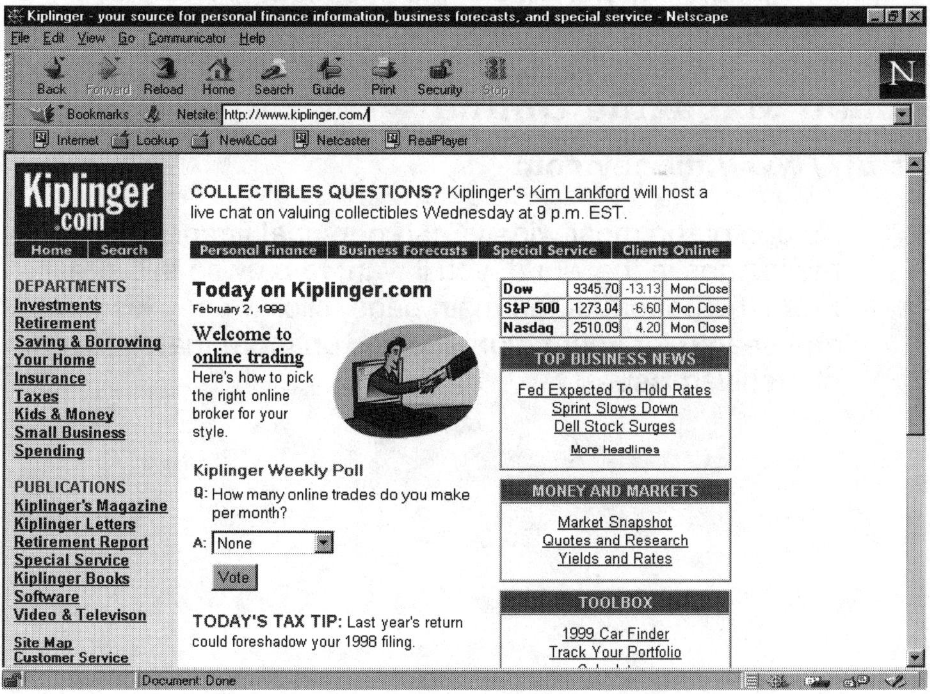

- In addition to market and economic news, this site provides articles and helpful tips on personal finance issues such as saving for college, retirement, and taxes.
- Informative reviews of the top-performing mutual funds and stock picks for the coming year can be found in the Investments Department.
- Kiplinger is also well-known for their Washington and Tax Letters. View samples and subscribe online to these weeklies from the Kiplinger Letters section.

Other Financial Super Sites

Finance Center

http://www.financecenter.com

- Very graphic and easy-to-use, this site provides personal financial advice and calculators for nearly every imaginable category, including budgeting, investing, insurance, credit lines, and autos.

Money Magazine Online

http://www.money.com

- As one of the most widely read personal finance magazines in the world, you'll want to browse this site. From the bottom of the main page, click Money Issues and search for your favorite topics on more than ten years of archived issues.

Index

O

P

Q

R

2/99 OD

Our One-Day Course has you using your software the next day

$18 ea.

Includes diskette

Here's how we do it

We struck out all the unnecessary words that don't teach anything. No introductory nonsense. We get right to the point—in "See spot run" language. No polysyllabic verbiage. We give you the keystrokes and the illustrated layout; step by simple step.

You learn faster because you read less

No fairy tales, novels, or literature. Small words, fewer words, short sentences, and fewer of them. We pen every word as if an idiot had to read it. You understand it faster because it reads easier.

Illustrated exercises show you how

We tell you, show you, and explain what you see. The layout shows you what we just explained. The answers fly off the page and into your brain as if written on invisible glass. No narration or exposition. No time wasted. **Each book comes with a practice disk to eliminate typing the exercises.**

DID WE MAKE ONE FOR YOU?

Cat. No.	Title
DC2	Access 97, Day 1
DC29	Access 97, Day 2
DC30	Access 97, Day 3
DC1	Access 7 for Windows 95
DC50	Basic Computer Skills
DC4	Excel 97, Day 1
DC27	Excel 97, Day 2
DC28	Excel 97, Day 3
DC39	Excel 2000
DC22	FrontPage
DC5	Internet E-mail & FTP w/Sim. CD
DC48	Internet for Sales People w/Sim. CD
DC49	Internet for Managers w/Sim. CD
DC6	Intro to Computers and Windows 95
DC51	Intro to Office 2000
DC21	Local Area Network
DC35	Lotus Notes 4.5
DC8	MS Explorer w/ Sim. CD

Cat. No.	Title
DC10	Netscape Navigator w/ Sim. CD
DC11	Outlook 97
DC52	Outlook 98
DC12	PageMaker 5
DC14	PowerPoint 97, Day 1
DC31	PowerPoint 97, Day 2
DC13	PowerPoint 7 for Windows 95
DC34	Upgrading to Office 97
DC47	Upgrading to Windows 98
DC56	Upgrading to Windows 2000
DC20	Visual Basics 3.0
DC16	Windows 95
DC24	Windows NT 4.0
DC18	Word 97, Day 1
DC25	Word 97, Day 2
DC26	Word 97, Day 3
DC36	Word 2000
DC17	Word 7 for Windows 95
DC19	WordPerfect 6.1

Preview any of our books at: http://www.ddcpub.com

DDC Publishing ***To order call 800-528-3897 fax 800-528-3862***
275 Madison Avenue • New York, NY 10016